National Approaches to Hydrocarbon Development

This book analyses the legal obstacles associated with the advancement of unitization processes and procedures at a national, domestic level.

It uses case studies of identified jurisdictions with relevant States practice and unitization experience in terms of the domestic legal framework and practices. For experience in unitization, the book will focus on the following countries: the United States, Canada, the United Kingdom, Norway, Brazil, Mexico, Ghana and Nigeria. Focusing on best practices which have influenced the development of the unitization concept, the book looks at the formulation of different models and operating agreements, and their potential impact on unexplored hydrocarbon resources, particularly in cases where unitization is necessary.

The book will be of interest to practitioners, scholars and students in the field of natural resource law, international law and unitization.

Eduardo G. Pereira is a globally recognized scholar specialising in natural resources and energy law. He has been active in the natural resources and energy industry for more than 15 years and is an international expert on oil, gas and energy contracts and regulations with practical experience in over 50 jurisdictions. He holds positions as a full-time, part-time, honorary, adjunct, research fellow and/or visiting scholar in a number of leading academic institutions around the world. He is also the author/editor of several leading oil and gas textbooks.

Marianthi Pappa is an associate professor at the University of Nottingham. She specializes in international law of the sea, and energy and natural resources law. She holds an LLB from Aristotle University of Thessaloniki, Greece, and an LLM in oil and gas law and a PhD in international law of the sea, both from the University of Aberdeen. Before joining academia, she practiced law in Greece and Cyprus in finance and energy. Marianthi is a fellow in the UK Higher Education Academy. She also delivers training workshops to governmental and business organizations on boundary disputes and energy law.

Damilola S. Olawuyi holds a doctorate (DPhil) in energy and environmental law from the University of Oxford and an LLM from Harvard University and the University of Calgary. He is an associate professor of energy and environment law at Hamad Bin Khalifa University College of Law; a visiting professor at Columbia Law School and China University of Political Science and Law; a senior visiting research fellow at the Oxford Institute for Energy Studies; and a Herbert Smith Freehills visiting professor at Cambridge University. He is also the Chancellor's Fellow and Director of the OGEES Institute, Afe Babalola University.

National Approaches to Hydrocarbon Development

Unitization and Unit Operating Agreements

Edited by Eduardo G. Pereira, Marianthi Pappa and Damilola S. Olawuyi

Routledge
Taylor & Francis Group
LONDON AND NEW YORK

First published 2025
by Routledge
4 Park Square, Milton Park, Abingdon, Oxon OX14 4RN

and by Routledge
605 Third Avenue, New York, NY 10158

Routledge is an imprint of the Taylor & Francis Group, an informa business

British Library Cataloguing-in-Publication Data
A catalogue record for this book is available from the British Library

ISBN: 978-1-032-75366-9 (hbk)
ISBN: 978-1-032-79266-8 (pbk)
ISBN: 978-1-003-49129-3 (ebk)

DOI: 10.4324/9781003491293

Typeset in Times New Roman
by Apex COVantage, LLC

Contents

List of Contributors *vii*

PART I
Concepts and Principles 1

1 Introduction 3
EDUARDO G. PEREIRA, MARIANTHI PAPPA, AND DAMILOLA S. OLAWUYI

2 Ownership of Resources, Rule of Capture and Government Approvals 9
EDUARDO G. PEREIRA, MARIANTHI PAPPA, AND DAMILOLA S. OLAWUYI

3 Unitisation and Unit Operating Agreements 26
EDUARDO G. PEREIRA, MARIANTHI PAPPA, AND DAMILOLA S. OLAWUYI

PART II
Case Studies 41

4 Unitization in Brazil: Conflicting Legal Regimes & Non-Unitized Areas Experience 43
ANDRÉ LEMOS AND EDUARDO G. PEREIRA

5 Unitization in Canada 55
CHI ILIYA-NDULE

6 Ghana 75
THOMAS KOJO STEPHENS

7 **Mexico** 102
DARIO G. LAMANNA

8 **Unitisation in the Nigerian Oil and Gas Industry** 110
DAMILOLA S. OLAWUYI AND OLUJOBI OLUSOLA JOSHUA

9 **Unitisation in Norway** 123
RUNE OMDAHL

10 **Unitization in the United Kingdom** 140
TOLULOPE O TAIWO

11 **United States of America** 158
KEITH B. HALL

PART III
Conclusion 181

12 **Negotiating Risk-Free Unitization and Joint Development Agreements: Summary and Options for Policymakers** 183
EDUARDO G. PEREIRA, MARIANTHI PAPPA, AND DAMILOLA S. OLAWUYI

Index *190*

Contributors

André Lemos holds a law degree from the PUC-Rio and is a candidate for an LLM in oil and gas at the University of Aberdeen. Holding more than 13 years of experience in project development, regulatory matters, and business transactions in all segments of the oil and gas industry, he is ranked as a star associate by Chambers and Partners (2024). A member of the oil and gas commission of the Brazilian Bar Association – Rio de Janeiro Chapter, he was shortlisted as a rising star in the Legal 500 Brazil Awards 2023.

Chi Iliya-Ndule is an associate in the Calgary office of Blake, Cassels, and Graydon LLP. Chi's practice focuses primarily on mergers, acquisitions and divestitures, and project development within the energy sector. Chi is currently the vice-chair of the Environmental, Energy, and Resources Law Section of the Canadian Bar Association. She holds an LLM in natural resources, energy, and environmental law from the University of Calgary, a BL from Nigerian Law School and an LLB from Olabisi Onabanjo University. She has been admitted as a Barrister and Solicitor in Alberta, Canada, and Nigeria.

Dario G. Lamanna is an international lawyer holding a JD, an LLM, and an MBA, specializing in oil and gas, energy, and merger and acquisitions law. Focusing on cross-border transactions in Latin America and the Caribbean, he has advised several corporations on business development, contract negotiations, and legal and regulatory matters. He has served as chief legal officer at several international energy companies and as a Board of Directors Member of the Association of International Energy Negotiators. He has authored a variety of publications such as the *Regime of Hydrocarbons in Latin America*, published by Ed. R. Depalma, 2007.

Keith B. Hall is a professor of Energy Law at Louisiana State University, a visiting professor at Baku University, Pittsburgh University, and Loyola School of Law, and the Director of the John P. Laborde Energy Law Center and the Mineral Law Institute. He teaches mineral rights, international petroleum transactions, energy law and regulation, and civil law property. He is a frequent speaker at international oil and gas conferences and has co-authored several leading books focusing on leases, unitization, hydraulic fracturing, induced seismicity, and the management of produced water that are used in law school and published by the American Bar. He is also a registered engineer (license status, inactive).

Olujobi Olusola Joshua is an associate professor at Afe Babalola University, Nigeria. He obtained his LLB Degree from the University of Ado-Ekiti, BL from the Nigerian Law School, and an LLM and PhD in jurisprudence and international law from the University of Lagos. He is an international legal consultant and the former sub-dean of the Faculty of Law at Elizade University. His experience is multidisciplinary, specializing in oil and gas law, recovery and repatriation of assets derived from grand corruption. His most recent book publications includes *Nigerian Petroleum, Energy and Gas Resources Law Petroleum Industry Act 2021 & Climate Change Act 2021* (Princeton and Associates Publishing Company Limited, Ikeja, Lagos).

Rune Omdahl is an international lawyer specialised in oil and gas, energy, field development, purchase and sale of petroleum products, LNG, M&A and related private equity and corporate finance. With experience from more than 20 jurisdictions, he is highly experienced in upstream issues and offers a deep knowledge of the corporate structures and contractual instruments in use in the offshore oil and gas sectors, including international treaties. He advises inter alia on international unitisation and cross-border issues (EEZ issues) and regularly works alongside governments on legislative and regulatory issues as well as energy companies. Omdahl is a partner at the law firm of Arntzen de Besche in Oslo and is a part of the firm's energy group.

Thomas Kojo Stephens obtained his BA in political science and philosophy from Emory University, LLB from the University of Ghana, QCL from the Ghana School of Law, and LLM from Cornell University. He obtained a PhD in petroleum law, policy and regulation from the University of Aberdeen. He is a senior partner at Stobe Law, and the Head of the Transactional and Energy Practice. He is an associate professor at the University of Ghana School of Law. He is an Advisory Board member of the International Energy Law Advisory Group, a principal trainer at the International Energy Law Training and Research Center, and was vice-chairman of Ghana's Public Interest and Accountability Committee in 2018–2020.

Tolulope O Taiwo holds a PhD in international oil and gas agreements, an LLM general from the University of Birmingham, and a First Class LLB from the University of Coventry. She worked in the Energy Practice of Aina Blankson, LP for several years, played a pivotal role in the establishment and operation of the ICE Energy Learning School, and regularly advised on joint venture agreements in the energy sector. She particularly provides her expertise in upstream oil and gas agreements, assisting clients on contractual, fiscal, and regulatory issues in licenses, PSCs, joint ventures, decommissioning, long-term gas contracts, and sales and distribution agreements.

Part I

Concepts and Principles

1 Introduction

Eduardo G. Pereira, Marianthi Pappa, and Damilola S. Olawuyi

1.1 Background and Context

This book examines the importance of the unitization agreement as a key contractual and fiscal tool for the management of oil and gas resources. It explores the legal challenges to the development of unitization processes and procedures both within a domestic context and internationally (cross-border unitization). It also looks at the best practices and to what extent such identified practices influence unitization and the joint development of oil and gas resources.

The impetus for the exploitation of petroleum is anchored on energy security.[1] In this context, the term *energy security* means 'to assure adequate, reliable supplies of energy at reasonable prices and in ways that do not jeopardise major national values and objectives'.[2] Petroleum is the pivot of energy security, given that it counts for 57% of the current global energy use.[3] The latter is regardless of the increased emphasis on cleaner energy sources like renewable energy. Thus, Nyman opines, 'the State's security of supplies at stable prices remains at the center of a debate dominated by fossil fuels'.[4] The efficient exploitation of petroleum is a driver of civilization and a wheel that delivers economic development.[5] As such, it does not come as a surprise that issues pertaining to the exploitation of petroleum are top priority in international discourse and national policies. The United Nations 2030 Agenda for Sustainable Development recognizes that fossil fuel development

1 Shahzada M Naeem Nawaz and Shahzad Alvi, 'Energy Security for Socio-Economic and Environmental Sustainability in Pakistan' (2018) 4(10) Heliyon e00854.

2 Daniel Yergin, 'Energy Security in the 1990s' (1988) 67(1) Foreign Aff 110, 111. For more commentaries, see Daniel Yergin, 'Ensuring Energy Security' (2006) 85(2) Foreign Aff 69–82.

3 The current global energy mix is oil (33%), natural gas (24%), coal (27%), renewables (11%), and nuclear power (4%). See also Robert Rapier, 'Fossil Fuels Still Supply 84 Percent of World Energy – and Other Eye Openers from BP's Annual Review' (2020) <http://www.forbes.com/sites/rrapier/2020/06/20/bp-review-new-highs-in-global-energy-consumption-and-carbon-emissions-in-2019/?sh=bbd332c66a16> accessed 16 September 2021.

4 J Nyman, 'Rethinking Energy, Climate and Security: A Critical Analysis of Energy Security in the U.S.' (2018) J Int Relat Dev 2.

5 Abdelrahman Azzuni and Christian Breyer, 'Definitions and Dimensions of Energy Security: A Literature Review' (2017) WIREs Energy Environ 1.

DOI: 10.4324/9781003491293-2

is crucial to attaining universal access to sustainable energy.[6] Some States have affirmed their commitment to achieving energy security through petroleum by adopting a specific policy. For instance, the Nigerian National Petroleum Policy 2017 reaffirms the commitment of the government to 'maximise production and processing of hydrocarbon'.[7] The UK's Oil and Gas Authority Strategy 2021 reaffirms the objective of maximizing the economically recoverable petroleum in its waters.[8] The Pakistan National Petroleum Exploration and Production Policy 2012 sets a target of accelerating the exploration and production of petroleum to attain energy security and sufficiency.[9] In the above context, there is the need to exploit petroleum to attain energy security while minimizing waste.

Petroleum is fugacious.[10] In many instances, a single reservoir will transcend the boundary of a defined owner[11] or even international boundaries.[12] In both cases, maximum efficiency in producing petroleum from a reservoir is best achieved when the operator treats the field as a single unit.[13] The latter is because the geological formations of a petroleum reservoir are such that there are limited points of efficient extraction.[14] As such, 'if the reservoir is exploited differently, the risk of inefficient exploitation is very high'.[15] In the words of McLaughlin, 'extraction from one point unavoidably affects conditions in the whole deposit and may result in other sharing parties not being able to extract the resources from their part of the deposit'.[16] Thus, it is necessary to negotiate with the adjacent owner to establish a

6 The United Nations 2030 Agenda for Sustainable Development, Goal 7.

7 The Nigerian National Energy Policy 2017, para 1.

8 The United Kingdom's OGA Strategy 2021, 5.

9 The Pakistan Petroleum Exploration and Production Policy 2012, section 1.3, para 1.

10 Bryan Clark, 'Migratory Things on Land: Property Rights and a Law of Capture' (2002) Elec J Comp L 10; M K Woodward, 'Ownership of Interests in Oil and Gas' (1965) 26(3) Ohio State Law J 353, 355.

11 David Edward Pierce, 'Coordinated Reservoir Development – An Alternative to the Rule of Capture for the Ownership and Development of Oil and Gas' (1983) 4 J Energy L Poly 1, 27.

12 Anne Hsiu-An Hsiao, 'Unilateral Actions and the Rule of Law in Maritime Boundary Disputes' (2016) 22 Asian Yearbook Int Law 237, 238.

13 Guillermo J Garcia Sanchez and Richard J McLaughlin, 'The 2012 Agreement on the Exploitation of Transboundary Hydrocarbon Resources in the Gulf of Mexico Confirmation of the Hydrocarbon Resources in the Gulf of Mexico Confirmation of the Rule or Emergence of a New Practice?' (2015) 37 Hous J Int'l L 681.

14 Guillermo J Garcia Sanchez and Richard J McLaughlin, 'The 2012 Agreement on the Exploitation of Transboundary Hydrocarbon Resources in the Gulf of Mexico Confirmation of the Hydrocarbon Resources in the Gulf of Mexico Confirmation of the Rule or Emergence of a New Practice?' (2015) 37 Hous J Int'l L 681. See Chukwuemeka Mike Okorie, 'Have the Modern Approaches to Unit Development of Straddling Petroleum Resources Extinguished the Applicability of the Primordial Law of Capture?' (2010) 18 Curr Int'l Trade LJ 41, 46.

15 Chukwuemeka Mike Okorie, 'Have the Modern Approaches to Unit Development of Straddling Petroleum Resources Extinguished the Applicability of the Primordial Law of Capture?' (2010) 18 Curr Int'l Trade LJ 41, 46.

16 Richard J McLaughlin, 'Establishing Transboundary Marine Energy Security and Environmental Cooperation Areas as a Method of Resolving Longstanding Political Disagreements and Improving Transboundary Resource Management in the Gulf of Mexico' (2008) 7 Issues Leg Scholarsh 1, 8.

system of joint development of such petroleum reservoir. The latter is where unitization comes in. The process of establishing an arrangement for a unified operation is called unitization and has been utilized in many oil and gas producing countries through regulations, agreements or some sort of arrangements. This process, when successful, prevents disputes between the parties, which could potentially hinder efficient exploitation. It also enables sharing economies of scale and making best use of technical information, means and equipment, thereby reducing costs and investments to develop fields as a single unit optimally.

The term *unitization* therefore means 'the joint, coordinated operation of a petroleum reservoir by all the owners of rights in the separate tracts overlying the reservoir'.[17] It has its root in the United States, where, primarily because of the common law rule of capture, it became necessary for regulatory authorities to encourage and mandate it in some cases.[18] It has gained popularity in other jurisdictions given its benefits, including lowering production costs, reducing waste, maximizing economic recovery, and giving relevant parties a fair share of the common reservoir.[19] A unitization and unit operating agreement (UUOA) refers to the agreement that underlies the unitization process.[20] The affected parties enter into a UUOA to detail the terms of the unitization process and how the common field will be governed or operated.[21] Unitization can be voluntary or compulsory. While voluntary unitization refers to a situation in which licence holders agree on their own to jointly development their petroleum reservoirs in a safe and efficient manner, compulsory unitization refers to a situation in which licence holders are mandated by law, court order or ministerial decision by the regulator to work together to develop the reservoir's oil and gas resources. Compulsory unitization may occur to achieve broad policy aims such as increasing production output through maximum recovery of available hydrocarbon resources; advancing a more coordinated and efficient development of fields; or ensuring resource conservation through the sharing of best available production technologies or production facilities.

While the concept of unitization is universal and widely practised, the global unanimity as to its definition, essential characteristics, the scope of its application,

17 Patrick H. Martin and Bruce M. Kramer, *Williams & Meyers Manual of Oil and Gas Terms* (12th edn 2003) 850. See also Damilola Olawuyi, *Extractives Industry Law in Africa* (Springer 2018) 1–25.

18 David Asmus and Jacqueline L Weaver, 'Unitizing Oil and Gas Fields Around the World: A Comparative Analysis of National Laws and Private Contracts' (2006) 28(1) Issues Leg Scholarsh 67, 68.

19 A Derman and K Vollus, 'Unitization' (2002) 215 ADVISOR, Ass Intern Petroleum Neg 5.

20 Danielle Beggs and Justyna Bremen, 'Unitisation and Unitisation Agreements' in Geoffrey Picton-Turbervill (ed), *Oil and Gas: A Practical Handbook* (Globe Law and Business 2009) 58.

21 Danielle Beggs and Justyna Bremen, 'Unitisation and Unitisation Agreements' in Geoffrey Picton-Turbervill (ed), *Oil and Gas: A Practical Handbook* (Globe Law and Business 2009) 58. In some jurisdictions like Canada, the agreement is divided into two, i.e. a unit agreement and a unit operating agreement. See Nina Howell and Lauren Kensall, 'Unitisation: Comments on 2020 AIPN Model International Unitization and Unit Operating Agreement' (2021) XI (38) Natl L Rev <https://www.natlawreview.com/article/unitization-comments-2020-aipn-model-international-unitization-and-unit-operating> accessed 18 September 2021.

and the content of the legislative framework underpinning it remains elusive. Nonetheless, academic literature has attempted to provide some analysis to provide a way forward. Worthington analysed the legal framework underpinning unitization in several jurisdictions, focusing on its core prescriptive elements.[22] His work extrapolates some uniform characteristics that are germane to an effective framework for unitization. However, Worthington's analysis lacks depth and does not cover cross-border unitization or a detailed analysis of a UUOA. MacLeod discussed the concept of unitization and analysed its use in the United Kingdom.[23] The latter study is limited to the United Kingdom and, like Worthington's work, does not cover cross-border unitization. Pereira and Carloni analysed the features of a UUOA in an intra-national context and compared it to a joint operating agreement (JOA).[24] Bastida et al. analysed the extent of the international framework for cross-border unitization and concluded that while there is no mandatory obligation to cooperate, it remains the most sensible option in the context of common petroleum reservoirs.[25] On the one hand, Bastida et al. did not attempt to marry their analysis with intra-national unitization practices, neither was their study preceded by a detailed discussion of the characteristics of a UUOA. While these and other previous works are limited in analysing the concluded agreements (especially joint development agreements [JDAs]), this book's distinctiveness is that it moves the debate forward by covering the issue of unitization and setting out the emerging trends, best practices and potential customary rules.[26]

In light of the above literature gaps, this book analyses unitization and the agreement underlying it (UUOA) from a domestic and international law perspective using selected case studies. In order to understand the legal challenges in developing hydrocarbon resources in unitized areas and/or disputed areas and how they are dealt by the concerned States, this book analyses the practice of States with significant experience in unitization and joint development. It further analyses the implications for countries with potential or significant hydrocarbon resources which might have to be developed through a unitization process. To that extent, first, the book raises and discusses the most suitable legal framework to regulate unitization developments where the concerned licensees are within the confines of a single jurisdiction and where the concerned licensees are located in more than one jurisdiction, and to what extent such legal framework provides a solid track record with proven positive experiences and what should be avoided. Secondly,

22 Paul F Worthington, *The Law on Petroleum Unitization: Legislating for Effective Regulatory* (Edward Elgar 2020).

23 Nicola MacLeod, 'Unitisation' in Greg Gordon and others (eds) *Oil and Gas Law – Current Practise and Emerging Trends* (2nd edn, Dundee University Press 2011) 413.

24 Eduardo G Pereira and Giulia Carloni, 'Unitisation and Unit Operating Agreements' in *Understanding Joint Operating Agreements* (Intersentia 2017) 45, 46.

25 Ana E Bastida and others, 'Cross-Border Unitization and Joint Development Agreements: An International Law Perspective' (2007) 29(2) Houston J Intern L 356, 373.

26 Ana E Bastida and others, 'Cross-Border Unitization and Joint Development Agreements: An International Law Perspective' (2007) 29(2) Houston J Intern L 356, 373.

it examines the main challenges and practical solutions to explore hydrocarbon resources in disputed areas (lessons learnt).

By bringing together the expertise of multiple authors and from different jurisdictions (Europe, the Americas, Asia and Africa), the book provides comparative and more complete discussion of the scope, application and guiding principles for the optimal development and application of unitization and JDAs in the petroleum sector.

1.2 Structure and Outline

This book is divided into three parts in line with the central research theme. Part I is the introductory part, which contains an analysis of the historical antecedents and legal justification for the UUOA. Concepts such as ownership, the rule of capture, government approvals and standard forms of a UUOA will be analysed. The standard form of a UUOA will be compared to similar arrangements like JOAs and pooling agreements to point out their similarities and differences. The introductory section concludes with a chapter that contains an analysis of the international law concerning cross-border unitization and joint development zones.

Part II contains case studies, including an analysis of unitization practices in Brazil Canada, Nigeria, Norway, the United Kingdom and the United States. The final part (Part III) contains a conclusion along with the lessons to be learnt from the book.

The originality of this book lies in its examination of issues that have not been addressed in the existing literature, including moving beyond concluded agreements to emerging trends, best practices and potential customary rules. The book is distinguishable from every other literature on the subject matter given its scope. It covers all the legal aspects of UUOA, to the extent that it can be rightly said that it covers the entire field of the subject matter. It looks at ancillary legal issues that precede unitization at the domestic and international levels. It contains an analysis of the legal framework and practices that inform the content of the UUOA in the domestic and international context. The scope covers current and emerging laws on UUOA. It also contains a comparison of the UUOA and similar arrangements like pooling, JOAs, JDAs and so on.

It is trite that 'the use of case studies is preferred to theoretical prepositions because it approaches a subject matter from the point of "lived reality"'.[27] As mentioned, this book contains a comparative analysis of the legal framework for unitization and UUOA using selected case studies that cut across several continents of the world. The lessons extrapolated from the case studies will be readily applicable. Regardless, the book still leverages the benefits of theoretical prepositions by employing them to analyse the emerging trends from current State practices in unitization (during negotiation and performance of the agreements) and the best

27 Ngozi Chinwa Ole, 'Review of Eduardo G Pereira and Tonje P Gormley (eds), *Local Content for the International Petroleum Industry*' (2019) 12 J World Energy Law B 198, 199.

practices in relation to that. Ultimately, this could determine whether a standard unitization model may arise or a set of customary rules could emerge in public international law.

1.3 Conclusion

The joint development of oil and gas resources in multiple units and wells is essential for the efficient, orderly and sustainable use of oil and gas resources. However, without adequate legal and contractual safeguards, unitization and JDAs may result in commercial disputes, tensions and risks, all of which may delay or undermine the maximization of petroleum resources needed to advance energy security. A comprehensive analysis and study of key legal and contractual risks and tensions that arise in the design, application and implementation of unitization and JDAs can help us plot a comprehensive path for effectively negotiating and implementing such agreements in a coherent manner.

The systemic and multijurisdictional survey of the unique and underlying features of unitization and JDAs in diverse jurisdictions offered by this book can simplify the task of negotiating transparent, collaborative and sustainable unitization, and JDAs. This book provides an invaluable compendium of analyses and resources for a wide range of audiences. For those in the academic field, it provides significant resources given that it touches upon every aspect of unitization and UUOA, including a view of its global use. It also provides a sturdy basis for further research in this subject matter. Countries and entities faced with the challenge of common petroleum reservoirs will also find this book resourceful. The book will also serve as a useful guide for anyone seeking to negotiate or draft a UUOA or a JOA. Overall, this book provides a strong starting and finishing point for anyone seeking to understand the subject matter of unitization.

2 Ownership of Resources, Rule of Capture and Government Approvals

Eduardo G. Pereira, Marianthi Pappa, and Damilola S. Olawuyi

2.1 Introduction

Issues pertaining to ownership and control of petroleum are inherently connected with the sovereignty of States.[1] If petroleum resources are properly harnessed and controlled, waste will be minimized and energy security strengthened.[2] What is more, issues of ownership and control of petroleum resources are recurring themes in policy discussion because they provide an avenue for external interferences with the sovereignty of a State.[3] The control and management of petroleum also have far-reaching implications for the economic development of a State. For instance, petroleum activities lead to the creation of valuable jobs for economic development.[4] In another instance, ownership and control of petroleum provides resource-rich States with a voice and leverage in international discourse.[5] A case at hand is the Organization of the Petroleum Exporting Countries (OPEC), which is currently a force to be reckoned with in international politics.[6] Another example is Russia's use of petroleum as tool to inform the narratives in their favour, following their ongoing war with Ukraine.[7] For the above reasons, the control and management of petroleum resources situated within a State is taken seriously.

In light of the above, this chapter analyses the theories and options for the ownership, control and management of petroleum resources around the world. It starts by discussing the nature of petroleum, which influences the extent to which the theories of ownership are applicable to it. It will identify that even though petroleum resources are fugacious elements, they are still the subject matter of absolute

1 Edith Penrose, 'Oil and International Relations' (1976) 2(1) Brit J Intern Stud 41, 42.

2 Samuel Chisa Dike, 'Energy Challenges and Insecurity in Nigeria: A Sectoral Perspective' (2018) 91 Readings Law Pol.

3 Norbert Edomah and others, 'The Role of Policy Makers and Institutions in the Energy Sector: The Case of Energy Infrastructure Governance in Nigeria' (2016) 8 Sustainability 829.

4 S A Madujibeya, 'Oil and Nigeria's Economic Development' (1976) 75 African Affairs 284.

5 Edith Penrose, 'Oil and International Relations' (n 1).

6 Andrew Chatzky and Anshu Siripurapu, 'OPEC in a Changing World' (2020) <OPEC in a Changing World | Council on Foreign Relations (cfr.org)> accessed 19 April 2021.

7 Sami Moisio, 'Geopolitics of Explaining Russia's Invasion of Ukraine and the Challenges of Small States' (2022) 97 Polit Geogr 102683.

DOI: 10.4324/9781003491293-3

and qualified ownership. It will be identified that very few States allow for the operation of absolute ownership of petroleum as modernization has given rise to restrictions on the latter. Following on from that, the rule of capture will be analysed. It will be argued that while the rule engendered sporadic development of the petroleum industry in the United States, it causes waste and low productivity. In the case of government ownership, the various vehicles through which private entities are engaged to explore and develop petroleum resources are explored. The vehicles include licenses, production sharing agreements and risk service contracts. The above-mentioned discussion is to set the stage for subsequent chapters of the book.

2.2 The Concept of Ownership

Before the emergence of organized society, the concept of ownership entailed absolute, total and unrestricted control and 'fullest amplitude of rights' over real property.[8] Prior to that time, the acquisition of ownership over real property was through first possession and conquest.[9] The first possession theory provided that if you were the first to discover a piece of land, you could take and own it.[10] Given that there were no organized rules governing such possession, the first possessor would enjoy the most significant possible latitude of rights over such land, including[11] but not limited to absolute use rights, control rights and transfer rights.[12] The use rights include grazing rights, farming and use of land for forestry.[13] The control rights are the rights to make decisions on how the land should be used.[14] Transfer rights cover the right to alienate or transfer other forms of interest in the land to others.[15]

However, the first possessor theory was criticized as morally wrong because 'most things already do have owners, and if you grab something originally possessed by someone else, you are not a first possessor . . . you have done something

8 Joseph Williams Singer, 'Original Acquisition of Property: From Conquest & Possession to Democracy & Equal Opportunity' (2011) 86 Indiana Law J 763–778. See also Robert A Simons, *When Bad Things Happen to Good Property* (Environmental Law Institute 2006) 31.

9 Richard A Epstein, 'Possession as the Root of Title' (1979) 13 Ga L Rev 1221. See also James E Krier, 'Evolutionary Theory and the Origin of Property Rights' (2009) 95 Cornell L Rev 139.

10 Joseph William Singer, 'Starting Property' (2002) 46 St Louis U LJ 565.

11 Clement C Chigbo, 'The Nature of Land Ownership and the Protection of the Purchaser' (2013) 1(1) J Sustain Dev L Pol 12.

12 Food and Agricultural Organisation, 'FAO Studies on Land Tenure' (2002) <Land Tenure and Rural Development (fao.org)> accessed 16 January 2020.

13 Food and Agricultural Organisation, 'FAO Studies on Land Tenure' (2002) <Land Tenure and Rural Development (fao.org)> accessed 16 January 2020. See also Elin Roos and others, 'Limiting Livestock Production to Pasture and By-products in a Search for Sustainable Diets' (2016) 58 Food Policy 1–13.

14 Elin Roos and others, 'Limiting Livestock Production to Pasture and By-products in a Search for Sustainable Diets' (2016) 58 Food Policy 1–13. See also James Karp and others, *Real Estate Law* (Dearborn Real Estate 2003) 47.

15 Ben O Nwabueze, *Nigerian Land Law* (Oceana Publications 1972) 7, 8. E A Taiwo, *The Nigerian Land Law* (Ababa Press 2011) 10.

wrong'.[16] What is more, the acquisition of land through the first possessor theory was cut short by conquest.[17] Conquest refers to the compulsory acquisition of ownership in a land through the extinction of the rights of the first possessor by force.[18] The acquisition of ownership through conquest is by no means limited to small portions of land.[19] The theory is applicable to the acquisition of territories through imperial colonization.[20] Even in the case of conquest, the ambit of rights exercisable over the land is unlimited.[21]

The emergence of the State has accompanied the imposition of restrictions on ownership to the extent that the concept of absolute ownership is fast diminishing in most jurisdictions.[22] Under the Anglo-American ownership system, there is no concept of absolute ownership, given that emphasis is on possession with restrictions imposed by law.[23] The underlying concept of ownership in such case is that a possessor of land will be deemed to have ownership of it against 'the person who does not have or who cannot rely on a better title'.[24] Another facet of the restrictions is that every act of transfer by the possessor must fall within the existing confines of the law.[25] Under the English System, the Crown is the owner of sub-surface resources within the jurisdiction.[26] Even the exercise of rights arising from the right to possession granted by the Crown must be within limits prescribed by law.[27] In the United States, a governmental authority, or an entity acting under the auspices of a governmental authority, may, in some cases, take property belonging to a private

16 Joseph William Singer, 'How Property Norms Construct the Externalities of Ownership' in Gregory S Alexander and Eduardo M Peñalver (eds), *Property and the Community* (Oxford University Press 2010).

17 Carol M Rose, 'Possession as the Origin of Property' (1985) 52 U Chi L Rev 86.

18 Richard A Epstein, 'Property Rights Claims of Indigenous Populations: The View from the Common Law' (1999) U Tol L Rev 3–5.

19 Dominic Alessio, 'Territorial Acquisitions are among the Landmarks of Our History': The Buying and Leasing of Imperial Territory' (2013) 3(1) IJIKM 74–96.

20 Dominic Alessio, 'Territorial Acquisitions are among the Landmarks of Our History': The Buying and Leasing of Imperial Territory' (2013) 3(1) IJIKM 74–96. See also Blanken Leo J, *Rational Empires: Institutional Incentives and Imperial Expansion* (University of Chicago Press 2012).

21 Walter C Neale, 'Property in Land as Cultural Imperialism: Or, Why Ethnocentric Ideas Won't Work in India and Africa' (1985) 19(4) J Econ Issues 951–958.

22 J H Merryman, 'Ownership and Estate' (1974) 48 Tulane L Rev 916, at 927; cited in S Panesar, *General Principles of Property Law* (Longman 2001) 113. It has been argued that the roman system of ownership is absolute. See Clement C Chigbo, 'The Nature of Land Ownership and the Protection of the Purchaser' (n 10) 12. However, it may be correct to say that it is near absolute given that it does have some restrictions. See Helen Scott, 'Absolute Ownership and Legal Pluralism in Roman Law: Two Arguments' (2011) Acta Juridica 23.

23 David A Thomas, 'Anglo-American Land Law: Diverging Developments from a Shared History: Part III: British and American Real Property Law and Practice – A Contemporary Comparison' (1999) 34(3) Real Prop Prob Trust J 443.

24 Luke Rostill, 'Relative Title and Deemed Ownership in English Personal Property Law' (2015) 35(1) Oxford J Legal Stud 44.

25 H H Rumble, 'Limitations on the Use of Property by Its Owner' (1918) 5(5) Va L Rev 297–315.

26 Clement C Chigbo, 'The Nature of Land Ownership and the Protection of the Purchaser' (n 10) 8.

27 Clement C Chigbo, 'The Nature of Land Ownership and the Protection of the Purchaser' (n 10) 8.

individual or entity through condemnation or eminent domain, albeit with compensation.[28] Similarly, in the United States, as with most other jurisdictions, an owner's absolute rights over land may be restricted or circumscribed for the public good.[29]

In summary, while the modern concept of ownership of real property may not be absolute, it confers certain rights and benefits above most interests. One of them is the superior right to use and control the real property therein subject to existing laws.[30] In the words of Bingham,

> they consist in the availability of legal remedies to the owner or possessor against others who interfere unlawfully with his use and control . . . and in the potential refusal of legal remedies in favor of others against him for his use and control.[31]

2.3 Ownership of Oil and Gas

2.3.1 Introduction

The point has been made that ownership of land confers on the beneficiary some rights over and above most. A tenet of ownership is the right to control and use what is in the land to the exclusion of others.[32] As a result, the right to control and use should ordinarily be applicable to mineral deposits situated in a given land.[33] However, the nature of oil and gas has made it a more complex object of ownership. Oil and gas are by nature fugacious to the extent that they may be plenteous in a particular land in a moment and be scarce in another time.[34] In instances where a land owner drills a well into a reservoir, it may deplete the quantity of oil and gas in a neighbouring well.[35] Accordingly, it is difficult to ascribe the general nature of control and use of the real property to oil and gas.

Some jurists have likened oil and gas to underground percolating water or wild animals, given its migratory nature.[36] However, such analogy was often rejected because while the movement of water was influenced by gravity, the migratory nature of oil was influenced by pressure.[37] It is often human activities that determine the migratory behavior of oil. It was also argued that the perambulating nature of water is not problematic for a land owner because water is naturally replenishable.

28 H E Willis, 'Due Process of Law under the United States Constitution' (1926) 74 U Penn L Rev 331.

29 Denise R Johnson, 'Reflections on the Bundle of Rights' (2012) 32 Vermont L Rev 247, 254.

30 Daniel B Klein and John Robinson, 'Property: A Bundle of Rights? Prologue to the Property Symposium' (2011) 8(3) Econ J Watch 193, 197.

31 Joseph W Bingham, 'The Nature and Importance of Legal Possession' (1915) 13(7) Mich L Rev 535.

32 George Gaines, *Florida Real Estate Principles, Practices and Laws* (Kaplan Publishing 1991) 40.

33 *Kier v. Peterson* (1861) 41 Pa. 357.

34 Bryan Clark, 'Migratory Things on Land: Property Rights and a Law of Capture' (2002) Elec J Comp L 10.

35 Bryan Clark, 'Migratory Things on Land: Property Rights and a Law of Capture' (2002) Elec J Comp L 10.

36 *Peoples Gas Co. v. Tyner* (1892) 131 Ind. 277, 31 N.E. 59; *Dark v. Johnston* (1867) 55 Pa. 164.

37 M K Woodward, 'Ownership of Interests in Oil and Gas' (n 37) 355.

In contrast, oil and gas are finite resources and, as such, an owner who has been disfavored by its migratory nature may be faced with a permanent situation of loss of expected benefits. Some other jurists have termed it 'mineral *ferae*' given that it roams about as the bird and wild beast do. According to a Kentucky court, oil and gas 'may be here today and gone tomorrow', justifying its comparison to wild animals.[38] In the case of *Wood County Petroleum Co. v. West Virginia Transp. Co.*,[39] the migratory nature of oil and gas was the subject of litigation. An owner of land assigned a lease solely for oil mining. In the process of drilling the oil, the lessee also recovered a more considerable amount of gas which he sold off. The owner/lessor sued the lessee for the value of the gas. The court held that since the gas was acquired as a natural consequence of the drilling of the oil, the lessor will not be entitled to damages. The court opined that natural gas shares some semblance to water, and as such, its ownership cannot be fully absolute in its literal sense.[40]

Private ownership of oil and gas can be absolute or qualified. The concept of absolute ownership as used in this context does not in any way connote the primitive concept of real property ownership.[41] In simple terms, an owner of the land also owns the petroleum reserve situated in the latter subject to restrictions imposed by law.[42] Thus, the person can by deed or reservation divest his interest to another or create other subsidiary interests.[43] In contrast, under qualified ownership, an owner does not have any title to the oil and gas situated under his land.[44] The person has only the exclusive right to extract and produce oil within the boundaries of land[45] after which he can become the bona fide owner of the oil and gas produced therein.[46] The various theories of ownership will be examined under the subsequent heading.

2.3.2 *Theories of Ownership*

2.3.2.1 *Absolute Ownership*

The point has already been made that under the absolute ownership theory, petroleum situated in a land also belongs to the owner of the land. Petroleum in situ is treated as running with the land for the purpose of ownership. The implication of the latter is that the owner has the right to explore, produce and dispose petroleum in his land as he deems fit.[47] Under the absolute theory, ownership of oil and gas is a real property interest. In the words of Veasey, 'it is well settled in every jurisdiction

38 *Hammonds v. Central Ky. Natural Gas Co.* (1934) 255 Ky. 685, 688, 75 S.W.2d 204, 205.

39 (1886) 28 W. Va. 210.

40 (1886) 28 W. Va. 210.

41 J R S Forbes and Andrew G Lang, *Australian Mining and Petroleum Laws* (Butterworths 1987) 27.

42 J H Laycraft and Ivan L Head, 'Theories of Ownership of Oil and Gas' (1953) 31 Can B Rev 382.

43 J H Laycraft and Ivan L Head, 'Theories of Ownership of Oil and Gas' (1953) 31 Can B Rev 382. For more commentaries, see Rufus S Garrett, 'Effect of Drilling Regulation upon the Law of Capture' (1950) 4 Sw LJ 469.

44 M K Woodward, 'Ownership of Interests in Oil and Gas' (n 37) 359.

45 *Barker v. Campbell-Ratcliff Land Co.* (1917) 64 Okla. 249, 167 P. 468.

46 *Barker v. Campbell-Ratcliff Land Co.* (1917) 64 Okla. 249, 167 P. 468.

47 Damilola S Olawuyi, *Extractives Industry Law in Africa* (Springer 2018) 87–107.

that oil and gas in place are minerals, and as such they are part of the realty'.[48] However, once the oil and gas is extracted from the land, it becomes personal property.[49]

The theory of absolute ownership of oil is the position in some parts of United States[50] and the common law position in England before the Petroleum Act 1934.[51] In most of the United States, the oil and gas beneath a land parcel belongs to the private owner.[52] Previously, all oil and gas beneath a given land in Scotland and England remains the property of the owner under the common law principle of *solum a caelo usque ad centrum.*[53] The principle simply means that whoever owns the land surface owns the sky and down to the depths of the earth. However, the Petroleum Act of 1934 reversed the common law position by introducing a domanial regime, where ownership of petroleum in its natural condition in strata in United Kingdom is vested in the Crown.[54] The domanial regime is currently the most typical type of ownership of petroleum in the world with the exception of the United States and Canada.[55]

An owner under the domanial and non-domanial regimes can divest their title in petroleum by creating other interests including leaseholds, mineral rights and royalty interests.[56] Under a leasehold arrangement, a land owner (lessor) will divest their exclusive right to explore and produce oil on their land to another called a lessee for a stipulated period of time.[57] Notably, an oil and gas lease in this context is functionally, and in some jurisdictions, actually, a determinable fee in the hydrocarbons underlying the land covered by the lease.[58] 'A mineral interest is created through a grant when a land owner conveys the mineral interest to another person through an instrument often referred to as a mineral deed'.[59] Such mineral interest may be full or partial. A royalty interest confers on the beneficiary an interest in the oil and gas removed from the land but generally not the right to explore and produce oil in the land.[60]

48 James A Veasey, 'Law of Oil and Gas' (1920) 18(6) Mich L Rev 459.

49 James A Veasey, 'Law of Oil and Gas' (1920) 18(6) Mich L Rev 459.

50 W L Summers, 'Property in Oil and Gas' (1915) Yale LJ 174, 174, 175. <PROPERTY IN OIL AND GAS (yale.edu)> accessed 20 February 2021.

51 Bryan Clark, 'Migratory Things on Land: Property Rights and a Law of Capture' (2002) 6(3) EJCL 1. <Article: Migratory Things on Land, vol. 6.3 (ejcl.org)> accessed 20 February 2021.

52 J S Adam, 'The Rights of a Land Owner to Oil and Gas in the Land' (1915) 63(6) U Penn L Rev 471.

53 Bryan Clark, 'Migratory Things on Land: Property Rights and a Law of Capture' (n 54).

54 The Petroleum Production Act 1934 (24 & 25 Geo.5c. 36) S.1(1).

55 Damilola S Olawuyi, *Extractives Industry Law in Africa* (n 50) 89.

56 M K Woodward, 'Ownership of Interests in Oil and Gas' (n 37) 367.

57 M K Woodward, 'Ownership of Interests in Oil and Gas' (n 37) 367. For more commentaries on oil and gas lease, see Earl A Brown, 'Elemental Principles of the Modern Oil and Gas Lease' (1955) 17(5) Mont L Rev 39–63.

58 Earl A Brown, 'Elemental Principles of the Modern Oil and Gas Lease' (1955) 17(5) Mont L Rev 39–63.

59 Dan Lefort and others, 'Legal Characteristics of the US Oil and Gas Interest' (2013) <Article-201308ShaleInvestmentEnglishtranslation.pdf (pillsburylaw.com)> accessed 20 February 2021.

60 Dan Lefort and others, 'Legal Characteristics of the US Oil and Gas Interest' (2013) <Article-201308ShaleInvestmentEnglishtranslation.pdf (pillsburylaw.com)> accessed 20 February 2021.

Notably, a State has near absolute ownership over the petroleum resources that is in situ within its territorial waters.[61] Article 2 of the United Nations Convention on the Law of the Sea (UNCLOS) defines the sovereignty of a coastal State over its territorial sea to stretch to its seabed and subsoil. Implicit in the sovereignty of the coastal State is ownership rights over its petroleum resources. In the words of Pappa,

> The principle of State ownership over natural resources emerges from the States' territorial sovereignty and is widely recognized in international community through numerous resolutions of the United Nations. In particular, it is acknowledged that all States have the 'inalienable right' to freely explore, develop, and dispose of their natural wealth in the name of their national development and for the well-being of their people. The so-called principle of permanent sovereignty over natural resources applies to petroleum and minerals situated in a State's land and Territorial Sea (TS) including the seabed and subsoil below that belt to an unlimited depth.[62]

An incidence of this ownership is the right to explore, develop and dispose of it in their national interest.[63] States can also confer the latter right to other parties, whether private or public entities including the grant of various concessionaires.[64] Like the modern idea of absolute ownership, State sovereignty over petroleum resources in its territorial waters is subject to international law.[65] For instance, the right of ownership enjoyed by a State over its territorial sea should not prejudice the right of innocent passage enjoyed by the ships of other States.[66]

2.3.2.2 Qualified Ownership

The theory of qualified ownership implies that the title to the petroleum in strata cannot be vested in the land owner until it is 'captured and reduced into possession'.[67] What the land owner has is the right to exploit and possess the petroleum in strata.[68]

61 Marianthi Pappa, 'Private Oil Companies Operating in Contested Waters and International Law of the Sea: A Peculiar Relationship' (2018) 16(1) Oil Gas Energy Law Intell 2. The territorial waters of a state for this purpose include its seabed, subsoil and airspace. See Ian Brownlie, *Principles of Public International Law* (7th edn, Oxford University Press 2008) 105.

62 Marianthi Pappa, 'Private Oil Companies Operating in Contested Waters and International Law of the Sea: A Peculiar Relationship' (2018) 16(1) Oil Gas Energy Law Intell 2. The territorial waters of a state for this purpose include its seabed, subsoil and airspace. See Ian Brownlie, *Principles of Public International Law* (7th edn, Oxford University Press 2008) 105.

63 Marianthi Pappa, 'Private Oil Companies Operating in Contested Waters and International Law of the Sea: A Peculiar Relationship' (n 64) 2.

64 The United Nations Convention on the Law of the Sea 1982 (n 65) Art 2(3).

65 The United Nations Convention on the Law of the Sea 1982 (n 65) Art 2(3).

66 The United Nations Convention on the Law of the Sea 1982 (n 65), Art 17.

67 Theodore Okonkwo, 'Ownership and Control of Natural Resources under the Nigerian Constitution 1999 and Its Implications for Environmental Law and Practice' (2017) 6(1) Intern L Res 164.

68 Theodore Okonkwo, 'Ownership and Control of Natural Resources under the Nigerian Constitution 1999 and Its Implications for Environmental Law and Practice' (2017) 6(1) Intern L Res 164.

Clarke has likened the qualified ownership as 'analogous with a profit *à prendre* under English common law or a servitude right to minerals under Scots law'.[69] In the words of Woodward,

> under this theory the owner of the land can have no 'title' to the oil and gas in place, but he does have the exclusive right to drill and produce from his own tract and to become the owner of the product when it is brought up to the surface.[70]

The principles of qualified ownership have been described in the case of *Rich v. Donaghey*[71] as thus:

> no absolute right or title to the oil or gas which might permeate the strata underlying the surface of their land, as in the case of coal or other solid minerals fixed in, and forming part of, the soil itself. But with respect to such oil and gas, they had certain rights designated by the same courts as a qualified ownership thereof, but which may be more accurately stated as exclusive right, subject to legislative control against waste and the like, to erect structures on the surface of their land, and explore thereof by drilling wells through the underlying strata, and *to take therefrom and reduce to possession, and thus acquire absolute title as personal property to such as might be found* and obtained thereby. This right is the proper subject of sale and may be granted or reserved.

The implication of the above is that an instrument of grant and reservation from a surface land owner under the qualified theory can only confer on the beneficiary the right to enter into the land, search for, exploit and possess and own the petroleum contained in the strata.[72]

The theory of qualified ownership captures the type of sovereign rights enjoyed by a State over the petroleum resources in its exclusive economic zone (EEZ) and continental shelf. With respect to the EEZ, the UNCLOS provides that sovereign rights of the State is 'for the purpose of exploring and exploiting, conserving and managing the natural resources'.[73] In similar vein, it provides that a State shall exercise sovereign rights over its natural resources including petroleum for the purpose of exploring and exploiting it.[74] While the latter provisions does not translate to the concept of near absolute ownership, it implies that in the event that a concerned State does not exercise the mentioned rights, another cannot without its express consent.[75] Just as stated, qualified ownership implies an exclusive right to explore and exploit oil. The latter captures the rights of a State over its petroleum

69 Bryan Clark, 'Migratory Things on Land: Property Rights and a Law of Capture' (n 54) 10.
70 M K Woodward, 'Ownership of Interests in Oil and Gas' (n 37) 359.
71 (1918) Okla. S.C.; 3 A.L.R. 352 at 355.
72 M K Woodward, 'Ownership of Interests in Oil and Gas' (n 37).
73 The United Nations Convention on the Law of the Sea 1982 (n 65) Art 56.
74 The United Nations Convention on the Law of the Sea 1982 (n 65), Art 77(1).
75 The United Nations Convention on the Law of the Sea 1982 (n 65), Art 77(2).

resources in its EEZ and continental shelf. The mentioned position resonates with that of Pappa, who opined that 'the States' right over those resources is not of full ownership but of a lesser – yet proprietary nature'.[76]

2.3.2.3 The Rule of Capture

The point has been made that ownership confers the right to exploit for and possess the petroleum situated below the land in question.[77] However, situations may arise where a private land owner or a lessee in the case of domanial regime exercise of his right to exploit petroleum in his land is indirectly affecting the equivalent right of adjourning land owners.[78] The latter mentioned is covered by the rule of capture.[79] Simply put,

> the traditional rule of capture in petroleum law provides that in the event A drills a well on his own land and produces oil or gas in a manner consistent with good industry practice, then if some of that oil or gas originates from under neighbouring lands, A becomes the owner of the oil or gas so produced and is not liable to his or her neighbour.[80]

The rule of capture is essentially a principle of non-liability for drainage. It allows a property owner or lessee to exploit and take as much petroleum as they can from their land without any regard for the equivalent right of adjourning property land owners.[81] The rule was initially applicable to groundwater but has become extended to percolating objects whose characteristics are peculiar and defies the ordinary property law principles.[82] Given the mentioned characteristics of petroleum as a percolating object, it is not surprising that the rule of capture is applicable to it in some jurisdictions. The rule is to the effect that title to petroleum will become legally vested in the owner of the land where they are recovered, regardless of their migration from the land of an adjourning neighbor.[83]

The rule of capture has become the bedrock of property rights as it pertains to petroleum in jurisdictions such as United States and Canada. It has become

76 Marianthi Pappa, 'Private Oil Companies Operating in Contested Waters and International Law of the Sea: A Peculiar Relationship' (n 64) 4.

77 J H Laycraft and Ivan L Head, 'Theories of Ownership of Oil and Gas' (1953) 31 Can B Rev 382.

78 David Edward Pierce, 'Coordinated Reservoir Development – An Alternative to the Rule of Capture for the Ownership and Development of Oil and Gas' (1983) 4 J Energy L Pol'y 1, 27.

79 Douglas G Caroom and Susan M Maxwell, 'The Rule of Capture – "*If It Ain't Broke. . .*"' (2006) 1 <Microsoft Word – 4 CH Caroom rme 6.doc (texas.gov)> accessed 11 March 2021.

80 Cecilia A Low, 'The Rule of Capture: Its Current Status and Some Issues to Consider' (2009) 46(3) Alberta L Rev 799, 800.

81 Joseph P Tomain, 'The Rule of Capture: Government and the Oil Industry' (1984) Faculty Articles and Other Publications, Paper 250, 228.

82 Matthew W Wagner and Urs P Krueter, 'Groundwater Supply in Texas: Private Land Considerations in a Rule-of-Capture State' (2003) 17(4) Soc Nat Res 349–357.

83 R Hardwicke, 'The Rule of Capture and its Implications as Applied to Oil and Gas' (1935) 13 Texas L Rev 391 at 393.

judicially recognised since 1886 in the case of *Wood County Petroleum Co. v. West Virginia Transp. Co.*[84] that the rule of capture is the basis of property rights in petroleum in the United States. The point was previously made that the United States operates a non-domanial regime where ownership of petroleum is vested in private property owners. Accordingly, private property owners may, and generally do, divide their interests in real property into many individual holdings.[85] Holders of petroleum rights are incentivized by the rule of capture to be the first to drill and produce, depleting the oil reserve under the land of other leaseholders.[86] The rule enables such the exercise of rights over petroleum in a manner that interferes with the equivalent right of a neighbour, without any legal liability.[87] It is also recognized as applicable to the ownership of petroleum in Canada. In the words of Low, 'the proposition that the rule applies in the oil and gas context in Canada has been widely accepted by the courts as well as regulators'.[88] Summarizing the rule of capture in the Canadian context, in the case of *Borys v. C.P.R.*,[89] the Privy Council states:

> The petroleum, in so far as is material to the present case, is found in a bed of porous rock underlying the plaintiff's land and the surrounding property, which contains at the bottom water, then the petroleum and on top a layer of gas. . . . The substances are fugacious and are not stable within the container although they cannot escape from it. If any of the three substances is withdrawn from a portion of the property which does not belong to the appellant but lies within the same container and any oil or gas situated in his property thereby filters from it to the surrounding lands, admittedly he has no remedy. So, also, if any substance is withdrawn from his property, thereby causing any fugacious matter to enter his land, the surrounding owners have no remedy against him. The only safeguard is to be the first to get to work, in which case, those who make the recovery become the owners of the material which they withdraw from any well which is situated on their property or from which they have the authority to draw.[90]

The rule of capture has been argued as historically underpinning the rapid development of the United States' petroleum industry and, the consequential low petroleum

84 (1886) 28 W. Va. 10. See also *Westmoreland & Cambria Natural Gas Co. v. De Witt* (1889) 130 Pa. 235 18 A. 724.

85 Gary D Libecap and James L Smith, 'The Economic Evolution of Petroleum Property Rights in the United States' (2002) 31(2) J Legal Stud S589.

86 Terence Daintith, 'The Rule of Capture: The Least Worst Property Rule for Oil and Gas' in Aileen McHarg and others (eds) *Property and the Law in Energy and Natural Resources* (Oxford University Press 2010) 140.

87 Terence Daintith, 'The Rule of Capture: The Least Worst Property Rule for Oil and Gas' in Aileen McHarg and others (eds) *Property and the Law in Energy and Natural Resources* (Oxford University Press 2010) 140.

88 Cecilia Low, 'The Rule of Capture: Its Current Status and Some Issues to Consider' (2009) 46(3) Alberta L Rev 800.

89 [1953] 2 D.L.R. 65 (P.C.) [Borys].

90 [1953] 2 D.L.R. 65 (P.C.) [Borys], at pp. 67, 68.

prices.[91] The reason for the latter is that the rule engenders competitive drilling, which means more production from different competing quarters.[92] The availability of petroleum from different competitive quarters translated to cheaper petroleum prices in the United States. In the words of Frankel, 'it may well be that these somewhat primitive methods were exactly what was required to make the young industry, in the first instance, aggressive and, in due course, great'.[93]

Regardless of the mentioned above benefit, the rule has attracted heavy criticism for 'over drilling and dissipation of the reservoir's natural energy'.[94] As stated, the rule of capture engineered competitive drilling from several leaseholders who were in a haste to be the first to drill as much petroleum as possible from their own property.[95] The latter led to excessive drilling which reduced the well pressure leading to low productivity.[96] What is more, the excessive drilling did not accommodate sustainable practices; rather it led to inefficient practices that wasted petroleum resources.[97] In the words of Budig, 'the rule of capture resulted in the loss of millions of dollars due to inefficient and unnecessary drilling'.[98]

Given the downsides of the rule, it is becoming quite unpopular in most jurisdictions. It is important to mention that the rule of capture is based in common law.[99] Thus, one would expect it to be widely applicable in the United Kingdom and other common law jurisdictions. Unfortunately, most common law jurisdictions have stifled the rule at its very root by embracing a domanial regime where ownership of petroleum resources is vested in the State.[100] As a corollary, the State exercises its rights of ownership in a manner that does not allow the rule of capture to thrive.[101] This can be seen in preventive legislation and clauses, some of which unify the property rights in a manner that capture will not be feasible. Similar to the United Kingdom's position, the Petroleum Act of Nigeria 2004 provides that the ownership of petroleum in the land and maritime zones of the State are vested in the latter.[102] Thus, the State can create various lease holdings from its ownership in the form of licenses and, recently production sharing

91 Lea VanderVelde, 'The Role of Captives in the Rule of Capture' (2005) University of Iowa Legal Studies Research Paper Number 05–23, 3.

92 Terence Daintith, 'The Rule of Capture: The Least Worst Property Rule for Oil and Gas' (n 89) 155.

93 P H Frankel, *Essentials of Petroleum: A Key to Oil Economics* (Francass and Co 2005) 19.

94 Bruce M Kramer and Owen L Anderson, 'The Rule of Capture: An Oil and Gas Perspective' (2005) 35 Environ Law 899, 902.

95 Danielle Beggs and John Stockdale, *Unitisation and Unitisation Agreements in Oil and Gas: A Practical Handbook* (Geoffrey Picton-Turbervill 2014) 81.

96 Danielle Beggs and John Stockdale, *Unitisation and Unitisation Agreements in Oil and Gas: A Practical Handbook* (Geoffrey Picton-Turbervill 2014) 81.

97 Jack Budig, 'The Co-Tenancy Act and the Modernization of West Virginia's Oil and Gas Law' (2019) 122(2) W Va L Rev 661.

98 Jack Budig, 'The Co-Tenancy Act and the Modernization of West Virginia's Oil and Gas Law' (2019) 122(2) W Va L Rev 661.

99 Ana Boswell Schepens, 'Prospecting for Oil at the Courthouse: Recovery for Drainage Caused by Secondary Recovery Operations' (1999) 50(2) Alabama L Rev 606.

100 Damilola S Olawuyi, *Extractives Industry Law in Africa* (n 50) 89.

101 Terence Daintith, 'The Rule of Capture: The Least Worst Property Rule for Oil and Gas' (n 89) 144.

102 The Petroleum Act 2004, Cap P.10 (NG) s.1(1)(2).

agreements.[103] In Trinidad and Tobago, ownership of petroleum resources is vested in the State and exercisable by the president.[104] The president[105] has the power to create leaseholds through the granting of various forms of licenses.[106] In the next section, the various interests created by the State pursuant to their right of ownership of petroleum will be discussed.

2.4 Government Approvals

2.4.1 Introduction

The point has been made that most jurisdictions favour the domanial system of ownership because it allows the State to retain 'absolute control and sovereign rights' over petroleum.[107] The implication is that the State has the right to exploit, explore and use petroleum resources beneath its land, land covered by water, and maritime areas either directly or through private parties.[108] The State's choice to confer its right of ownership of petroleum on a private party may be informed by the idea of controlling and achieving energy security.[109] It might also be the case that the State does not have the risk capital and technical capacity to make the most of its right of ownership of petroleum in situ.[110] The legal instruments by which the State confers the right to explore and explore petroleum on a private party include licenses, petroleum sharing agreements and risk service contracts.[111]

2.4.2 License

In simple terms, a license refers to an authorization to do a thing which ordinarily would have been unlawful.[112] In this context, 'a license (referred to in some

103 Eghosa Osa Ekhator, 'Public Regulation of the Oil and Gas Industry in Nigeria: An Evaluation' (2016) 12(1) Ann Survey Int Comp Law 43, 58.

104 The Petroleum Act of Trinidad and Tobago 2010, Cap 10 (T & T) s.3.

105 Section 6(3) of the Petroleum Act of Trinidad and Tobago gave the Minister for Petroleum the powers to create and grant various forms of licenses.

106 Eduardo G Pereira and others, 'Addressing Residual Liability and Insolvency in Disused Oil and Gas Infrastructure Left in Place: The Cases of Brazil, Nigeria, and Trinidad and Tobago' (2020) 11(2) J Sustain Dev Law Policy 351.

107 Damilola S Olawuyi, *Extractives Industry Law in Africa* (n 50) 90.

108 Damilola S Olawuyi, *Extractives Industry Law in Africa* (n 50) 90. See also Yinka Omorogbe and Peter Oniemola, 'Property Rights in Oil and Gas under Dominial Regime' in A McHarg and others (eds) *Property and the Law in Energy and Natural Resources* (Oxford University Press 2010) 115.

109 Jubilee Easo, 'Licenses, Concessions, Production Sharing Agreements and Service Contracts' in Geoffrey Picton-Turbervill (ed), *Oil and Gas: A Practical Handbook* (Globe Law and Business 2009) 27.

110 Jubilee Easo, 'Licenses, Concessions, Production Sharing Agreements and Service Contracts' in Geoffrey Picton-Turbervill (ed), *Oil and Gas: A Practical Handbook* (Globe Law and Business 2009) 27.

111 Taiwo Adebola Ogunleye, 'A Legal Analysis of Production Sharing Contract Arrangements in the Nigerian Petroleum Industry' (2015) 5(8) J Energ Technol Policy 1–6.

112 Greg Gordon, 'Petroleum Licensing' in Greg Gordon and others (eds), *Oil and Gas Law-Current Practice and Emerging Trends* (2nd edn, Dundee University Press 2011) 67–69.

countries as a lease) is essentially a permission granted by a State to an IOC (international oil company) to exploit petroleum in a certain geographical area in return for a fee or a royalty'.[113] The power of the State to grant a license emanates from its right of ownership over the petroleum within its jurisdiction.[114] The interest conferred through the license is not the entirety of the State's interest because the latter retains the ownership of the petroleum in situ.[115] The State also has the right to re-license the same acreage upon the expiration of the licensing period. On the other hand, a license implies that the ownership of the extracted petroleum is transferred to the licensee at the well head. Also implicit in most petroleum licenses (especially production) is that the State is precluded from issuing further licenses to other parties with respect to the same geographical area.[116] In the words of Taverne, 'so long as the license is valid, no person other than the licensee itself is authorised to exercise the rights conferred'.[117]

Licenses are used to express government approvals in the context of the right to explore and exploit petroleum in situ. In the United Kingdom, while the Crown has all rights to petroleum, the authority to grant licenses for petroleum activities is exercised by the Oil and Gas Authority (OGA).[118] The OGA has the power to grant production and exploration licenses which may be seaward or landward.[119] The exploration license is non-exclusive in nature and enables the licensee to search for petroleum in a particular area.[120] The production license is an exclusive license granted for the searching and getting of petroleum situated in the seaward or landward area.[121] The United Kingdom's model of license is a hybrid model being both

113 Jubilee Easo, 'Licenses, Concessions, Production Sharing Agreements and Service Contracts' (n 112) 29.
Jubilee Easo, 'Licenses, Concessions, Production Sharing Agreements and Service Contracts' (n 112) 29.

114 Jubilee Easo, 'Licenses, Concessions, Production Sharing Agreements and Service Contracts' (n 112) 29.

115 Bernard G Taverne, *Petroleum, Industry and Governments: A Study of the Involvement of Industry and Governments in Exploring for and Producing Petroleum* (3rd edn, Wolters Kluwer 2013) para 5.2.1.

116 Bernard G Taverne, *Petroleum, Industry and Governments: A Study of the Involvement of Industry and Governments in Exploring for and Producing Petroleum* (3rd edn, Wolters Kluwer 2013) para 5.2.1.

117 Bernard G Taverne, *Petroleum, Industry and Governments: A Study of the Involvement of Industry and Governments in Exploring for and Producing Petroleum* (3rd edn, Wolters Kluwer 2013) para 5.2.1.

118 OGA, 'Licensing Regime' (2020) <Oil and Gas Authority: Licensing regime – Regulatory framework (ogauthority.co.uk)> accessed 27 March 2021. See also Olusola Joshua Olujobi, 'Analysis of the Legal Framework Governing Gas Flaring in Nigeria's Upstream Petroleum Sector and the Need for Overhauling' (2020) 9 Soc Sci 132, 142.

119 Yanal Abul Failat, 'Licensing Regime: United Kingdom' in Eduardo G Pereira and Henrik Bjørnebye (eds), *Regulating Offshore Petroleum Resources: The British and Norwegian Models* (Edward Elgar 2019) 214.

120 Greg Gordon, 'Petroleum Licensing' (n 105) 88.

121 Greg Gordon, 'Petroleum Licensing' (n 105) 88.

a contractual[122] and regulatory instrument[123] normally awarded for value called royalties and rental. The royalties and/or rentals are normally extracted through a taxation regime.[124] In Norway, the Ministry of Petroleum and Energy has the authority to issue licenses.[125] Similar to the practice in the United Kingdom, the Ministry of Petroleum can award survey[126] and production licenses which allows petroleum activities to be carried for a period of ten years at first instance with chances of extension for another 30 years.[127] The license is normally used in jurisdictions that can effectively use their tax regimes to make the most revenue from their petroleum resources.[128]

2.4.3 Production Sharing Agreements

Another vehicle through which the State confers on a private party, the right to explore and exploit petroleum in situ is the production sharing agreement (PSA). The PSA is a contractual instrument between a host government and an international oil company (IOC) or 'contractor', where the latter will undertake the exploration and exploitation of petroleum in exchange for a share in the latter.[129] The contractor is normally granted the exclusive rights to explore and exploit petroleum within the given field.[130] In turn, the contractor assumes all the risks of the

122 It is a contractual instrument given that it is an agreement made between the government represented by the Secretary of State on one hand and, the companies who are the licensees. See T Daintith, G Willoughby and A Hill, *United Kingdom Oil and Gas Law* (3rd edn 2000) para 1–344 <https://www.sweetandmaxwell.co.uk/Product/Energy-Law/United-Kingdom-Oil-and-Gas-Law/Looseleaf/30792605>.

123 Some terms of the license evidence that it is also a regulatory instrument. For instance, the Secretary of State reserves the right to revoke the license in event of the breach of the terms of the license. Moreover, some portion of the license is excluded from the arbitration clause with the Secretary having the sole rights to determine the interpretation of such terms. See Greg W Gordon, 'Production Licensing on the UK Continental Shelf: Ministerial Powers and Controls' (2015) 4(1) LSU J Energy L Res 75, 77.

124 John Paterson, 'Production Sharing Agreements in Africa: Sovereignty and Relationality' (2019) University of Aberdeen, Center for Energy Working Paper 001/19, 5.

125 Jubilee Easo, 'Licenses, Concessions, Production Sharing Agreements and Service Contracts' (n 112) 31.

126 The Petroleum Act 29, 1996 No. 72 relating to Petroleum Activities (Norway) s. 2–1. See Tina Hunter, 'The Offshore Petroleum Regulatory Frameworks of Australia and Norway' (2010) 8(4) Oil Gas Energy Law Intell 11.

127 The Petroleum Act 29, 1996 No. 72 relating to Petroleum Activities (Norway) s. 2–1. See Tina Hunter, 'The Offshore Petroleum Regulatory Frameworks of Australia and Norway' (2010) 8(4) Oil Gas Energy Law Intell 11, s. 3–3.

128 Vincent P Wangelow, 'Petroleum Licensing in the European Union: The Allocation of E&P Rights in Denmark' (2018) 11(2) J World Energy Law B 145.

129 Central Bank of Russia, 'Production Sharing Agreements' (2011) <Production Sharing Agreements: Paper by the Central Bank of Russia (BOPCOM-11/17) – Twenty-Fourth Meeting of the IMF Committee on Balance of Payments Statistics, Moscow, Russia, 24–26 October 2011> accessed 28 March 2021.

130 Central Bank of Russia, 'Production Sharing Agreements' (2011) <Production Sharing Agreements: Paper by the Central Bank of Russia (BOPCOM-11/17) – Twenty-Fourth Meeting of the IMF Committee on Balance of Payments Statistics, Moscow, Russia, 24–26 October 2011> accessed 28 March 2021.

exploration and production activities.[131] Unlike the license, the contractor does not have the title to the petroleum at the well head.[132] However, the contractor is only entitled to the portion of oil allotted to them under the PSA as cost oil and profit oil, respectively.[133] The distinction between license and PSA lies in the way through which the State derives revenue from such petroleum activities.[134] In the case of license, the State derives revenue through the taxation of the profits of the IOC.[135] For the PSA, 'the State derives value principally by receiving a share of the oil and gas produced (or the equivalent in cash where the operator is required to dispose of the hydrocarbons on the State's behalf)'.[136]

The PSA is fast growing in popularity as a vehicle for conveying government approval for the exploration and exploitation of petroleum in situ especially in developing countries. In sub-Saharan Africa, the PSA is the predominant method for conveying the right to explore and exploit petroleum.[137] Some developing countries outside sub-Saharan Africa, like Indonesia and Malaysia, also use PSAs.[138] In some instances like Azerbaijan, the PSA is first a contractual document and is subsequently given the status of legislation through State approval.[139] Arguably, the benefit of the latter is that it affords the terms of the PSA better protection against subsequent changes in law compared to the situation where the PSA takes effect merely as a contract.[140] In brief, the preference for PSAs has been attributed to its feature of allowing the State to have greater control over the petroleum resources extracted in comparison to the licensing model.[141]

2.4.4 Risk Service Contracts

The risk service contract is an arrangement under which an IOC agrees for a valuable consideration to provide a host State with services or technical information for exploration and/or development.[142] In the contract, the ownership of the petroleum

131 Sola Adepetun, 'Production Sharing Contracts: The Nigerian Experience' (1995) 13(1) J Energy Nat Res Law 21.
132 S M Lavlinskii, 'Techniques of Developing the Economic Clauses of a Production Sharing Agreement for Oil and Gas Projects' (2007) 18(1) Stud Russ Econ Develop 68.
133 S M Lavlinskii, 'Techniques of Developing the Economic Clauses of a Production Sharing Agreement for Oil and Gas Projects' (2007) 18(1) Stud Russ Econ Develop 68.
134 John Paterson, 'Production Sharing Agreements in Africa: Sovereignty and Relationality' (n 127) 5.
135 John Paterson, 'Production Sharing Agreements in Africa: Sovereignty and Relationality' (n 127) 5.
136 John Paterson, 'Production Sharing Agreements in Africa: Sovereignty and Relationality' (n 127) 5.
137 John Paterson, 'Production Sharing Agreements in Africa: Sovereignty and Relationality' (n 127) 5.
138 Sani Saidu, 'A Comparative Analysis of Production Sharing Contracts of Selected Developing Countries: Nigeria, Indonesia, Malaysia and Equatorial Guinea' (2014) 2(2) J Financ Account 34.
139 Nurlan Mustafayev, 'Production-Sharing Agreements in the Petroleum Industry of Azerbaijan' (2015) 8(4) J World Energy Law B 362.
140 Nurlan Mustafayev, 'Production-Sharing Agreements in the Petroleum Industry of Azerbaijan' (2015) 8(4) J World Energy Law B 362.
141 Nurlan Mustafayev, 'Production-Sharing Agreements in the Petroleum Industry of Azerbaijan' (2015) 8(4) J World Energy Law B 362.
142 Abbas Ghandi and C Y Cynthia Lin, 'Oil and Gas Service Contracts Around the World: A Review', 3 (2014) <service_contracts_review_paper.pdf (cornell.edu)> accessed 11 April 2021.

in situ or extracted is vested in the State while the IOC (contractor) assumes the technical and financial risk for petroleum exploration and development.[143] Such compensation may be monetary in form usually from petroleum proceeds realized by the State.[144] It may be in the form of a percentage share in the market value of the petroleum produced within a specified period of time.[145] In the latter instance, the share of petroleum may be provided in kind similar to the terms of a PSA.[146] In other cases, the contractor acts as an agent of the State for marketing the petroleum recovered, with the authorization to take some of the proceeds from the oil sales as their compensation for services rendered.[147] In a pure service risk contract, the petroleum host State assumes all the risk associated with the petroleum exploration and development.[148] The IOC is merely contracted to perform specified services in exchange for a fee.[149] In all instances, the compensation of the contractor is contingent on the recovery of commercial quantities of petroleum.

The risk service contract is preferred by some States in comparison to other arrangements because the State in all instances retains title to ownership of petroleum. It is normally adopted by States who perceive title to petroleum as being inherent to their sovereignty.[150] For instance, the Iranian Constitution prohibits the granting of licenses or ownership interest in petroleum on private companies.[151] Thus, it is the State through the national oil company that is the holder of every concession.[152] The Iranian government contracts an IOC to assume the financial and technical risk of the petroleum exploration and development in exchange for remuneration.[153] Some other countries like Iraq, Saudi Arabia, Ecuador, Bolivia and Mexico are using one variant of service risk contract or another in order to explore and develop their petroleum resources.[154] Venezuela and Kuwait signed their first batch of service risk contracts in 1991 and 1992 respectively.[155]

143 Ernest E Smith, 'From Concession to Service Contract' (1992) 27(4) Tulsa L Rev 493, 519.
144 Ernest E Smith, 'From Concession to Service Contract' (1992) 27(4) Tulsa L Rev 493, 519.
145 Jubilee Easo, 'Licenses, Concessions, Production Sharing Agreements and Service Contracts' (n 112) 38.
146 Jubilee Easo, 'Licenses, Concessions, Production Sharing Agreements and Service Contracts' (n 112) 38.
147 Jubilee Easo, 'Licenses, Concessions, Production Sharing Agreements and Service Contracts' (n 112) 38.
148 Alejandro Ibarra Yúnez and Fidel Flores Chapa, 'Oil Risk Contracts, Business Conduct and Performance Patterns: Data Panel Analysis' (2017) 62 Contaduría y Administración 1538, 1542.
149 Alejandro Ibarra Yúnez and Fidel Flores Chapa, 'Oil Risk Contracts, Business Conduct and Performance Patterns: Data Panel Analysis' (2017) 62 Contaduría y Administración 1538, 1542.
150 Ernest E Smith, 'From Concession to Service Contract' (n 146) 519.
151 The Constitution of the Islamic Republic of Iran 1979, Art 44.
152 The Constitution of the Islamic Republic of Iran 1979, Art 44.
153 Mahdi Haddadi, 'The Nature of Iranian Petroleum Contracts in Upstream Section' (2015) 44 Int Let Soc Human Sci 45–52.
154 Abbas Ghandi and C Y Cynthia Lin, 'Oil and Gas Service Contracts Around the World: A Review', 3 (2014) <service_contracts_review_paper.pdf (cornell.edu)> accessed 11 April 2021.
155 Abbas Ghandi and C Y Cynthia Lin, 'Oil and Gas Service Contracts Around the World: A Review', 3 (2014) <service_contracts_review_paper.pdf (cornell.edu)> accessed 11 April 2021. See also

2.5 Conclusion

It has been established that petroleum is fugacious in nature. As such, they cannot be subject to the general principles of ownership applicable to real property. There are two theories of ownership applicable to petroleum: absolute and qualified ownership. Under the absolute ownership theory, petroleum in situ is treated as same with the land for the purpose of ownership. Thus, the owner of a land possesses the ownership and control of the petroleum in situ. The theory of absolute ownership is said to be widely applicable in some US states. It was explained that the qualified ownership theory is widely applicable to the ownership of petroleum resources in most jurisdiction. Under it, the ownership of petroleum resources in situ is not vested in the land owner until it is extracted and reduced to possession.

The rule of capture was discussed as applicable in some parts of the world which operate a non-domanial ownership regime. The rule allows a land owner to drill and produce oil in his land in a manner that can deplete that of his neighbour without incurring any legal liability. It was argued that the rule introduces competition which may contribute to the sporadic development of the petroleum industry. Regardless, it also leads to waste and low productivity occasioned by competitive drilling. In domanial regimes, the various methods through which the government involves private party to explore and develop petroleum in their land were analysed. The instruments were identified as licenses, production sharing agreements and risk service contracts. It was stated that the license which minimizes State participation in exploration and development is used where the State has a sturdy tax regime to extract the most resources from petroleum activities, while production sharing agreements and risk service contracts are used by States with a greater need or desire to remain in ownership and control of their petroleum.

Mahdi Nooruldeen M Nory, 'International Contracts in Developing Countries about Oil and Gas: For Instance, Kurdistan and Kuwait' (2017) 61 J Law Policy Global 83.

3 Unitisation and Unit Operating Agreements

Eduardo G. Pereira, Marianthi Pappa, and Damilola S. Olawuyi

3.1 Introduction

In the preceding chapter, the rule of capture was extensively discussed. As Daintith puts it,

> the legal rule of non-liability for (a) causing oil and gas to migrate across property lines and (b) producing oil or gas which was originally in place under the land of another, so as long as the producing well does not trespass.[1]

While the rule was said to precipitate the rapid development of the US petroleum industry, it also led to competitive drilling and waste,[2] as well as unnecessary and avoidable duplication of expenditure.[3] MacLeod criticises the rule as leading to protracted court proceedings, an experience which is not beneficial to concerned land owners.[4] Some of the protracted cases involving the rule of capture include *Kelly v. Ohio Oil*[5] and *Barnard v. Monongahela Natural Gas Co.*[6] Most of the cases ended in favour of the rule of capture.[7] In the case of *Barnard*, the court reiterated that the only option available for an adjoining land owner whose oil was depleted as a result of this rule was to go and do likewise.[8]

1 T Daintith, G Willoughby and A Hill, United Kingdom Oil and Gas Law (3rd edn, Sweet and Maxwell 2000) Para 1–724.
2 Steven N Wiggins and Gary D Libecap, 'Oil Field Unitization: Contractual Failure in the Presence of Imperfect Information' (1985) 75(3) American Economic Review 368, 369.
3 Nicola MacLeod, 'Unitisation' in Greg Gordon and Others (eds) Oil and Gas Law – Current Practise and Emerging Trends (2nd edn, Dundee University Press 2011) 413.
4 Nicola MacLeod, 'Unitisation' in Greg Gordon and Others (eds) Oil and Gas Law – Current Practise and Emerging Trends (2nd edn, Dundee University Press 2011) 413. See also E Poitevent, 'Oil-Proceeds from Unitised Field' (2000) IELTR N10.
5 (1897) 49 N.E. 399.
6 65 A. 801 (Sup. Ct. Pa. 1907).
7 Cecilia Low, 'The Rule of Capture: Its Current Status and Some Issues to Consider' (2009) 46(3) Alberta L Rev 799.
8 Cecilia Low, 'The Rule of Capture: Its Current Status and Some Issues to Consider' (2009) 46(3) Alberta L Rev 799., 803.

DOI: 10.4324/9781003491293-4

In the light of the above, some States have developed rules to curb the excesses of the rule of capture. For instance, the UK's Petroleum Licensing (Production) (Seaward Areas) Regulations 2008 contain provisions against the rule of capture.[9] First, it provides that except with the permission of the minister, a licensee is prohibited from drilling a well in any part of the field that is less than 125 m from the boundaries of the licensed area.[10] It will be difficult to envisage that the minister will consent to the drilling of a well very close to the boundaries of the field in cases where it will engender the unsustainable practices of the rule of capture. Again, the Petroleum Regulations empower the minister to mandate unitisation in circumstances where it is expedient.[11] While the Petroleum Regulations did not expressly define such circumstances, it is presumed that it would encapsulate instances where the rule of capture would undermine the maximisation of economic recovery which is at the heart of UK petroleum policy.[12] A country like Yemen provides against the excesses of the rule of capture by stipulating in its Production Sharing Agreement 1992 that the contractor shall 'take all proper measures, according to generally accepted methods in the Petroleum Industry to prevent loss or waste of Petroleum above or under the ground in any form'.[13]

In the preceding paragraph, it was mentioned that unitisation is one of the ways through which various States avoid the risks of the rule of capture. *Unitisation* is a process through which licensees or producers of an oil field which spans several licence areas concede to developing the field as a single unit in accordance with its geophysical area as opposed to developing the field piecemeal as separate but competing developments within each licence area as specified in their individual licenses.[14] Under unitisation, adjourning licensees can produce hydrocarbons from their individual licensed area jointly, eliminating competitive drilling with its negative ramifications.[15] Notably, unitisation enables the parties to develop and use one set of infrastructure, pipelines and procession kits which will enable the economics of the field. Unitisation can also be used in the international context, where a petroleum reserve is straddling the maritime boundaries of two States.[16] In this instance, the States can opt for some form of unitisation termed a *joint development agreement*.[17] However, unitisation as a process in international context is not the focus

9 Nicola MacLeod, 'Unitisation' (n 3) 417.

10 The Petroleum Licensing (Production) (Seaward Areas) Regulations 2008, Sch, Model Clause 20.

11 The Petroleum Licensing (Production) (Seaward Areas) Regulations 2008, Sch, Model Clause 28.

12 Sean Rush, 'Unitization and Redetermination' in Peter Roberts (ed), *Oil and Gas Contracts: Principles and Practises* (Sweet and Maxwell 2019) para 4–08.

13 Jacqueline L Weaver, 'Unitizing Oil and Gas Fields Around the World: A Comparative Analysis of National Laws and Private Contracts' (2006) 28(1) Issues Leg Scholarsh 26.

14 Danielle Beggs and Justyna Bremen, 'Unitisation and Unitisation Agreements' in Geoffrey Picton-Turbervill (ed), *Oil and Gas: A Practical Handbook* (Globe Law and Business 2009) 58.

15 Danielle Beggs and Justyna Bremen, 'Unitisation and Unitisation Agreements' in Geoffrey Picton-Turbervill (ed), *Oil and Gas: A Practical Handbook* (Globe Law and Business 2009) 58.

16 Paul F Worthington, 'Contemporary Challenges in Unitization and Equity Redetermination of Petroleum Accumulations' (2010) 3(1) *SPE Econ Mgmt* 10–17.

17 Paul F Worthington, 'Contemporary Challenges in Unitization and Equity Redetermination of Petroleum Accumulations' (2010) 3(1) *SPE Econ Mgmt* 10–17.

of this chapter. In contrast, this chapter contains an exposition of the process of unitisation and the terms of the unitisation and unit operating agreement (UUOA). For this purpose, it is divided into four sections in addition to the introduction. Section 3.2 discusses the meaning of unitisation and UUOA, the rationale behind it and a fair example of the jurisdictions where it is practiced. Section 3.3 provides a comparison between UUOA and other contractual arrangements like pooling and joint operating agreements (JOAs). Section 3.4 discusses common clauses that are peculiar to the UUOA. The final section is the conclusion.

3.2 Unitisation and Unit Operating Agreements

Unitisation is the 'the joint, coordinated operation of a petroleum reservoir by all the owners of rights in the separate tracts overlying the reservoir'.[18] Unitisation was an answer to two challenges which confronted the petroleum industries in the early '90s. Hardwicke identifies the first problem to wit: 'What could be done to increase efficiency in oil and gas development and production, or how could recovery of oil and gas be materially increased and the expense of operation materially decreased?'[19] The second challenge has already been identified as initiated by the rule of capture.[20] Unitisation is becoming increasingly popular among petroleum States owing to several reasons.[21] First, recent development in petroleum geology has made it feasible for common petroleum reservoirs to be identified.[22] Additionally, the maturation of petroleum provinces implies that smaller petroleum fields are now considered for production.[23] As a result of the latter, more petroleum licenses are issued and more shared fields are identified for potential exploitation.[24] In all, the benefit of unitisation is that it lowers production costs, reduces waste, maximises economic recovery and gives each licensee a fair share of the common reservoir.[25]

18 Patrick H. Martin and Bruce M. Kramer, *Williams & Meyers Manual of Oil and Gas Terms* (12th edn, LexisNexis 2003) 850.

19 Robert E Hardwicke, Anti-Trust Laws et al. vs Unit Operation of Oil and Gas Pools cited in Bruce A Landis, 'A Summary of Unitization and the Engineering Functions in Unitization' (1959) J Petrol Technol 30.

20 Robert E Hardwicke, Anti-Trust Laws et al. vs Unit Operation of Oil and Gas Pools cited in Bruce A Landis, 'A Summary of Unitization and the Engineering Functions in Unitization' (1959) J Petrol Technol 30.

21 Eduardo G Pereira and Giulia Carloni, 'Unitisation and Unit Operating Agreements' in *Understanding Joint Operating Agreements* (Intersentia 2017) 45, 46.

22 Eduardo G Pereira and Giulia Carloni, 'Unitisation and Unit Operating Agreements' in *Understanding Joint Operating Agreements* (Intersentia 2017) 45, 46.

23 Eduardo G Pereira and Giulia Carloni, 'Unitisation and Unit Operating Agreements' in *Understanding Joint Operating Agreements* (Intersentia 2017) 45, 46. See also J Lang Weaver and D F Asmus, 'Unitizing Oil and Gas Fields Around the World: A Comparative Analysis of National Laws and Private Contracts' (2006) 28(1) Issues Leg Scholarsh 12.

24 J Lang Weaver and D F Asmus, 'Unitizing Oil and Gas Fields Around the World: A Comparative Analysis of National Laws and Private Contracts' (2006) 28(1) Issues Leg Scholarsh 12.

25 J Lang Weaver and D F Asmus, 'Unitizing Oil and Gas Fields Around the World: A Comparative Analysis of National Laws and Private Contracts' (2006) 28(1) Issues Leg Scholarsh 12. See also A Derman and K Vollus, 'Unitization' (2002) 215 ADVISOR, Ass Intern Petroleum Neg 5.

A UUOA is an agreement that underlies the unitisation process. It is entered into by the affected licensees in order to detail the terms of the unitisation process and how the common field will be governed or operated.[26] In some jurisdictions like Canada and Brazil, the agreement is divided into two: a unit agreement and a unit operating agreement.[27] For such jurisdictions, a reason for splitting the UUOA into two agreements is to protect certain details from the public. That is, in instances where the UUOA will typically be submitted to the government, the unit agreement will be presented and the unit operating agreement will be kept private. The unit agreement normally covers issues like the respective interests of the party in the unitised field and the general terms for the formation of the unit.[28] The unit operating agreement governs the operation of the units and hence provides for the appointment of the operator such issues as the appointment and removal of unit operators, the location and extent of the reservoir, definition of operational terms like test wells and injection wells and so on.[29]

Unitisation and UUOAs have become common practice in several jurisdictions. The United Kingdom provides against the rule of capture by empowering the secretary of state to mandate unitisation where it is in the interest of maximisation of economic recovery.[30] In Algeria, the Hydrocarbon Law of 2005 provides that the National Development of Hydrocarbon Resources (ALNAFT) has the power to mandate affected contractors to draw up a unitisation plan in the event of a common reservoir that straddles two or more licensed areas.[31] The unitisation plan shall be submitted to the ALNAFT for approval before implementation. In the event of a non-adoption or approval of the unitisation plan by the relevant contractors or ALNAFT respectively, the latter may appoint an independent expert at the expense of the contractors to draw up a unitisation plan which will come into force.[32] Unlike the UK, the Algerian Hydrocarbon Law mandates unitisation in every instance where a common reservoir is discovered at the instance of the ALNAFT.

26 Danielle Beggs and Justyna Bremen, 'Unitisation and Unitisation Agreements' (n 14).

27 Nina Howell and Lauren Kensall, 'Unitization: Comments on 2020 AIPN Model International Unitization and Unit Operating Agreement' (2021) XI (38) Natl L Rev <https://www.natlawreview.com/article/unitization-comments-2020-aipn-model-international-unitization-and-unit-operating> accessed 18 May 2021.

28 Nina Howell and Lauren Kensall, 'Unitization: Comments on 2020 AIPN Model International Unitization and Unit Operating Agreement' (2021) XI (38) Natl L Rev <https://www.natlawreview.com/article/unitization-comments-2020-aipn-model-international-unitization-and-unit-operating> accessed 18 May 2021.

29 Nina Howell and Lauren Kensall, 'Unitization: Comments on 2020 AIPN Model International Unitization and Unit Operating Agreement' (2021) XI (38) Natl L Rev <https://www.natlawreview.com/article/unitization-comments-2020-aipn-model-international-unitization-and-unit-operating> accessed 18 May 2021.

30 W English, 'Unitisation Agreements' in M David (ed), *Upstream Oil and Gas Agreements* (Sweet and Maxwell 1997) 98.

31 Michael Polkinghorne, 'Unitisation and Redetermination: Right or Obligation?' (2007) 25(3) J Energy Nat Resour Law 303, 305.

32 Michael Polkinghorne, 'Unitisation and Redetermination: Right or Obligation?' (2007) 25(3) J Energy Nat Resour Law 303, 305.

In Australia, the law provides for flexibility in the context of entering into a UUOA.[33] A licensee can voluntarily enter into a UUOA for the joint development of a common reservoir in Australia, subject to the authorisation of the Joint Authority.[34] The Joint Authority can also mandate concerned licensees to enter into a UUOA 'for the purpose of securing the more effective recovery of petroleum from the petroleum pool'.[35]

In most jurisdictions, a pre-unitisation agreement may be entered into by the parties before the UUOA.[36] The rationale for a pre-unitisation agreement is that a UUOA involves a lot of complex issues which cannot be agreed to in haste.[37] Thus, the UUOA may take one or more years to negotiate.[38] The pre-unitisation agreement is adopted preliminarily as a legal umbrella to enable initial evaluation work for the unitisation pending the formal conclusion of the UUOA.[39] It binds the parties to the process which will establish their tract participation for the purpose of a future unitisation agreement. It normally defines how parties will evaluate the common reservoir in order to develop a common field and unitisation plan.[40] The agreement covers operational issues like the appointment of pre-unit operator, pre-unit operating committee, development plan and so on. In the pre-unitisation agreement, parties stipulate the initial unit interest that each would have.[41] Such interest is normally tentative pending the conclusion of the UUOA after a full evaluation of the field. The parties also stipulate legal issues in the pre-unitisation agreement like termination provisions and so on.[42] The scope of pre-unitisation agreement varies from one jurisdiction to another. The pre-unitisation agreement in Papua New Guinea is about 50 pages long, while the one used in Indonesia is

33 Emily Tsokos, 'A Comparative Review of Unit Development under the Commonwealth Petroleum (Submerged Lands) Act 1967' (2007) 26 ARELJ 396, 403.

34 Emily Tsokos, 'A Comparative Review of Unit Development under the Commonwealth Petroleum (Submerged Lands) Act 1967' (2007) 26 ARELJ 396, 403. The Joint Authority for each petroleum area is the responsible State minister and Commonwealth minister of that state. Amongst other things, they have the responsibility for the grant or refusal of offshore petroleum licenses. They can also vary the title given. They can also cancel or suspend petroleum licenses. See the Offshore Petroleum and Greenhouse Gas Storage Act 2006.

35 Emily Tsokos, 'A Comparative Review of Unit Development under the Commonwealth Petroleum (Submerged Lands) Act 1967' (2007) 26 ARELJ 396, 403.

36 Hunton Andrews Kurth, 'Unitisation – The Oil and Gas Industry's Solution to One of Geology's Many Conundrums' (2014) <https://www.lexology.com/library/detail.aspx?g=69912ce0-127d-447e-8a47-50f5d235dcfa> accessed 17 May 2021.

37 Hunton Andrews Kurth, 'Unitisation – The Oil and Gas Industry's Solution to One of Geology's Many Conundrums' (2014) <https://www.lexology.com/library/detail.aspx?g=69912ce0-127d-447e-8a47-50f5d235dcfa> accessed 17 May 2021.

38 David Asmus and Jacqueline L Weaver, 'Unitizing Oil and Gas Fields Around the World: A Comparative Analysis of National Laws and Private Contracts' (2006) 28(1) Issues Leg Scholarsh 67, 68.

39 David Asmus and Jacqueline L Weaver, 'Unitizing Oil and Gas Fields Around the World: A Comparative Analysis of National Laws and Private Contracts' (2006) 28(1) Issues Leg Scholarsh 67, 68.

40 Micheal P G Taylor and Sally M Tyne, *Taylor and Winsor on Joint Operating Agreements* (Longman 1992) 113.

41 Johnson Wilkinson, *Introduction to Oil and Gas Joint Ventures* (Oil Field Publications 1997) 47.

42 Johnson Wilkinson, *Introduction to Oil and Gas Joint Ventures* (Oil Field Publications 1997) 47.

about 14 pages long.[43] The pre-unitisation agreement is terminated by the adoption of a unitisation agreement.[44]

In all, the UUOA is beneficial given that it fosters maximisation of economic recovery, minimises waste and reduces competitive drilling. However, it is not without its own drawbacks. It is usually a complex procedure which requires serious funding and technical considerations which may not be easily glossed over.[45] One set of licensee(s) may be more advanced and experienced than the others. Thus, the experienced ones may have the upper hand in negotiating better interests in the unitised field to the disadvantage of the other party(ies). The situation is worsened by the general reduction in the percentage interest in the licensed area. For instance, a licensee who has a 100% interest in their licensed area, will be entitled to lesser percentage in the unitised area, though it may be justifiable in some instances by the maximisation of recovery, reduction of waste and wider nature of the unitised area which may cumulatively translate to bigger petroleum dividends.

3.3 Unitisation and Unit Operating Agreements Compared to Similar Contractual Arrangements

The UUOA has similar features with some other contractual agreements like pooling and the JOAs. In some instances, the UUOA is influenced and influences such contractual agreements. This section contains an analysis of the relationship between UUOA and related contractual arrangements such as pooling contract and JOA.

3.3.1 UUOA and Pooling

The UUOA shares some commonalities with a pooling arrangement or agreement. In the North American usage, the term *pooling* refers to an agreement or understanding pursuant to which the working interests for different contiguous tracts (geographical locations) are combined within the area of a drilling spacing unit.[46] It is the joining of different individual interests in several tracts into one tract in order to have adequate acreage for the purpose of getting the needed acreage to receive government approval for petroleum activities.[47] A pooling arrangement is commonly used in the United States and some parts of Canada.[48] The UUOA is

43 David Asmus and Jacqueline L Weaver, 'Unitizing Oil and Gas Fields Around the World: A Comparative Analysis of National Laws and Private Contracts' (2006) 28(1) Issues Leg Scholarsh 67, 68.

44 David Asmus and Jacqueline L Weaver, 'Unitizing Oil and Gas Fields Around the World: A Comparative Analysis of National Laws and Private Contracts' (2006) 28(1) Issues Leg Scholarsh 67, 68.

45 Austin T Lee, 'Pooling and Unitisation' (2017) <https://bracewell.com/sites/default/files/news-files/Pool ing%20and%20Unitization.pdf> accessed 30 May 2021.

46 Nigel Bankes, 'Pooling Agreements in Canadian Oil and Gas Law' (1995) 33(3) Alberta L Rev 493, 494.

47 Nigel Bankes, 'Pooling Agreements in Canadian Oil and Gas Law' (1995) 33(3) Alberta L Rev 493, 494.

48 C T Mullane and A P G Walker, 'The Pooling Clause and the Effects of Unitization on the Oil and Gas Lease' (1965) Alberta L Rev 250.

similar to pooling arrangements given that it is the coming together of petroleum interests for the joint coordination of the petroleum reservoir.[49] Both the UUOA and pooling arrangements are largely necessitated by regulation. The two types of arrangements may be initiated voluntarily or compulsorily. Pooling agreements are sometimes entered into voluntarily by some owners of small tracts to obtain the acreage required by law to obtain a permit to drill a well.[50] Likewise, unitisation may be voluntarily initiated for the joint operation of a common reservoir to maximise economic recovery and reduce waste.[51]

Nonetheless, UUOA is different from a pooling agreement in several respects. For one, the two are distinguishable by the rationale behind their existence. A pooling agreement is necessitated by the need to get adequate acreage in order to qualify for a permit to drill a well.[52] Conversely, the impetus for the UUOA agreement is the need to avoid competitive drilling and maximise economic waste.[53] A pooling agreement is generally relevant to small acreage owners who want to join their interests together for the purpose of getting a drilling permit.[54] The UUOA is predominantly used by licensees who have existing interests in designated, generally large license areas.[55] In most instance, the UUOA is entered into by existing licensees after a field has been identified but before development commences. Pooling agreements and declarations generally apply to something less than an entire reservoir. By contrast, UUOA is formed for the development of an oil reservoir or field.

3.3.2 UUOA and Joint Operating Agreements

The UUOA also shares similar attributes with a JOA. Petroleum exploration and development are highly risky and capital intensive yet rewarding for the successful parties.[56] In the words of Mathews and Pereira, 'In short, it is a challenging business characterized by high upfront costs and substantial risk'.[57] The burden of the

49 C T Mullane and A P G Walker, 'The Pooling Clause and the Effects of Unitization on the Oil and Gas Lease' (1965) Alberta L Rev 250.

50 Raymound Myers, 'Problems of Pooling, Unitization, and Secondary Recovery' (1959) U Ill LF 543. See also, e.g. 16 Tex Admin Code 3.37, 3.38.

51 Joseph J French and Frank Elliot, 'Legal Effect of Voluntary Pooling and Unitization: Theories and Party Practise' (1957) 35 Tex L Rev 401, 402–405.

52 Thomas K Dougherty, 'Pooling and Unitization in Texas' (2001) Annual of the Arkansas Natural Resources Law Institute 72.

53 C T Mullane and A P G Walker, 'The Pooling Clause and the Effects of Unitization on the Oil and Gas Lease' (1965) Alberta L Rev 250.

54 C T Mullane and A P G Walker, 'The Pooling Clause and the Effects of Unitization on the Oil and Gas Lease' (1965) Alberta L Rev 250.

55 C T Mullane and A P G Walker, 'The Pooling Clause and the Effects of Unitization on the Oil and Gas Lease' (1965) Alberta L Rev 250.

56 Nkaepe Etteh, 'Joint Operating Agreements: Which Issues Are Likely to be the Most Sensitive to the Parties and How Can a Good Contract Design Limit the Damage from Such Disputes?' (Centre for Energy, Petroleum and Mineral Law and Policy 2010) <http://www.dundee.ac.uk/cepmlp/gateway/index.php?news=31272> accessed 7 June 2021.

57 Christopher Mathews and Eduardo G Pereira, 'Joint Operating Agreements: Understanding Different Interests and Concerns in the Wake of *Reeder v. Wood County Energy*' (2017) <https://www.duo.

upfront cost on a party can be ameliorated and the risk mitigated by the pooling resources with other parties through a JOA.[58] A JOA is a contractual arrangement where two or more parties come together to undertake the risk of petroleum exploration and development, whilst sharing the dividends according to the participating interests of each party.[59] The UUOA is akin to the JOA to the extent that the former has been termed 'a bigger JOA'.[60] Kenneth Barnhill sums the similarity between UUOA and JOA as follows:[61]

> Joint operations is the term generally used to refer to the procedure whereby co-owners of mineral properties agree upon the development and operations of such properties by one or more of the co-owners for the benefit of the other co-owners. Unitized operations denote a similar arrangement, but generally on a larger scale, such as for the exploration, development, and operation of an entire pool, structure or field, or a substantial portion thereof.

It is not surprising that the UUOA has similar content as the JOA. Like the JOA, the parties to the UUOA normally appoint an operator which is responsible for the daily management of the exploration and development from the unitised field.[62] The dividends of the parties to the UUOA are also defined according to the interests in the unitised field. The latter is termed a tract participation, while that of JOA is called a participating interest. Other commonalities that it shares with the JOA include default provisions, dispute resolution, sole risk, assignment and decommissioning.[63]

However, the UUOA is distinguishable in several respects from the JOA. In the first remove, the JOA is the constitution that governs a joint venture between participants that have one or more petroleum licenses or concession agreements. It is mostly applicable to a licensed area/block which is smaller in comparison to an entire oil reservoir, the subject matter of unitisation.[64] On the other hand, the UUOA is a separate constitution, in a sense a 'supra-constitution' agreed between several licensees which may include several joint ventures governed by separate

---

uio.no/bitstream/handle/10852/61603/Joint-Operating-Agreements-Post-Reeder-CXM-edits-minus bibliography.pdf?sequence =4&is Allowed=y> accessed 7 June 2021.

58 Christopher Mathews and Eduardo G Pereira, 'Joint Operating Agreements: Understanding Different Interests and Concerns in the Wake of *Reeder v. Wood County Energy*' (2017) <https://www.duo.uio.no/bitstream/handle/10852/61603/Joint-Operating-Agreements-Post-Reeder-CXM-edits-minus bibliography.pdf?sequence =4&is Allowed=y> accessed 7 June 2021. See Eduardo G Pereira, *Encyclopaedia of Oil and Gas Law 1* (Globe Law and Business 2014) 103, 104.

59 Scott Styles, 'Joint Operating Agreements' in Greg Gordon and others (eds), *Oil and Gas Law – Current Practise and Emerging Trends* (n) 359.

60 Eduardo G Pereira and Giulia Carloni, 'Unitisation and Unit Operating Agreements' in Understanding Joint Operating Agreements (n) 51.

61 K E Barnhill Jr, 'Taxation of Oil and Gas Operating Agreements. The Scope and Application of I.T. 3930' (1953–1954) 26 Rocky Mt L Rev 133.

62 Gary D Libecap and James L Smith, 'The Self-Enforcing Provision of Oil and Gas Unit Operating Agreements: Theory and Evidence', NBER Working Paper No. 7142 (1999) 5 <https://www.nber.org/system/files/working_papers/w7142/w7142.pdf> accessed 7 June 2021.

63 Danielle Beggs and Justyna Bremen, 'Unitisation and Unitisation Agreements' (n 14) 58.

64 Eduardo G Pereira and Giulia Carloni, 'Unitisation and Unit Operating Agreements' (n 61) 44.

JOAs, which applies exclusively to the area of a field straddling the licence areas awarded to those joint ventures. While the UUOA is motivated partly by the need to eliminate competitive drilling between licensees, the latter is not the case with the JOA, which is predicated on the need to share risks and ameliorate the capital burden of petroleum activities on a given company. Another exclusive feature of the UUOA is the provision on redetermination. In the case of a JOA, the participating interest of the relevant parties is determined from the initial stage of the contract and it remains constant until it elapses save for transfer, assignment and so on.[65] For the UUOA, the parties will normally provide for redetermination, a mechanism which allows the parties to readjust their original unit equity to reflect any change in the field data especially as it relates to the estimated production.

In all, the UUOA normally exists simultaneously with all the underlying JOAs.[66] Its provisions reflect those of the underlying JOAs. In event that there is a clash between the provisions of the two, the parties to the JOA will make such necessary adjustments that will make it at par with the UUOA.

3.4 Common Clauses in a Unitisation and Unit Operating Agreement

As mentioned above, the UUOA details the basis for the operation of a unitised field. Some of the issues addressed in the UUOA include the parameters for the commencement of the unitised relationship, the extent of the interests of each group in the unitised field and the readjustment of such interests in line with changing realities or increased knowledge. Other common clauses which it also shares with JOAs are non-unit operations, general decision-making mechanisms, assignment of unit interests, decommissioning and dispute resolution. The Association of International Energy Negotiators (AIEN) has developed a model form of international UUOA.[67] The AIEN model form of UUOA was designed to incorporate the needed flexibility that will enable it to be used in most jurisdictions subject to peculiar circumstances.[68] The AEPN UUOA is a model that is meant for use in a unitised arrangement within one jurisdiction; it is not fit for cross-border unitisation.[69] The Association of International Petroleum Negotiators (AIPN) UUOA

65 Eduardo G Pereira and Giulia Carloni, 'Unitisation and Unit Operating Agreements' (n 61) 44. For more commentaries, see J Lang Weaver and D F Asmus, 'Unitizing Oil and Gas Fields Around the World: A Comparative Analysis of National Laws and Private Contracts' (2006) 28(1) Houston J Int Law 12; A Derman and K Vollus, 'Unitization' (2002) 215 ADVISOR, Ass Intern Petroleum Neg 5.

66 J Lang Weaver and D F Asmus, 'Unitizing Oil and Gas Fields Around the World: A Comparative Analysis of National Laws and Private Contracts' (2006) 28(1) Houston J Int Law 12; A Derman and K Vollus, 'Unitization' (2002) 215 ADVISOR, Ass Intern Petroleum Neg 5.

67 The first model agreement was developed in 2006 and has been updated in 2020. See AIPN, 'Model Contracts' (2020) <Search Results for Product: AIPN> accessed 14 June 2021.

68 AIPN, 'Guidance Notes to AIPN Model Form International Unitization and Unit Operating Agreement' (2020) 1, 2 <https://www.aipn.org/forms/store/ProductFormPublic/unitization-and-unit-operating-agreement-2006> accessed 14 June 2021.

69 AIPN, 'Guidance Notes to AIPN Model Form International Unitization and Unit Operating Agreement' (2020) 1, 2 <https://www.aipn.org/forms/store/ProductFormPublic/unitization-and-unit-operating-agreement-2006> accessed 14 June 2021.

will form the basis for the following analysis of the common clauses in a typical UUOA. The clauses that will be analysed include unit creation, determination and redetermination.

3.4.1 Unit Creation

The initial clauses of the UUOA provide for the creation of a unitised area out of a union of licensed areas called tracts. In the words of the model contract,

> all rights and interests of the parties under the Tract A Contract and the Tract B Contract in so far as they relate to the Unit Interval, Unit Substances and the Conduct of Unit Operations are hereby unitised effective as of the effective date, in accordance with the terms of this agreement.[70]

In some instances, the effectiveness of the agreement is dependent on some conditions. In the model contract, an example of such condition includes the obtaining of all the necessary government consents as stipulated by law.[71] Where the consents are not obtained, it may lead to the termination of the agreement especially in the case of a consent which is a condition subsequent. The UUOA also stipulates the licensed areas that are unitised and the parties involved.[72] The licensed area which forms part of the unitised field is called a tract.[73]

It is also typical to include a clear definition of the unitised substances and the scope of the agreement. The AIPN Model UUOA defines the unitised substances as 'all substances produced from or attributable to the Unit Interval which the Parties are entitled to produce' under the underlying tract contract forming the unitisation agreement.[74] The substances in the context of this chapter are usually hydrocarbons. It is also germane for the parties to detail the scope of the agreement. The latter is necessitated by the need to avoid unnecessary overlap between the UUOA and the underlying JOAs.[75] The scope of the UUOA does not just stop

70 The AIPN Model Form International Unitization and Unit Operating Agreement 2020, Clause 4(1) <Microsoft Word – AIPN Model Form UUOA 2020 – Final Issued Version.docx> accessed 14 June 2021.

71 The AIPN Model Form International Unitization and Unit Operating Agreement 2020, Clause 4(1) <Microsoft Word – AIPN Model Form UUOA 2020 – Final Issued Version.docx> accessed 14 June 2021. Clause 4(1)(D). For further commentaries on the Model Unitisation Contract, see A Timothy Martin, 'Model Contracts: A Survey of the Global Petroleum Industry' (2016) <Model Contracts-Survey of Global Petroleum Industry (FINAL) (timmartin.ca)> accessed 14 June 2021.

72 A Timothy Martin, 'Model Contracts: A Survey of the Global Petroleum Industry' (2016) <Model Contracts-Survey of Global Petroleum Industry (FINAL) (timmartin.ca)> accessed 14 June 2021, initial part. For more commentaries, see Paul F Worthington, *The Law on Petroleum Unitization: Legislating for Effective Regulation* (Edward Elgar Publishing 2020) 136.

73 Paul F Worthington, *The Law on Petroleum Unitization: Legislating for Effective Regulation* (Edward Elgar Publishing 2020) 136. Danielle Beggs and Justyna Bremen, 'Unitisation and Unitisation Agreements' (n 14) 63.

74 Danielle Beggs and Justyna Bremen, 'Unitisation and Unitisation Agreements' (n 14) 63. Clause 1.146.

75 AIPN, 'Guidance Notes to AIPN Model Form International Unitization and Unit Operating Agreement' (n 69).

at the production of the unitised substances but also may cover transportation of the substances.[76] In some instances, it may cover an option for joint marketing of unitised substances.[77] However, as rightly noted in the AIEN Guidance Notes, care must be taken to couch the option of joint marketing in order not to prejudice any party in terms of giving the other undue advantage in competition.[78] The latter is mostly applicable in jurisdictions with antitrust laws.

3.4.2 Determination

The UUOA is made by a conglomerate of groups who are holders of their individual licenses. It usually defines the relative working interests of its participants in a specific field which overlaps the areas to which the JOAs typically applies. Similar to a JOA, each group must determine the percentage interest that it would have in the unitised field. Mostly, each group will aspire to have the percentage of unit equity that is proportionate to the hydrocarbons beneath its tract. In the same vein, each party in each group will aspire to have a percentage of unit equity that represents its JOA working interest in the tract applicable to that JOA. As captured in the AIEN Model UUOA, 'Each Party's Unit Interest is determined by multiplying that Party's Group Interest in each Group by the Tract Participation for that Group and adding the results'.[79] By way of illustration, where a group has a tract participating interest of 45%, and the group is made up of three parties holding a 60%, 30% and 10% interest in the underlying JOA, respectively,[80] their respective equity interests will be 27%, 13.5% and 4.5%, respectively.[81] For a group that has a 20% tract participating interest and is made of three parties holding 40%, 25% and 35%, respectively, in the underlying JOA, their equity interests will be 8%, 5% and 7%, respectively.[82]

The determination of the tract participation and unit interests of each group and parties respectively is often very technical and complex.[83] As such, there are several methods developed for the latter purpose. The methods include stock tank oil originally in place (STOOIP), recoverable reserves, and moveable oil originally in place (MOOIP). The STOOIP method is reputed to be the easiest. When STOOIP is used,

76 The AIPN Model Form International Unitization and Unit Operating Agreement 2020, Clause 3.1(A) (n 71).

77 The AIPN Model Form International Unitization and Unit Operating Agreement 2020, Clause 3.1(A) (n 71).

78 AIPN, 'Guidance Notes to AIPN Model Form International Unitization and Unit Operating Agreement' (n 69) 1, 2.

79 The AIPN Model Form International Unitization and Unit Operating Agreement 2020, Clause 5.2 (B) (n 71).

80 Eduardo G Pereira and Giulia Carloni, 'Unitisation and Unit Operating Agreements' (n 61) 54, 55.

81 Eduardo G Pereira and Giulia Carloni, 'Unitisation and Unit Operating Agreements' (n 61) 54, 55.

82 Eduardo G Pereira and Giulia Carloni, 'Unitisation and Unit Operating Agreements' (n 61) 54, 55.

83 M Taylor and S Tyne, *Taylor and Windsor on Joint Operating Agreements* (Sweet & Maxwell 2nd edn 1992) 114.

the participating and unit interests are calculated based on the total volume of oil estimated to be in the reservoir. While STOOIP is very basic and reputed to be the easiest method, it has also been criticised as being inequitable. In the words of MacLeod, 'this method may not be completely equitable, as some of the oil will never actually be produced. In addition, it makes no distinction between the reserves that are produced and those which are left in the reservoir'.[84] The recoverable reserves method allows for unit and participating interests to be determined by the recoverable hydrocarbons.[85] Unlike STOOIP, it is equitable yet difficult to use because it is impossible to determine the recoverable hydrocarbons unless the reservoir has been depleted. The MOOIP allows for calculation of unit and participating interests based on an estimation of the oil originally in place minus the hypothetical oil left after the reservoir has been depleted.[86] While it appears more equitable than the STOOIP, its fairness is greatly reduced by the uncertainties surrounding the estimation of the oil originally in the reservoir and the oil left after the reservoir has been depleted.

3.4.3 Redetermination

The point was made that the determination of tract participation and unit interests are mostly based on estimation. Thus, it is very common that the basis for the calculation of tract participation and unit interests may change. The latter may necessitate a need to change the existing tract participation and unit interests. Redetermination is the process for the review and revision of the tract participation and unit interests.[87] The UUOA will normally detail the terms and trigger for parties to initiate a redetermination at certain points of the development stage. The circumstances that may trigger the initiation of a redetermination includes the availability of a new geological data. This was captured in the AIPN Model UUOA as follows:

> it is recognized that the tract participations are based on the data available at the time, that the redeterminations . . . are to reflect additional or better data, that adjustments made . . . are corrections of each party's respective share of costs incurred for the unit account, and that the adjustments to entitlement to unit substances made . . . are corrections to the entitlements of the respective parties based on such corrected tract participations.[88]

The UUOA will specify the exact period when redetermination will be permitted. It may be after production has reached a certain level or after a period of time has

84 Nicola MacLeod, 'Unitisation' (n 4) 423.

85 Nicola MacLeod, 'Unitisation' (n 4) 423.

86 Nicola MacLeod, 'Unitisation' (n 4) 423.

87 The AIPN Model Form International Unitization and Unit Operating Agreement 2020 (n 71) Clause 1.98.

88 The AIPN Model Form International Unitization and Unit Operating Agreement 2020 (n 71) Clause 5.4.

elapsed.[89] In other instances, it may be permitted when a certain number of wells have been drilled.

The process of redetermination is generally time-consuming and expensive. It is time-consuming because it has a direct bearing on the value of the assets of the group given that it may cause the tract participation and unit interests of the parties to decrease and increase accordingly. Thus, parties take considerable time to ensure that they get the best out of the redetermination process. Mechanisms are usually incorporated to ensure that the groups do not bear the weight of the readjustment disproportionately.[90] This may entail that the group whose tract participation had increased will defray their higher share gradually in subsequent productions.[91] It has been reported that an average redetermination would cost up to US$2 million.[92] Thus, appropriate care must be taken to incorporate provisions that will deter the unnecessary initiation of the process. Against the background, the UUOA will normally provide that where the redetermination is triggered unnecessarily, the concerned group would bear the cost of some or all of the other group's expenditure for the process.[93] Disputes arising from a redetermination are normally referred to an independent expert provided for in a dispute resolution clause.[94]

3.5 Conclusion

Unitisation is necessitated by the need to eliminate competitive drilling, and it is also a tool for maximisation of economic recovery. It is for this reason that it has become common practice. It was noted that a downside of unitisation is that it is a lengthy, expensive and complex process. As such, the group with the financial and technological wherewithal may have the upper hand in negotiations and outcomes. The UUOA was compared with the pooling agreement. It was argued that the UUOA is similar to a pooling agreement given that it brings together petroleum interests for the joint coordination of the petroleum reservoir. It was stated that both the UUOA and pooling arrangements are necessitated by some form of regulatory intervention. The differences between UUOA and pooling arrangements were analysed, one of them being the rationale for their existence. In the same vein, the UUOA was compared with the JOA and found to have similarities. One of them is that they both have similar clauses like the default provisions, dispute resolution, sole risk, assignment and decommissioning. Amongst others, a dissimilarity between the JOA and UUOA is that the former details the relationship between parties to a joint venture, while the latter governs the relationship between the several

89 P Deemer, 'Unitisation Agreements', Conference Paper, University of Dundee, September 2004, 7.
90 Nicola MacLeod, 'Unitisation' (n 4) 427.
91 Nicola MacLeod, 'Unitisation' (n 4) 427.
92 Michael P G Taylor and Sally M Tyne, *Taylor and Winsor on Joint Operating Agreements* (n 40) 116.
93 Michael P G Taylor and Sally M Tyne, *Taylor and Winsor on Joint Operating Agreements* (n 40) 116.
94 Paul F Worthington, 'Use and Misuse of Pendulum Arbitration in Expert Redetermination of Tract Participation' (2007) 7(1) SPE Econ Mgmt 29–34.

licensees which may include joint ventures with respect to a common reservoir straddling between license areas.

In conclusion, the clauses unique to the UUOA were analysed, using the model AIPN UUOA as an example. The unit creation clauses were first in consideration. The preliminary clauses detail when the UUOA will become effective. It was stated that sometimes the effectiveness is contingent on other conditions like the obtaining of relevant government consent(s). It also sets out the scope of the agreement. The scope may sometimes include transportation, in which care must be taken in defining its scope. The determination clause contains the tract participation of each group and unit interests of each party. It was stated that the process of determination is complex and technical, and three methods have been developed for that purpose: STOOIP, MOOIP and recoverable reserves. The recoverable reserves method was noted as the most equitable yet was criticised as difficult to use because it is impossible to determine the recoverable hydrocarbons unless the reservoir has been depleted. The redetermination clause was analysed. It is the process for the review and revision of the tract participation and unit interests. As its definition suggest, it is very complex, thus, extra provisions are made to deter a group initiating it frivolously.

Part II

Case Studies

4 Unitization in Brazil

Conflicting Legal Regimes & Non-Unitized Areas Experience

André Lemos and Eduardo G. Pereira

Introduction

Brazilian Federal Constitution of 1988, which is still in force, established the State monopoly over the upstream, importation and exportation of oil and its by-products, oil refining and maritime and pipeline transportation activities. This monopoly was exercised by Petrobras – a mixed capital company controlled by the Brazilian State – until the constitutional amendment #9 (dated of 1995), which loosened it by allowing the Brazilian government to contract with private parties to conduct these activities in the country. The constitutional amendment # 9 (dated of 1995) was further regulated by Law #9,478/1997 ('Petroleum Law'), which created the current Brazilian oil and gas regulator – the National Agency of Petroleum, Natural Gas and Biofuels ('ANP'), set forth the possibility of awarding new blocks through competitive bid rounds and under the concession contract regime and terminated with the Petrobras' monopoly.

ANP Round Zero (dated of 1998) ratified and regulated under proper concession contracts Petrobras' rights over the producing fields and areas with commercial discoveries or exploration investments made by Petrobras.[1] Between 2006 and 2007, the giant offshore discoveries of Tupi (Santos basin) and Caraxéu (Campos basin) were made in the pre-salt layer (more than 2,000 meters of water depth and approximately 300 kilometers off the coast). The following years were marked by debates within the Brazilian Congress in order to increase the State's control over such reserves, though the concession contract regime had successfully attracted new players (including majors, national and foreign independent oil companies and private equity funds) and investments to Brazil.[2] In 2010, Law #12,351/2010 ('Pre-Salt Law') was enacted establishing the production sharing contract regime for all of the pre-salt polygon and other strategic areas.[3] The

1 www.gov.br/anp/pt-br/rodadas-anp/rodadas-concluidas/rodada-zero

2 Website of the Brazilian Ministry of Mines and Energy (http://www.mme.gov.br/documents/36212/447336/Linha_do_tempo.pdf/b55bbdd3-08e6-f86e-dac3-2bb532f312f7).

3 Pursuant art. 2, item V, of the Pre-Salt Law, strategic area is defined as the region of interest for the national development characterized by the low exploration risk and high production potential.

DOI: 10.4324/9781003491293-6

geographic coordinates of the pre-salt polygon areas are defined in an exhibit to the Pre-Salt Law. The National Council of Energy Policy ('CNPE') may classify other areas as strategic or from the pre-salt polygon.[4] Such pre-salt and strategic areas may be awarded in competitive bids or directly contracted with Petrobras under the production sharing contract regime in both cases.[5] CNPE defines the blocks that will be directly contracted with Petrobras or that will be bid for.[6] It is important to be noted that no blocks have been directly contracted to Petrobras so far.

In parallel, Law #12,276/2010 ('Transfer of Rights Law') provided a mechanism whereby the Brazilian State directly transferred to Petrobras the right to produce up to 5 billion barrels of oil equivalent (boe) in a specific prolific area of the pre-salt province (areas of Búzios, Sépia, Atapu, North of Berbigão, South of Berbigão, North of Sururu, South of Sururu, Itapu, South of Lula and South of Sapinhoá). In exchange, the Brazilian State increased its participation in the Petrobras' stock capital through the issuance of public debt bonds. The transfer of rights agreement had a revision mechanism on the declaration of commerciality of the relevant fields. It was discovered that such transfer of rights agreement areas held far more than 5 billion barrels of oil and natural gas. Petrobras was reimbursed by the Federal Government in USD 9.058 billion and the relevant surplus volumes were offered in a bid round in 2019 under the production sharing contract regime.[7]

Thus, the current Brazilian E&P legal framework comprises: (i) the production sharing contract regime for the pre-salt and strategic areas; (ii) the transfer of rights agreement for specific fields of the pre-salt area; and (iii) the concession contract regime for all other areas.[8]

Unitization Regulation in Brazil

Pursuant to article 27 of the Petroleum Law, which was later revoked by the Pre-Salt Law, the concessionaires of the different blocks where the same field extends should execute a unitization agreement. If the parties did not reach an agreement within the term determined by the ANP, the oil and gas regulator would determine how the rights and obligations under such blocks will be equally appropriated, based on an arbitration award and on the applicable general law principles. Such principles include the conservation rational use of oil and natural gas

4 Article 9, item V, of the Pre-Salt Law.

5 Article 8 of the Pre-Salt Law.

6 Article 9, items II and III, of the Pre-Salt Law.

7 Petrobras' website (https://petrobras.com.br/fatos-e-dados/tudo-o-que-voce-precisa-saber-sobre-cessaoonerosa.htm#:~:text=Cess%C3%A3o%20Onerosa%20%C3%A9%20um%20regime,com%20a%20Uni%C3%A3o%20em%202010.&text=Pelo%20contrato%2C%20a%20revis%C3%A3o%20seria,o%20valor%20inicial%20do%20c ontrato).>.

8 Although there are services risk agreements executed with Petrobras still in force, they are not significant.

reserves and reservoirs, as per the articles 8, item IX,[9] and article 44, item I,[10] of the Petroleum Law.

The concession contracts of the Brazil Round Zero, as duly amended, Round 1 (dated 1999) and Round 2 (dated 2000) provided that, in case a discovery extends outside of the concession area, the concessionaire should promptly inform the ANP. Then, ANP must notify the concessionaire(s) of the adjacent block so that they may commence negotiating a unitization agreement. The unitization agreement should contain, among other provisions commonly used in similar agreements: (i) the rights and obligations of the concessionaires; (ii) the unit area; (iii) the appointed Operator; (iv) participating interests of the parties; (v) the relevant term for the submission of the development plan; and (vi) government take and other third-party revenues. If requested, ANP can act as a mediator in the relevant negotiations. ANP would have a 60 day period to request revisions on the submitted unitization agreement and the concessionaires would have the same period to discuss the requested revisions with ANP and comply with them. Development and production operations in the unit area are suspended while the unitization agreement is not approved by the ANP, unless ANP, at its own criteria, approved such activities and since the unanimous approval of all concessionaires for such continuation is obtained.[11]

Subject to the terms of the relevant concession agreement, the ANP may act as the virtual concessionaire of any open acreage for the purpose of negotiating unitization with the concessionaire whose field extends into such open acreage. In any event, this open acreage could be subject to a bid at any time and the future concessionaire(s) would assume the rights and obligations under the executed unitization agreement. In case of open acreage and/or of insufficient appraisal to allow significant discussions on the unitization, the concessionaire(s) could proceed with the declaration of commerciality and submit a development plan as it (they) understood that the development operations could be performed in line with the best petroleum industry practices and the applicable regulation/legislation.

Under the form of concession contract for Brazil Round 3 (2001), any operators involved in a potential unit area may conduct appraisal activities, subject to the authorization of the ANP and the unanimous consent of all operators, regardless of whether unitization has formally taken place. The concession contract of the Brazil Round 4 (2002) excluded the obligation to set forth a specific deadline for the submission of the development plan in the unitization agreement.[12]

As to the Brazil Round 5 (dated of 2003), ANP adopted smaller polygons for the delimitation of the blocks resulting in the increase of the likelihood of unitization

9 Article 8, item IX, of the Petroleum Law provides that, as one of the ANP's attributions, ANP must "guarantee the compliance with the good practices for the conservation and rational use of oil, natural gas, its by-products and biofuels, as well as for environmental preservation."

10 Article 44, item I, of the Petroleum Law provides that the concessionaire must "adopt in all of its operations the required measures fir the conservation of the reservoirs and other natural resources for the safety of the people and equipment, as well as for the environmental protection."

11 ANP's website (http://rodadas.anp.gov.br/pt/concessao-de-blocos-exploratorios-1).

12 ANP's website (http://rodadas.anp.gov.br/pt/concessao-de-blocos-exploratorios-1).

cases. The concession contract of such bid round established: (i) the concessionaires are obliged to notify ANP of the extension of any reservoir across a polygon boundary within 72 hours of such extension coming to their knowledge; and (ii) that ANP, when acting as a mediator in the negotiations of the unitization agreement, should determine the term for the execution of such an agreement.[13]

The concession contract of the Brazil Round 6 (dated of 2004) required the concessionaires to submit to the ANP the negotiations' schedule and to allow ANP to participate in such negotiations, as an observer. After the conclusion of the appraisal operations, ANP would set forth the obligations related to the concession contracts and government take within 60 days from the submission of the discovery appraisal final report. In case ANP believes that a proper appraisal of the joint reservoir was made, the ANP may request the operations in the unit area to go on. In case of different terms for the exploration or production phases of the concession contracts where the common reservoir straddles into, ANP could also extend the exploration or production phase exclusively as to the unit area.

The concession contract of the Brazil Round 7 (2005) is similar to the Brazil Round 6, but established a 10 days' notice period as of the verification that the reservoir extends beyond the concession area. In addition, the possibility of moving forward with the operations could also occur in case one of the concession areas is in the production phase, as previously authorized by ANP. There were only minor changes in the concession contract of the Brazil Round 8 (2006) in comparison with the one from the Brazil Round 7. It provided that the joint evaluations of unit area could also be performed through a proper development plan, in addition to the possibility of a joint appraisal plan, as provided in the past concession contracts. There was no substantial revisions in the concession contracts of the Brazil Rounds 9 (2007) and 10 (2008).[14]

The Pre-Salt Law, dated of 2010, revoked the unitization provisions of the Petroleum Law. Likewise in the Petroleum Law, under the Pre-Salt Law, unitization is not voluntary in Brazil, but rather mandatory.[15] ANP Resolution #867/2022, as amended, further regulated the unitization provisions of the Pre-Salt Law.

The unitization clauses of the concession contracts of the Brazil Rounds from 11 to 17 and the production sharing contracts of the Pre-Salt Rounds from 1 to 6 do not regulate the unitization procedures in detail, but only provide that, whenever it is identified that a reservoir extends beyond the contract area, an oil and gas unitization procedure must take place in accordance with the applicable Brazilian legislation.[16] In addition, such concession contract and production sharing contract models allow for the partial assignment or transfer of the contract area as an alternative, if unitization negotiations are not successful.

13 ANP's website (http://rodadas.anp.gov.br/pt/concessao-de-blocos-exploratorios-1).

14 ANP's website (http://rodadas.anp.gov.br/pt/concessao-de-blocos-exploratorios-1).

15 Article 33 of the Pre-Salt Law.

16 ANP's website (http://rodadas.anp.gov.br/pt/concessao-de-blocos-exploratorios-1).

According to the ANP Resolution #867/2022, the Operator must promptly notify ANP of the identification of a shared reservoir. Then, ANP shall notify the other party(ies) (of the adjacent blocks or fields) so that it or they can either confirm or reject the existence of a common reservoir within 180 days.[17] ANP will determine the term for the negotiation and execution of the unitization agreement in line with the CNPE's guidelines.[18] The parties will inform the ANP, on a quarterly basis, the status of the negotiations, including: (i) the negotiations schedule; (ii) the division of the rights and obligations of the parties that may have impacts on the Federal Government or on the public interest; and (iii) the performed studies.[19]

The unitization agreement will be added as an exhibit to the relevant E&P granting instruments involved in the unitization by means of proper amendments to them[20] and will contain, at least: (i) the identification of the shared reservoir; (ii) the definition of the unit area with the delimitation of the relevant polygon; (iii) the appointed Operator; (iv) the rights and obligations of the parties that will have impacts on the Federal Government; (v) the participating interests of the parties; (vi) the possibility of redeterminations – including the criteria, conditions, periods and limits; (vii) the local content commitments; (viii) the obligations regarding the government take; (ix) the dispute resolution mechanism; and (x) the development plan. More than one shared reservoir may be included in the same unitization agreement.

For purposes of defining the parties' participating interests, the ratio between the original volumes of equivalent oil in each area will be preferably used, although other criteria may be submitted for ANP's analysis and approval. In case there are different terms for the exploration or production phases of the relevant areas, ANP, at its own criteria, may extend such phases.[21, 22] Usually, the companies in Brazil only include the required minimum clauses in the unitization agreement that will be submitted to ANP and then internally further regulate their joint operations in a unit operating agreement ('UOA'), ANP and works similarly to a joint operating agreement ("JOA") in relation to the E&P granting instrument.

Redeterminations of the parties' participating interest must be technically grounded by the contractor(s) and/or concessionaire(s) and previously approved by ANP. ANP may also request redeterminations when technically grounded.[23]

ANP will approve or request clarifications or revisions within 60 days counted from the receipt of the draft unitization agreement, and the contractor(s) and/or concessionaire(s) must comply with such requests of revisions or clarification within the same period.[24]

17 Article 3 of the ANP Resolution #867/2022.
18 Article 8 of the ANP Resolution #867/2022.
19 Article 9 of the ANP Resolution #867/2022.
20 Article 12 of the ANP Resolution #867/2022.
21 Article 13 of the ANP Resolution #867/2022.
22 Article 33 of the Pre-Salt Law.
23 Articles 29 and 30 of the ANP Resolution #867/2022.
24 Article 12 of the ANP Resolution #867/2022.

In the absence of sufficient data and information to appraise the shared reservoir, the parties may jointly perform the relevant appraisal activities – under a proper appraisal plan – and execute a pre-unitization agreement.[25]

Development and production operations will be suspended while the unitization agreement is not approved by ANP, unless the possibility of moving forward with the activities is technically grounded and authorized by ANP.[26, 27]

If the common reservoir extends into areas where the contractor(s)/ concessionaire(s) or joint ventures have the same composition and participating interests, a unitization commitment must be executed.[28] Such a commitment will contain: (i) the delimitation of the shared reservoir; (ii) the tracts' participating interests; (iii) local content commitments; and (iv) the government take and third parties' participations. The draft unitization commitment must be submitted to ANP along with the studies that led to conclusions of the tracts' participating interests, using preferably the original volumes of oil equivalent.[29]

In case the parties do not voluntarily execute the relevant unitization agreement under the term defined by ANP, ANP will define the rights and obligations of the parties under the shared reservoir through a technical opinion that will be based on the petroleum industry best practices.[30] The involved parties will submit to ANP a detailed and clear description of the issues that prevented the conclusion of the negotiations regarding the unitization agreement and suggest proposals for solving such issues within 60 days from the termination of the term established by ANP for the preparation of the unitization agreement, as well as data and information for the ANP's analysis. ANP may request additional data and information and the parties will have a 30 days period for submitting them. ANP, at its own discretion, may accept the hiring of a third party for the preparation of such technical opinion and, in this case, the contractors and/or concessionaires will reimburse ANP for the relevant costs.[31] ANP will have a term of 120 days for determining the rights and obligations of the parties under the relevant unit area. The counting of this period will be halted whenever ANP requests additional information and/ or data.[32] The technical opinion, as duly grounded, will be submitted for the prior approval of the ANP's Board of Directors.[33] After the approval by the ANP's Board of Directors, the parties will have a 60-day period for the execution of the relevant unitization agreement.[34]

25 Article 7 of the ANP Resolution #867/2022.
26 Article 11 of the ANP Resolution #867/2022.
27 Article 41 of the Pre-Salt Law.
28 Article 4 of the ANP Resolution #867/2022.
29 Article 13, paragraph 2nd of the ANP Resolution #867/2022.
30 Article 33 of the ANP Resolution #867/2022.
31 Article 34 of the ANP Resolution #867/2022.
32 Article 36 of the ANP Resolution #867/2022.
33 Article 35 of the ANP Resolution #867/2022.
34 Article 37 of the ANP Resolution #867/2022.

Unitizations Involving Conflicting Legal Regimes in Brazil

Challenging unitizations involving blocks or fields granted under different E&P regimes are quite usual in Brazil – especially due to the existence of three E&P legal regimes in force and to the geological characteristics of the pre-salt area.[35]

Before the enactment of the ANP Resolution #867/2022, the existence of conflicting E&P legal regimes in unitization procedures resulted in regulatory uncertainty and hours of discussions among the regulators, in-house and external lawyers and management of oil and gas companies. In order to face this challenging situation, ANP understands that there are divisible obligations, which may be separately fulfilled in accordance with the specific provisions of each relevant granting instrument involved in the unitization, and indivisible obligations, which cannot be separately complied with and will need to be regulated in detail in line with the petroleum industry best practices, public interest and equality principles.[36, 37] This theory is grounded in articles 257 and 258 of the Brazilian Civil Code. The article 257 of the Brazilian Civil Code provides that 'if there is more than one debtor or more than one creditor in a divisible obligation, it is assumed to be divided into as many obligations, either equal or different, as there are creditors or debtors' and the article 258 of the Brazilian Civil Code set forth that 'the obligation is indivisible when the benefit has as its object a thing or fact that cannot be divided, due to its nature, economic reasons or the reason for the legal transaction.'

The harmonization of the local content commitments/percentages for the development phase – even in unitizations involving the same E&P regime (e.g., local content commitments may vary in the same bid round depending on the sector and operational environment of the areas) – is a key issue, because, as the development and production operations are jointly performed in the unit area, the local content commitments for the development phase cannot be separately fulfilled.

As an indivisible obligation, under the ANP Resolution #867/2022, the local content commitments for the development phase in case of unitizations should be initially complied with by the concessionaire(s) and/or contractor(s) in line with the following specific formula: (i) the original volumes of oil equivalent for the area under unitization divided by (ii) the relevant local content commitments in contracts that cover the unitization area.

However, as reflected in the ANP Resolution #833/2020 and based on ANP's experience throughout the years, its studies and the opinions of the relevant players, ANP's Local Content Superintendence understood that the best regulatory option for the harmonization of the local content commitments for the development phase would be to offer to the contracting parties of the unit area the possibility of choosing the entirely local content clause (commitments and percentages) of one of the E&P granting instruments involved in the unit area with the retroactive effect

35 Contrato de partilha da produção: comentado (livro eletrônico) / Alexandre B. Calmon [et al.], – São Paulo: Blucher, 2018, p. 110.

36 ANP Legal Opinion No. 237/2012PF-ANPPGFAGU, p. 48.

37 Article 13, paragraph 6, of the ANP Resolution #867/2022.

to all investments made since the beginning of the development phase, in other words, as of the declaration of commerciality.[38]

Differently, considering that the unit operations do not include exploration activities, the local content commitments for such a phase, as a divisible obligation, will be separately fulfilled in accordance with the provisions of each E&P granting instrument involved in the unit area.[39, 40]

The government take and third-party revenues – mainly special participation tax and royalties – are deemed as divisible obligations, so that the parties must follow the provisions of each relevant E&P granting instrument.[41]

ANP Resolution #870/2022 set forth that in case of unitizations involving concession contract areas and production sharing contract areas and/or transfer of rights areas, the special participation tax will be assessed only on the portion allocated to the field under the concession contract regime.[42] It should also be highlighted that, in case of changes in the government take obligations as a result of redeterminations, the effects on payments of the government take will be produced as of the effective date of the redetermination, without any retroactive effect.[43]

Royalties are due by both concessionaires under the concession contracts and contractors under the production sharing contracts. The due value is applicable on a certain percentage of the hydrocarbons production, and it is deemed as a financial compensation to the federal, state and city governments for the oil and natural gas exploration and production activities. The royalties' percentages may vary even for blocks awarded in the same bid round and may be reduced, considering the geological risks, the forecasted production (in case of marginal or mature fields) and other relevant factors.[44]

Likewise, the cost oil, as a divisible obligation – which is only applicable to the production sharing contracts and is defined as a portion of hydrocarbons production that is only due in case of a commercial discovery and correspondent to the costs and investments made by the contractor(s) in the performance of the exploration, appraisal, production and decommissioning activities subject to the limits, terms and conditions provided in the relevant production sharing contract[45] – will be separately calculated based on the portion of the unit area related to the production sharing contract.

The conduct of unit operations by the Operator is an example of indivisible obligation. Each individual block included in a proposed unit generally has a single operator. However, there generally cannot be multiple operators for an individual

38 ANP Local Content Superintendence's Technical Note No. 15/2020/SCL/ANP-RJ.
39 Article 39 of the ANP Resolution #867/2022.
40 Article 3 of the ANP Resolution #833/2020.
41 Article 25, paragraph 4th of the ANP Resolution #867/2022.
42 Article 9 of the ANP Resolution #870/2022.
43 Article 31, sole paragraph, of the ANP Resolution #867/2022.
44 Article 47, paragraph 1, of the Petroleum Law.
45 Article 2, item II, of the Law #12,351/2010.

field. Thus, the ANP's regulation provides that the parties must appoint a single Operator for the unit area.[46]

Unitizations with Open Acreages in Brazil

Due to the huge size of the reservoirs located in the pre-salt layer of the Brazilian offshore basins and the geological characteristics of such areas, there is a great likelihood of unitizations with open acreages in the Brazilian pre-salt polygon.

If the shared reservoir extends into an open acreage, the Operator and Non-Operator(s) (if applicable) of the contracted area will mandatorily execute a unitization agreement with the Federal Government, as duly represented by either PPSA[47] – in case the open acreage is located in the pre-salt polygon and in the areas deemed as strategic – or ANP – in all other areas. The relevant contractor(s) and/or concessionaire(s) will submit to ANP a preliminary proposal for the joint appraisal of the shared reservoir and ANP will inform to other involved party(ies) within 180 days how the shared reservoir will be assessed. ANP – on behalf of the Federal Government – may either directly perform such activities or hire Petrobras.[48, 49]

Any future contractor(s) or concessionaire(s) of the open acreage will assume the rights and obligations under the unitization agreement executed with the Federal Government – either by PPSA or ANP. In any event, such future contractor(s) or concessionaire(s) along with the ones of the adjacent tract may request ANP's approval for revisions on the executed unitization agreement.

It is important to highlight that the open acreage will not necessarily be subject to bids under the same E&P regime or granting instrument of the adjacent area. However, the same commitments (e.g. local content) of the contracted area will be applied to the open acreage until it is awarded in a future bid round.

The companies in the adjacent area to the open acreage may request (i) the suspension of the E&P granting instrument term; or (ii) continuity of the activities, provided that ANP authorizes it and under the conditions set forth by the oil and gas regulator while the open acreage is not awarded in a certain ANP's auction.[50] Under the most recent versions of the concession contract and production sharing contract, the contractors may be authorized by the ANP for the drilling of wells beyond the contract areas in case of unitizations.[51]

The operator of the adjacent contracted area will also be the operator of the unitized area, for so long as the open acreage area is not awarded in a certain bid

46 Article 13, item III, of the ANP Resolution #867/2022.

47 PPSA is a state owned company in charge of the production sharing contracts management and the marketing of the Federal Government's share of oil and natural gas produced in such areas.

48 Article 14 of the ANP Resolution #867/2022.

49 Articles 36, 37 and 38 of the Pre-Salt Law.

50 Article 17 of the ANP Resolution #867/2022.

51 Clause 19.10 of the production sharing contract of the Pre-Salt Round 6 and Clause 15.19 of the concession contract of the Brazil Round 16.

round.[52] PPSA or ANP – on behalf of the Federal Government – cannot be the operator of the unit area. As soon as the open acreage is awarded to a company or joint venture, the parties may freely appoint the new operator of the unitized area.

If the production of the shared reservoir commences before the effective date of the relevant unitization agreement involving an open acreage, which is the first day of the month following the approval of the unitization agreement by the ANP, the Operator and Non-Operator(s) (if applicable) of the contracted area will be entirely entitled to the produced oil and natural gas, including the production of any drill stem tests.[53]

The costs related to the period before the effective date of the unitization agreement involving an open acreage may only be reimbursed by the Federal Government: (i) in case of commerciality of, at least, one of the discovered areas; and (ii) up to the limit of the production that the Federal Government is entitled. Costs related to the payment of signature bonuses and to the fulfillment of the minimum exploration program, as well as for activities that have not produced data and information on the shared reservoir, cannot be reimbursed.[54]

The reimbursement of costs and investments related to the exploration phase is usually a point of discussion during the negotiations of the relevant unitization agreement. The reimbursement could be grounded under the prohibition of unjust enrichment, in other words, the rule preventing a party from receiving a benefit without a proper compensation to the other party.

ANP's legal department understands that the reimbursement of the exploration costs and investments in the unit area in case of unitizations involving production sharing contract areas would result in a double payment by the Federal Government, taking into consideration that the contractors will already be reimbursed by cost oil earned in relation to the contracted area.[55]

If the production of the shared reservoir commences before the award of the open acreage, but after the effective date, the monetization of all produced oil and natural gas will be divided in accordance with the participation interest of the Federal Government and the other parties.[56]

The Federal Government will participate in the operating expenditures related to the production and capital expenditures in connection with the development – in the ratio between the hydrocarbon production prior to the award of the open acreage and the total recovery of hydrocarbons forecasted in the relevant development plan. However, the Federal Government will not pay such costs in cash, but rather in discounts of its entitlements of the hydrocarbons production, which may not be greater than 20% of the monthly production.[57] As explained by ANP during the discussions of the draft version of the ANP Resolution #867/2022, this 20%

52 Article 16, item I of the ANP Resolution #867/2022.
53 Article 17 of the ANP Resolution #867/2022.
54 Article 18 of the ANP Resolution #867/2022.
55 ANP Legal Opinion No. 2372012PF-ANP-PGF-AGU.
56 Article 17 of the ANP Resolution #867/2022.
57 Article 18, paragraph 3rd of the ANP Resolution #867/2022.

limit was based on the fact that the average percentage of the aggregated costs in exploration, appraisal, production and decommissioning activities over the gross revenues of the five largest Brazilian oil fields in the period between 2007 and 2009 was 22.38% with a standard deviation of 7.92%.[58]

Conclusion

Unitizations in Brazil may turn out to be very complex and challenging, as they could potentially involve different E&P legal regimes (e.g., concession contract, production sharing contract and transfer or right agreement regimes).

Between the enactment of the Pre-Salt Law (dated of 2010) and the issuance of the ANP Resolution #867/2022 (dated of 2013), there was a great deal of regulatory uncertainty in unitizations in Brazil involving conflicting E&P legal regimes, which resulted in the postponement of investments in some projects.

A key issue dealt by ANP Resolution #867/2022 was the harmonization of different obligations provided in the E&P granting instruments involved in a certain unitization. This regulation adopts the rationale that there are indivisible obligations (e.g., local content commitments for the development phase and operatorship) – that may not be separately fulfilled due to their nature or economic reasons – and divisible obligations (e.g., local content commitments for the exploration phase, royalties, special participation tax and cost oil) which may be separately fulfilled in accordance with each E&P granting instrument. In the former case, such obligations will be regulated in detail, by the ANP, in line with the petroleum industry best practices, public interest and equality principles. This aspect of the ANP Resolution #867/2022 was crucial to grant regulatory certainty to the players in the Brazilian upstream industry.

On the other hand, there are certain privileges to the Federal Government in case of unitizations involving open acreages that may result in regulatory uncertainty to the contractors. The Federal Government will only reimburse costs and expenditures related to the period before the effective date of the unitization agreement involving an open acreage in case of commerciality of, at least, one of the discovered areas. The reimbursement will not include costs related to the payment of signature bonuses and to the fulfillment of the minimum exploration program, as well as for activities that have not produced data and information on the shared reservoir. It could be argued that, because of such provisions, the Federal Government would be carried by the relevant contractors. Furthermore, the Federal Government participation in the capital and operational expenditures in connection with the development activities is capped to 20% of the monthly production.

Thus, further improvements in the applicable regulation are still necessary to increase the attractiveness of the Brazilian upstream market to the investors (NOCs, majors, IOCs, Brazilian independent companies and private funds), especially

58 ANP's website (http://www.anp.gov.br/consultas-audiencias-publicas/concluidas/2150-aviso-de-consulta-eaudiencia-publicas-n-5-2013).

taking into consideration that, due to the geological characteristics and huge size of the pre-salt reservoirs plus the great number of offshore areas that were still not offered for bids by the Brazilian Government, there is a great likelihood of unitizations in Brazil.

Four (4) Key Findings of this Chapter

1. Due to its geological characteristics, unitizations are quite common in Brazil.
2. Unitizations in Brazil may be very challenging, considering the potential coexistence of different E&P legal regimes (e.g., concession contract, production sharing contract and transfer or right agreement regimes).
3. Current regulation has provided certainty to the companies operating in Brazil, especially regarding indivisible obligations in different legal regimes (e.g., local content obligations).
4. Certain privileges given to the Federal Government may be criticized, including caps on the payment of capital and operational expenditures and absence of reimbursement obligations in the case of areas where there were no commercial discoveries. Therefore, further improvements to the applicable regulation are still needed.

5 Unitization in Canada

Chi Iliya-Ndule

5.1 Introduction

This chapter reviews the law relating to unitization in Canada, federally, and in Alberta. Canada is a federation divided into ten provinces and three territories. Governmental power is distributed between the federal government and the provincial governments.[1] The majority of the mineral rights within Canada's boundaries are owned by the government, with a minority being held by private individuals and corporations.[2] Each province regulates the exploration, development, conservation and management of oil and gas within its boundaries, excluding federally managed lands,[3] while inter-provincial and international oil and gas operations, and operations in Canada's frontier lands are regulated federally.[4]

According to Natural Resources Canada, Canada is the fourth largest producer of crude oil and the fifth largest producer of natural gas in the world, with the province of Alberta producing the largest amount of crude oil and marketable gas within Canada.[5] Canada relies heavily on its oil and gas sector[6] and is committed

1 Constitution Act, 1867 (U.K), 30 & 31 Vict., c. 3 [Constitution Act, 1867], ss. 91, 92, 92A. The government of the three territories are subordinate to the federal parliament – Northwest Territories Act, R.S.C 1985, c N-27; Nunavut Act, S.C 1993, c. 28; Yukon Act, S.C. 2002: See Peter Hogg, *Constitutional Law of Canada* (5th edn, Carswell 2007).

2 Alberta, 'Freehold Minerals in Alberta' <https://www.alberta.ca/freehold-minerals-in-alberta.aspx>.

3 Federally managed lands include national parks and Indian reserves.

4 Constitution Act, 1867, *supra* note 1. Frontier Lands include lands in the Northwest Territories, Nunavut, Sable Island and submarine areas located outside of a province in the internal waters, territorial sea or the continental shelf of Canada for which the Government of Canada has the right to dispose of or exploit petroleum resources: Canadian Petroleum Resources Act, RSC 1985, c. 36 (2nd Supp.), s. 2.

5 Energy Fact Book 2022–2023, Natural Resources Canada <Section 6: Oil, natural gas and coal (nrcan.gc.ca)>. In 2021, Alberta produced 62% of Canada's natural gas and 85% of Canada's oil and equivalent: Alberta Energy Regulator, 'Alberta Energy Outlook: ST98 Executive Summary' (2022) Alberta Energy Regulator <Alberta Energy Outlook – ST98 2022 Executive Summary (aer.ca)>.

6 Statistics published by Statista Research Department on 6 October 2022, shows that the mining and oil and gas extraction sector added 151.58 chained 2012 Canadian dollars to Canada's total GDP in 2021, which is the fourth largest contributor by industry to the GDP: Real Value Added to the Gross

DOI: 10.4324/9781003491293-7

to promoting conservation and the orderly and responsible production of its oil and gas resources.[7]

This chapter is divided into five sections. Section 5.2 will provide a general overview on the concept of unitization. Sections 5.3 and 5.4 will examine the legal and regulatory regime governing unitization federally and in Alberta, respectively. Section 5.5 will set out the conclusion.

5.2 Unitization

Oil and gas resources accumulate in natural underground pools.[8] Each pool is a homogenous whole, with the substances moving freely within it.[9] Oil and gas leases rarely cover an entire pool; as a result, it is typical for multiple parties to hold various oil and gas rights in a pool. The migratory nature of oil and gas and the rule of capture[10] provided an incentive for the various owners of the oil or gas rights in a pool to drill and drain competitively.[11] The race to drill numerous wells in order to capture oil and gas resources as quickly as possible led to unrestricted drilling, excessive production and rapid depletion of oil and gas resources.[12] The economic and physical waste and the desire to obtain maximum recovery of oil and gas resources led to oil and gas conservation practices and legislation.[13]

Unitization is one means by which the effects of the rule of capture can be avoided.[14] Unitization "is the joint, coordinated operation of an oil or gas reservoir by all the owners of rights in the separate tracts overlying the reservoir or reservoirs."[15] It is the development and production of oil or gas resources in a

Domestic Product (GDP) of Canada in 2021, by Industry" (2022) Statista <https://www.statista.com/statistics/463290/real-value-added-to-canada-gdp-by-industry/>.

7 Canada Oil and Gas Operations Act, RSC 1985, c O-7 [COGOA], s. 2.1; Oil and Gas Conservation Act, RSC 2000, c O-6 [OGCA], s. 4; Responsible Energy Development Act, SA 2012, c R-17.3, [REDA], s 2(1).

8 John B Ballem, *The Oil and Gas Lease in Canada* (4th edn, University of Toronto Press 2008) 251.

9 John B Ballem, *The Oil and Gas Lease in Canada* (4th edn, University of Toronto Press 2008) 251.

10 The rule of capture effectively assigns property rights to oil and gas resources upon extraction: Gary D Libecap and Steven N Wiggins, 'The Influence of Private Contractual Failure on Regulation: The Case of Oil Field Unitization' (1985) 93(4) J Polit Econ 690 at 693. For the history and current state of the rule of capture in Canada, see Cecilia A Low, 'The Rule of Capture: Its Current Status and Some Issues to Consider' (2009) 46(3) Alta L Rev 799.

11 Gary D Libecap and Steven N Wiggins, 'The Influence of Private Contractual Failure on Regulation: The Case of Oil Field Unitization' (1985) 93(4) J Polit Econ 690 at 693. For the history and current state of the rule of capture in Canada, see Cecilia A Low, 'The Rule of Capture: Its Current Status and Some Issues to Consider' (2009) 46(3) Alta L Rev 799.

12 Bob Galbraith and Al Skeet, 'Production of Oil and Gas' in A T Main and J Denis McGrath (eds), *Introduction to Oil & Gas Law* (Canadian Association of Petroleum Landmen 1992) 93.

13 Cecilia Low, *supra* note 10 at 799, 816–822; John Ballem, *supra* note 8 at 224.

14 Cecilia Low, *supra* note 10 at 821.

15 Jacqueline Lang Weaver and David F Asmus, 'Unitizing Oil and Gas Fields Around the World: A Comparative Analysis of National Laws and Private Contracts' (2006) 28 Hous J Int'l L 3 at 11.

common field or pool, or part thereof, that crosses different spacing units[16] and ownership interests so that operations are conducted as a single unit and as if there is only one operator.[17] Unitization promotes efficiency of the operations and maximizes recovery from the pool. In Canada, two agreements are used to govern unit operations: a unit agreement, which is the agreement between all the interests owners to unitize their interests, and a unit operating agreement, which is the agreement providing for the management and operation of a unit area or unitized zone.[18] As unitization results in the development and production of a pool as a single unit, it modifies the relationship between the lessor and lessee of the various leases and the lessors are typically called royalty owners and the lessees, working interest (WI) owners.[19]

Pooling, which involves combining, through agreement, the WIs for different contiguous tracts of land within a spacing unit,[20] is another conservation process that is often wrongly used interchangeably with unitization. Unlike pooling, which is limited to a spacing unit and is required in order to obtain a well license,[21] unitization encompasses an entire pool or part thereof, and involves the joint operation and development of the pool by the different WI and royalty owners without regard to surface boundary lines and is often utilized after the primary production phase of a pool.[22]

Unitization mitigates wasteful operations, and promotes the organized, cost-effective, and efficient exploitation of oil and gas reserves. However, the usefulness or success of unitization can be limited or maximized by legislation or a lack thereof.[23] Unitization may be voluntary or compulsory. Unitization is voluntary where the owners are required to agree amongst themselves to enter into a unitization arrangement, and it is compulsory when the unitization arrangement is forced on all the owners by legislation.

16 A spacing unit or drilling spacing unit is the minimum area established by the relevant regulatory authority for the purpose of drilling for or producing oil and gas: COGOA, s. 29. See also Cecilia Low, *supra* note 10 at 821. Oil and Gas Conservation Rules, AR 151/1971 [OGCR], s. 4.010(1) defines a drilling spacing unit as the surface area and the subsurface vertically beneath that area, or where the spacing unit is prescribed with respect to a specified pool, geological formation, member or zone, the pool, geological formation, member or zone vertically beneath that area. In Alberta, unless the Alberta Energy Regulator prescribes otherwise, the surface area of a spacing unit for an oil well is one quarter section and for a gas well is one section: OGCR, s. 4.010(3). A section of land is 1 mile square.

17 OGCA, s. 78.

18 COGOA, ss. 29, 40; OGCA, s. 79(2).

19 Galbraith & Skeet, *supra* note 12 at 98.

20 Cecilia Low, *supra* note 10 at 821.

21 All producing jurisdictions in Canada effectively require pooling in order to license a well where there is more than one tract in a spacing unit. Cecilia Low, *supra* note 10 at 821.

22 Patrick H Martin and Bruce M Kramer, *Williams & Meyers, Oil and Gas Law Abridged Seventh Edition*, sec no. 901 (LexisNexis Matthew Bender 2018); Government of Alberta, *Guide for Unit Agreement* (updated 2020) <https://training.energy.gov.ab.ca/Guides/Guide_For_Unit_Agreements.pdf>; Michael P Simms and Carole Chan, 'Onshore Oil and Gas Regimes in Atlantic Canada' (2014) 37 Dalhousie LJ 87 at 111; Cecilia Low, *supra* note 10 at 821.

23 Cecilia Low, *supra* note 10 at 821.

5.3 Legal and Regulatory Framework Governing Unitization Federally

5.3.1 Primary Legislation and Regulatory Body

The Canadian Energy Regulator (hereinafter Canadian Regulator) is the primary regulator responsible for oil and gas operations federally.[24] The Canadian Regulator was established under the Canadian Energy Regulator Act in 2019,[25] replacing the National Energy Board, which was formed in 1959. The Canadian Regulator, together with its predecessor, have over 60 years' experience overseeing oil and gas activities in Canada.[26] It is responsible for making decisions, orders and giving directions with respect to federal oil and gas interests, production and conservation.[27] The Canadian Regulator has regulatory responsibilities over oil and gas activities in Nunavut, parts of Northwest Territories (NWT) and Canada's offshore that are not regulated by other provincial or federal regulations.[28]

The Canadian Oil and Gas Operations Act (COGOA)[29] is the primary legislation governing unitization of oil and gas tracts federally, while the Oil and Gas Operations Act (OGOA)[30] governs unitization in the NWT. The Canadian Regulator administers both the COGOA and the OGOA.[31]

24 Canadian Energy Regulator Act, SC 2019, c 28, s. 10 [CERA].

25 Canadian Energy Regulator Act, SC 2019, c 28, s. 10 [CERA].

26 Canada Energy Regulator, *Our History*, Canada Energy Regulator <https://www.cer-rec.gc.ca/en/about/who-we-are-what-we-do/our-history.html>.

27 *CERA*, s. 11.

28 Canada Energy Regulator, *What We Regulate in the North and Offshore*, Canada Energy Regulator <https://www.cer-rec.gc.ca/en/about/north-offshore/what-we-regulate.html>. See also the Services Agreement between the Government of the Northwest Territories as represented by the Office of the Regulator of Oil and Gas Operations and the Majesty the Queen in Right of Canada as represented by the Canada Energy Regulator dated 10 March 2020: Canada Energy Regulator, *Government of the Northwest Territories as Represented by the Office of the Regulator of Oil and Gas Operations – Service Agreement*, Canada Energy Regulator <https://www.cer-rec.gc.ca/en/about/acts-regulations/other-acts/cooperative-agreements/government-northwest-territories-as-represented-office-regulator-oil-gas-operations-service-agreement.html>. Areas offshore the east coast of Canada are regulated by the Canada-Newfoundland and Labrador Offshore Petroleum Board and Canada–Nova Scotia Offshore Petroleum Board: Canada Energy Regulator, *Offshore Drilling*, Canada Energy Regulator <https://www.cer-rec.gc.ca/en/about/north-offshore/offshore-drilling.html>. The Canadian Regulator also performs services for Yukon and provides advice to Yukon with respect to energy matters, including matters related to unitization: see the Services Agreement between the Government of Yukon as represented by the Minister of Energy, Mines and Resources and the Majesty the Queen in Right of Canada as represented by the Canada Energy Regulator dated 2 September 2020: Canada Energy Regulator, *Services Agreement between the Government of Yukon and the Canada Energy Regulator*, Canada Energy Regulator <https://www.cer-rec.gc.ca/en/about/acts-regulations/other-acts/cooperative-agreements/yukon-government-services-agreement.html>.

29 RSC 1985, c O-7.

30 SNWT 2014, c 14.

31 The CER administers the OGOA in respect of the Inuvialuit Settlement Region within NWT's onshore: OGOA, s. 1.

5.3.2 Legal and Regulatory Framework

The COGOA and the OGOA promote, in respect of the exploration for and exploitation of oil and gas, the conservation of oil and gas resources.[32] Under the COGOA and OGOA, unitization may either be voluntary or compulsory.[33] Research indicates that the Canadian Regulator has not invoked the unitization of oil and gas tracts.

5.3.2.1 Voluntary Unitization

Any one or more WI and royalty owners in a pool or in a part of a pool that exceeds a spacing unit may enter into a unit agreement and operate their interests in accordance with the unit agreement, as long as a copy of the unit agreement is filed with the chief conservation officer.[34] No party may conduct operations under a unit agreement without the requisite approval.

5.3.2.2 Compulsory Unitization

The COGOA and OGOA authorize each of their Oil and Gas Committee[35] (hereinafter Committee) to order the unitization of oil and gas tracts in certain instances and despite the objection of minority interest holders. The minister[36] may enter into a unit agreement on any terms and conditions that the minister deems fit.[37]

5.3.2.2.1 COMPULSORY UNITIZATION ON APPLICATION OF THE CHIEF CONSERVATION OFFICER

In order to prevent waste, the chief conservation officer may apply to the Committee for a unitization order requiring WI owners in a pool or part thereof to enter into

32 COGOA, s. 2.1; OGOA, s. 2.1.

33 See COGOA, s. 38. Unitization may be voluntary or compulsory in other jurisdictions in Canada except Alberta, see Canada–Newfoundland and Labrador Atlantic Accord Implementation Newfoundland and Labrador Act, RSNL 1990, c C-2, s. 169; Canada–Nova Scotia Offshore Petroleum Resources Accord Implementation (Nova Scotia) Act, SNS 1987, c 3, s. 170; Exploration, Drilling and Production Regulation, O Reg 245/97, ss. 15, 16 (Ontario); Oil and Gas Act, CCSM c 034, s. 135 (Manitoba); Oil and Gas Act, RSY 2002, c. 162, s. 87 (Yukon); Oil and Gas Activities Act, SBC 2008, c 36, s. 72 (BC); Oil and Gas Conservation Act, RSS 1978, c O-2, s. 35 (Saskatchewan); and Oil and Gas Operations Act, SNWT 2014, c. 14, ss. 75 (NWT).

34 COGOA, s. 37(1); OGOA, s. 74(1). The Chief Conservation Officer is appointed by the CER: COGOA, s. 3.1; OGOA, s. 105. The Minister may enter into a unit agreement on terms and conditions that the Minister deems advisable: COGOA, s. 37(2); OGOA, s. 74(2).

35 The Oil and Gas Committee is a committee established by the Governor in Council or Executive Council, as applicable, and the Oil and Gas Committee is under the direction of the Minister: COGOA, ss. 6(1)(2); OGOA, ss. 27(1)(2).

36 The Minister means in relation to any area in respect of which the Minister of Northern Affairs or the Minister of Natural Resources have administrative responsibility for the natural resources therein, the Minister of Northern Affairs or the Minister of Natural Resources, as applicable: COGOA, s. 2.

37 COGOA, s. 37(2); OGOA, s. 74.

a unit agreement and a unit operating agreement (together, the Unitization Agreements) in respect of that pool.[38]

The Committee will hold a hearing with all interested parties to consider the chief conservation officer's application.[39] After the hearing and if the Committee is of the opinion that unitization of the applicable tracts will prevent waste, the Committee may order that the pool, or part thereof, be operated as a unit and that all the WI owners enter into the Unitization Agreements within a specified period, not exceeding six months.[40]

If the WI and royalty owners fail to enter into the Unitization Agreements within the time specified in the unitization order, all drilling and producing operations in the pool will cease until the Unitization Agreements have been entered into and approved by the Committee.[41] However, the Committee may permit the owners to continue operations if the Committee is convinced that the owners are in the course of entering into the Unitization Agreements.[42]

5.3.2.2.2 COMPULSORY UNITIZATION ON APPLICATION OF THE WORKING INTEREST OWNERS

One or more WI owners who are parties to the Unitization Agreements (in the case of an application for a variation) or proposed Unitization Agreements, and who own a total of 65% or more of the WIs in a unit may apply for a unitization order with respect to such agreements.[43] The unit operator or proposed unit operator may also make the unitization order application on behalf of the majority WI owners.[44] The application for a unitization order must contain[45]:

a. a plan showing the proposed unit area;
b. a copy of the unit agreement, which must include:
    i. a description of the unit area and the unit tracts;
    ii. the share of production from a unit area that has been allocated to a unit tract and deemed to have been produced from that unit tract;
    iii. an allocation to each unit tract of a share of production from the unitized zone not required, consumed or lost in the unit operation; and
    iv. a termination clause;

38 COGOA, s. 38(1); OGOA, s. 75(1).
39 COGOA, s. 38(2); OGOA, s. 75(2).
40 COGOA, s. 38(3), (4); OGOA, s. 75(3), (4).
41 COGOA, s. 38(4); OGOA, s. 75(4).
42 COGOA, s. 38(5); OGOA, s. 75(5).
43 COGOA, s. 39(1); OGOA, s. 76(1). The percentage of interests is determined with respect to: (a) WI, on the basis of tract participations shown in the unit agreement, and (b) royalty interests, on a prorated area basis: COGOA, s. 47(1); OGOA, ss. 84(1).
44 COGOA, s. 39(3); OGOA, s. 76(3).
45 COGOA, s. 40; OGOA, s. 77.

c. a copy of the unit operating agreement, which must include:

    i. the contribution or transfer to the unit of investment in wells and equipment in the unit area; and any adjustment among the WI owners;
    ii. the costs and expenses of the unit operation to the WI owners;
    iii. the determination of the percentage value of each WI owner's vote;
    iv. the determination of the method of voting before the operating committee and the percentage value of votes required to make a decision;
    v. a supervisory unit operating committee that consists of representatives of the WI owners; and
    vi. the appointment of a unit operator that is responsible for carrying out the unit operation under the direction and supervision of the operating committee;

d. the nature of operations to be carried out;
e. the unit tracts; and
f. the names and addresses of the WI and royalty owners in each proposed unit tract.

The application is to be made to the minister, who shall transfer the application to the Committee.[46] The Committee will hold a hearing with all interested parties to consider the application.[47]

After the hearing, the Committee may make an order that the Unitization Agreements are valid contracts, binding on and enforceable against all owners if the Commission finds that:

a. at the commencement of the hearing:

    i. the Unitization Agreements were executed by one or more WI owners holding a total of 65% or more of the total WIs in the unit area; and
    ii. the unit agreement was executed by one or more royalty owners owning a total of 65% or more of the royalty interests in the unit area; and

b. the unitization order would result in the more efficient or more economical production of oil or gas or both from the unitized zone.[48]

The Committee may, on application, make a unitization order varying the terms of the Unitization Agreements.[49] A variation will become ineffective if, before its effective date, the applicant on behalf of all WI owners withdraws the application for a variation or a statement of written objection is signed by (1) in the case of a unit agreement, one or more WIs and royalty owners holding more than 25% of

46 COGOA, s. 39(2); OGOA, s. 76(2).
47 COGOA, s. 41(1); OGOA, s. 78(1).
48 COGOA, s. 41(2); OGOA, s. 78(2).
49 COGOA, s. 41(3); OGOA, s. 78(3).

the total WIs in the unit area, and (2) in the case of a unit operating agreement, one or more WI owners holding more than 25% of the total WIs in the unit area.[50] The Committee will revoke a variation that becomes ineffective.[51] The WIs and/or royalty owners who sign the statement of written objection must belong to the same group of WI and/or royalty interest owners holding 65% or more of the total WIs in the unit area who signed the Unitization Agreements.[52]

The effective date of the unitization order must be at least 30 days from the date on which the order was made.[53] A unitization order may be amended on the application of a WI owner, except that no amendment can be made that will alter the ratio of tract participation in the unit agreement contained in the unitization order.[54] The Committee shall hold a hearing before amending a unitization order.[55] However, an amendment hearing may be dispensed with where one or more WI and royalty interest owners holding a total of 65% or more of the total WIs in the unit area consent to the proposed amendment.[56]

Once a unitization order is made and while it is in effect, all drilling and production operations from the unitized zone must be in accordance with the provisions of the approved Unitization Agreements.[57]

Unlike the unitization order made upon the application of the chief conservation officer, which is based on the prevention of waste, a unitization order made upon the application of WI owners focuses on efficiency and economical production of oil and gas resources and requires the buy-in of a majority of the WI and royalty owners.

5.3.2.3 Unitization of Straddling Resources

Under the COGOA and OGOA, a single oil and gas pool in the Inuvialuit Settlement Region that straddles the offshore and onshore may be exploited as a single pool and shall, to the extent possible, be managed by a single exploration or drilling program.[58]

The owners may enter into the Unitization Agreements and, upon approval by the minister and the government of NWT, operate their interests in accordance with the Unitization Agreements.[59] The Unitization Agreements may only be approved if all owners are parties to the agreements. No exploitation authorization

50 COGOA, s. 42(2); OGOA, s. 79(2).
51 COGOA, s. 42(3); OGOA, s. 79(2).
52 COGOA, s. 42; OGOA, s. 79(2).
53 COGOA, s. 42(1); OGOA, s. 79(1).
54 COGOA, ss. 44(1), 45; OGOA, ss. 81(1), 82.
55 COGOA, ss. 44(1), 45; OGOA, ss. 81(1), 82.
56 COGOA, s. 44; OGOA, s. 81(2).
57 COGOA, s. 46; OGOA, s. 83.
58 COGOA, s. 48.04; OGOA, s. 89. The Minister or the Government of the NWT may require the other to make an order that a pool that is a straddling resource be exploited as a single pool: COGOA, s. 48.06; OGOA, s. 91.
59 COGOA, s. 48.07; OGOA, s. 92.

or development plan will be approved until the Unitization Agreements have been approved.[60]

Where a straddling resource is required to be exploited as a unit and the WI owners have not entered into the Unitization Agreements, the minister shall make an order requiring the WI owners to enter into the Unitization Agreement in the portion of the pool that is within the minister's jurisdiction.[61] However, the minister or the government of NWT may require of the other that a straddling resource be exploited as a singled pool or field.[62] If the WI and/or royalty owners cannot enter into the Unitization Agreements, within 90 days of the minister's order, the minister or the government of NWT may refer the matter to an independent expert, and the minister shall issue a unitization order in accordance with the expert's final decision.[63] The joint approval of the minister and the government of NWT is required for a unitization order to be effective.[64]

Unitization Agreements for straddling resources shall remain in force until the later of the day commercial production ends or the day there are no outstanding decommissioning or abandonment obligations.[65]

5.4 Legal and Regulatory Framework Governing Unitization in Alberta

5.4.1 Primary Legislation and Regulatory Body

In 1930, the government of Canada transferred the ownership of crown minerals within its borders to Alberta.[66] Alberta Energy manages and administers legislation governing ownership and administration of Alberta's oil and gas resources. Alberta Energy's mission is to "assure sustained prosperity in the interests of Albertans through the stewardship of energy and mineral resource systems, responsible development and wise use of energy."[67]

In 1932, in order to promote conservation and reduce the wasteful flaring of natural gas, Alberta enacted the Turner Valley Conservation Act and the Turner Valley Conservation Board, which are the forerunners of Alberta's current conservation legislation and the energy regulator.[68] In 1938, Alberta created its energy regulator, the Petroleum and Natural Gas Conservation Board. Over the years, the role

60 COGOA, s. 48.09; OGOA, s. 94.

61 COGOA, s. 48.08; OGOA, s. 93.

62 COGOA, s. 48.06; OGOA, s. 91.

63 COGOA, ss. 48.091, 48.092; OGOA, s. 96.

64 COGOA, s. 48.092; OGOA, s.96.

65 COGOA, s. 48.07(1); OGOA, s. 92(3).

66 See An Act Respecting the Transfer of the Alberta Natural Resources of Alberta, SA 1930, c 21.

67 Alberta, *Energy*, Alberta <https://www.alberta.ca/energy.aspx#:~:text=Energy's%20mission%20is%20to%20assure,and%20wise%20use%20of%20energy>.

68 Gordon Jaremko, *Steward: 75 Years of Alberta Energy Regulation* (Energy Resources Conservation Board 2013) 159 <https://static.aer.ca/prd/documents/about-us/Steward_Ebook.pdf>; Bob Galbraith and Al Skeet, *supra* note 12 at 93.

of the Petroleum and Natural Gas Conservation Board evolved and it has undergone several name changes: the Oil and Gas Conservation Board (1957–1971), the Energy Resources Conservation Board (1971–1995), the Alberta Energy and Utilities Board (1995–2007), once again the Energy Resources Conservation Board (2008–2013) and now the Alberta Energy Regulator (AER).[69]

The AER is the sole regulator of all aspects of oil and gas development in Alberta.[70] It was created under the Responsible Energy Development Act in 2013. The AER is responsible for ensuring that oil and gas resources are developed in an efficient, orderly and environmentally responsible manner.[71]

Accordingly, Alberta Energy issues leases and licences and grants the right to drill for and recover oil and gas while the AER regulates drilling and production operations of both Crown and freehold minerals.

The Oil and Gas Conservation Act[72] and the Mines and Minerals Act[73] are the primary legislation governing unitization in Alberta. The AER administers the Oil and Gas Conservation Act. The purposes of the Oil and Gas Conservation Act are to ensure (1) the conservation, and prevention of waste, of oil and gas resources; (2) that efficient and responsible practices are observed in the production of oil and gas resources; and (3) that each oil and gas interest owner obtains its fair share of the production of oil or gas from any pool.[74]

The Mines and Minerals Act governs the management and disposition of Crown-owned mineral rights, and is administered jointly by Alberta Energy, the Ministry of Environment and Parks, and the AER. However, the provisions that deal with unitization are administered by Alberta Energy.

5.4.2 Legal and Regulatory Framework

Alberta Energy administers three types of unit agreements: standard unit agreements, production allocation unit agreements and gas storage unit agreements.[75] Alberta Energy owns its model production allocation and gas storage unit agreements, and uses the Petroleum Joint Venture Association's (PJVA) model Unitization Agreements.[76] This section focuses on the PJVA's model Unitization Agreements.

69 Alberta Energy Regulator, *What Is the AER*, Alberta Energy Regulator <https://www.aer.ca/providing-information/news-and-resources/enerfaqs-and-fact-sheets/enerfaqs-what-is-the-aer>.

70 Alberta Energy Regulator, *How Does the AER Regulate Energy Development in Alberta?*, Alberta Energy Regulator <https://www.aer.ca/protecting-what-matters/holding-industry-accountable/how-does-the-AER-regulate-energy-development-in-alberta>.

71 REDA, s. 2(1).

72 RSA 2000, c O-6.

73 RSA 2000, c M-17.

74 OGCA, s. 4.

75 Alberta Government, *Petroleum and Natural Gas Tenure in Alberta* (2016) 15, Alberta <https://open.alberta.ca/dataset/6ba11381-43d7-4d64-a0e4-e594d9cb8b10/resource/4ad12ed6-fb9d-4067-b12c-11d34c0c482b/download/Tenure-Brochure-PRINTABLE-VERSION-February-15-2016-Version-for-Print-Shop.pdf> (PNG Tenure in Alberta).

76 Guide for Unit Agreements, *supra* note 22. The production allocation unit agreement is a unit-type agreement for a single well that crosses multiple spacing units of mixed ownership, while the gas

In Alberta, unitization is voluntary; the AER cannot compel owners to enter into Unitization Agreements.[77] Owners of oil and gas interests in a common pool may choose to unitize their operations to achieve a more efficient and economical operation or to meet the AER's requirements for common ownership to implement a secondary recovery scheme.[78] The AER has the statutory duty to encourage unitization negotiations/efforts initiated by owners for the purpose of accomplishing a more efficient and economical development and production of the oil and gas resources in a common pool.[79] However, in practice, the AER may exert substantial pressure on owners to enter into Unitization Agreements, by its power to impose production penalties and adjust allowables.[80]

The minister enters into unit agreements on behalf of the Crown.[81] The Crown only participates in units that contain Crown-leased mineral rights and where there is diversity of ownership, either at lessee or lessor level.[82] Crown-owned minerals are subject to the unit agreement only so long as the Crown is a party to the unit agreement.[83]

The unit operator facilitates and coordinates the negotiation of the unit among the owners. A proposal for a unit agreement can be submitted at any time but cannot be finalized without Alberta Energy's authorization.[84] A proposal must include technical data that explains the proposed calculation of tract participation factors, the pool being unitized such as engineering and geophysical data and the extent of the pool, the presence of a gas cap, and AER water flood application and project area approval.[85]

When reviewing a unit agreement proposal, Alberta Energy considers whether:

1. The petroleum and natural gas (PNG) agreements have been continued indefinitely,

---

storage unit agreement is an agreement that establishes a reservoir as one in which natural gas may be stored after it was produced from its native reservoir: Guide for Unit Agreements, *supra* note 22 at 3, 4.

77 Except for unitization in Turner Valley Field, which may be mandatory. Owners of tracts holding over 50% with respect of a part of the pool who are unable to enter into a unit agreement may apply to the AER to make an order that the part of the pool in respect of which the application was made be operated as a unit operation: Turner Valley Unit Operations Act, RSA 2000, c T-9.

78 PNG Tenure in Alberta, *supra* note 75 at 14.

79 This duty is mandated irrespective of whether or not the purpose is accomplished by the unit operation: OGCA, s. 79(1).

80 Allowables are production rate controls applied mainly to oil pools or oil reserves according to an AER order: AER Directive 007-1: Allowables Handbook – Guidelines for the Calculation of Monthly Production Allowables in Alberta. Meyers, *supra* note 22 at s. 933; See also Alastair Lucas and Constance Hunt, *Oil and Gas Law in Canada* (Carswell 1990) 215.

81 MMA, s. 102(2). The Crown only participates as a royalty owner in units that contain Crown leased mineral rights: PNG Tenure in Alberta, *supra* note 75 at 5.

82 A proposed unit with only one lessor and the same lessees will be rejected by Alberta Energy as being unnecessary: Guide for Unit Agreements, *supra* note 22 at 7.

83 MMA, s. 104(1).

84 Guide for Unit Agreements, *supra* note 22 at 1.

85 Guide for Unit Agreements, *supra* note 22 at 1.

2. The PNG agreements have expired,
3. The unit includes non-producing lands contrary to Alberta's tenure policies,
4. The unit covers an entire pool or has a "window,"
5. Owners of any adjacent lands that could be adversely affected by the unit have been offered participation in the unit upon reasonable terms,[86]
6. The basis for determining tract participation factors is equitable and technically justifiable,[87]
7. The unit comprises complete spacing units for the unitized substances,
8. All leases included in the unit are in good standing, and
9. If the unit is being formed for a particular purpose such as to implement an enhanced recovery project that requires AER approval, the unit contains all of the lands included in the approval.[88]

Two copies of the Unitization Agreements must be filed within one month of the agreements becoming effective.[89] A unit agreement becomes effective on the first of the month after it has been executed by all the owners.[90] When the Unitization Agreements have been filed and are in effect, the unit operator is required to notify the AER of the tracts that qualified for inclusion in the unit area, the appointment of the unit operator, and any changes to the unit area, unit ownership and unit operator.[91]

When a pool is subject to the Unitization Agreements, the AER, on application, may vary or suspend any relevant legislative and regulatory provision regarding the development and production of the oil or gas resources as it relates to the pool for the duration of the unit operation.[92] Any operations carried on in accordance with the unit operating agreement are deemed to be carried on each tract and the portion of unit production allocated to each tract, and only that portion, is, for all purposes, deemed to have been produced from that tract within the meaning of the terms and provisions of each lease or other contract applicable to that tract.[93]

86 In order for the unitization to proceed without these lands, letters from these owners declining participation in the unit is normally required: Guide for Unit Agreements, *supra* note 22 at 7.

87 Equitable tract factors are typically based upon a combination of two or three factors such as hydrocarbon pore volume, remaining recoverable reserves and productivity; a formula that heavily penalizes undrilled lands or that is based on surface area is not acceptable to Alberta Energy; lands that have not been drilled at the time of the formation of the unit will retain a reduced tract factor; and no lands be allocated a tract factor of zero. If the tract factors are determined to be inequitable in a unit that is comprised entirely of Crown land, Alberta Energy will inform the operator but will not ask for any adjustment: Guide for Unit Agreements, *supra* note 22 at 7.

88 Guide for Unit Agreements, *supra* note 22 at 7, 8.

89 OGCA, s. 79(2).

90 Guide for Unit Agreements, *supra* note 22 at 2.

91 OGCA, ss. 79(3), 91. When changes are made to unit tract ownership, Exhibit A must be revised and a new effective date, which must be on the first day of the month must be filed: Guide for Unit Agreements, *supra* note 22 at 2.

92 OGCA, s. 79(4).

93 OGCA, s. 87.

Upon unitization, royalty payments or deliverables due under any lease shall be calculated based on the amount of unitized petroleum substances deemed to be produced from the applicable unit tract, and the payment or delivery of the royalty so calculated shall satisfy the royalty payment or delivery obligation under any such lease or other contract.[94] Each lease is continued by operations on or production from the unitized zone, regardless of the location within the unit of such operations.[95]

A spacing unit that is subject to a pooling order may be included in a unit area as a single unit tract, in which event the provisions of the pooling order will be replaced by the provisions of the unit operation, but the share of all unit production, costs and expenses allocated to the spacing unit will be shared by owners in accordance with the pooling order.[96]

According to the Mines and Minerals Act, a unit agreement may provide:

a. for the appointment of a unit operator,
b. for participation in the development of the mineral,
c. for compensation for interests that are adversely affected,
d. for the variation of any agreement to the extent necessary to give effect to the unit agreement,
e. for deemed operations for tracts within the unit operation,
f. that the product allocated to a tract be deemed to have been produced from the tract,
g. deemed production in commercial quantity from any unit tract for the purpose of extending or renewing a lessee's agreement, and
h. for any other matters the Minister considers necessary.[97]

In addition, the following technical data must be provided: geological and structural mapping of the pool, structural and/or stratigraphic cross-sections to support the mapping, detailed information on the methods used to calculate the tract factors, well data, copies of applications and approvals made to the AER for enhanced recovery schemes or other operations to be conducted on the unit, reservoir information and surveys that support the size and continuity of the reservoir and productivity of the unit lands, seismic information (if applicable), written confirmation from any owners not included in the unit indicating that they do not wish to be a part of the unit, and a clear and properly labelled copy of the well log.[98]

The minister may, upon giving three months' notice to the unit operator and the WI owners, withdraw from a unit agreement if no unit operations have been

94 C T Mullane and A P G Walker, 'The Pooling Clause and the Effects of Unitization on the Oil and Gas Lease' 4 (2) Petroleum Law Suppl: Oil Gas Lease at 250; Section 703 of the PJVA model unit agreement.
95 Petroleum and Natural Gas Tenure Regulation, s. 15(1).
96 OGCA, s. 84(1).
97 Mines and Minerals Act (MMA), s. 102(3).
98 Guide for Unit Agreements, *supra* note 22 at 8, 9.

conducted for 12 consecutive months.[99] Within the three-month notice period, the unit operator may apply to the minister to withdraw its withdrawal notice. The application must include evidence showing that unit operations had not ceased, unit operations had recommenced or unit operations were suspended as a result of force majeure.[100] The minister may either extend the three-month notice period or withdraw from the unit agreement.[101]

5.4.3 Key Terms of the PJVA's Model Unit Agreement and Unit Operating Agreement

5.4.3.1 Cooperation and Sharing Resources

Article 3 of the model unit agreement provides for the unitization of the royalty and WI owners' interests in respect of the unitized petroleum substances and zones and the effect of such unitization. It provides that the WI owners are granted the right to develop, produce and operate the unitized zone without regard to the boundary lines or lease, and each lease is continued by the operations or production from the unitized zone, irrespective of the location of such operations within the unit; provided that where a lease or other agreement requires shut-in royalty payments in the absence of actual production of unitized substances from the unit area as a condition to continuing such lease or other agreement, such payment requirement shall continue to apply notwithstanding the above deemed production provisions of the unit agreement. It also confirms that the unitization does not result in any transfer of exchange of interest in the applicable leases, tracts, unitized zones or unitized substances before production.

Article 5 of the model unit agreement deals with the inclusion and qualification of tracts. It provides for the requisite qualifications to be met before a tract can be included in the unit area as of the effective date of the unit agreement.

Article 7 of the model unit agreement provides for the allocation of unitized substances among tracts. Produced unitized substances shall be allocated among each tract in accordance with the respective tract participations and the quantity allocated shall be deemed to have been produced from the unitized zone in such tract regardless of whether or not the unitized substances were produced from a well or wells on such tract.

Each party owns an undivided interest in the unit facilities that is equal to its unit participation and the unit operator shall hold such interests in trust for the owners.

5.4.3.2 Restrictions

Pursuant to Article 5 of the model unit operating agreement, a WI owner may conduct operations on its tract for the discovery and production of petroleum

99 Petroleum and Natural Gas Tenure Regulation, s. 24(2).
100 Petroleum and Natural Gas Tenure Regulation, s. 24(3), (4).
101 Petroleum and Natural Gas Tenure Regulation, s. 24(5), (6).

substances, other than the unitized substances, as long as the party protects the unitized zone and prevents interference with unit operations. A party exercising this right must indemnify all other WI owners against all actions, liabilities and expenses that may arise as a result of the party exercising this right. Unlike model joint operating agreements that include extensive provisions on the conduct of exclusive/sole operations, the PJVA unit operating agreement leaves the details of how a WI owner will exercise its right to conduct sole operations to the WI owner.

5.4.3.3 Management

Article 4 of the model unit operating agreement deals with supervision and control of the unit operations by the operating committee and how the operating committee operates. The operating committee provides an avenue for the non-unit operators to exert some control over the unit operator's activities.

An operating committee made up of the WI owners' representatives shall supervise and control all unit operations, except matters specifically designated to be within the exclusive jurisdiction of the unit operator or specifically excluded from the jurisdiction of the operating committee. Each WI owner shall also appoint an alternative representative who will act when the primary representative is absent. Also, representatives of the WI owners may attend meetings with a reasonable number of advisors, which should allow representatives to obtain expert opinion as needed during meetings.

All matters before the operating committee are decided by an agreed upon percentage of affirmative votes, and any decision by vote is binding on all WI owners. WI owners may vote by proxy or by notice. Each WI owner's voting interest is equal to its unit participation. Any WI owner who does not vote or abstains from voting on any matter shall be deemed to have voted in the affirmative on the matter. The unit operating agreement is silent on how WI owners should exercise their votes, i.e., whether votes should be cast in accordance with individual preference or in the best interest of the unit.

In addition to deciding the percentage of affirmative votes required to decide general matters, the WI owners have the option to decide the percentage of affirmative votes that will be used to decide specific matters, such as removal of the unit operator, issues dealing with qualification of tracts, enlargement of unit area and termination of the agreement.

Where there are only two WI owners for voting purposes, all matters before the operating committee shall be determined by unanimous approval, and the failure of the WI owners to reach a unanimous approval will be treated as a dispute and resolved in accordance with the dispute resolution provisions, discussed below.

5.4.3.4 Operatorship

Articles 6 through 9 of the model unit operating agreement clearly set out the duties, obligations, rights and liabilities of the unit operator. The WI owners designate a unit operator from amongst themselves that shall be responsible for managing the unit facilities on their behalf. The unit operator is responsible for holding and maintaining all licenses and approvals, and title to the unit facilities on behalf of the WI owners. The unit operator is not authorized to conduct unit operations without the approval of the operating committee. The unit operator is also required to consult with the operating committee from time to time with respect to the conduct of unit operations, which are to be conducted in a good and workmanlike manner, and in accordance with good oil field and environmental practice.

The unit operator retains all of its rights and obligations as an owner with respect to its unit participation. Subject to the operating committee's approval, the unit operator may subcontract all or substantially all of its duties and responsibilities to a third-party subcontractor or to an affiliate, provided that the unit operator retains full control and supervision of the subcontractor or affiliate. The unit operator is an independent contractor and is responsible for the employees and contractors utilized to conduct the unit operations. With the approval of the operating committee, the unit operator may enter into agreements with any person for the use or joint use by any person or by the unit operator of any of the unit facilities or any facilities, respectively, and all costs and expenses recovered or incurred pursuant to said agreements shall be for a joint account established and maintained by the unit operator for the benefit and risk and at the expense of the owners (the Joint Account).

The unit operator will cease to be unit operator if (1) the unit operator becomes bankrupt or insolvent or is unable to pay its debts as they become due; (2) the unit operator assigns or attempts to assign its general powers and responsibilities of supervision and management, unless the assignment is to an affiliate who is also an owner; (3) the operating committee votes to remove the unit operator; (4) the unit operator ceases to be an owner; or (5) the unit operator resigns upon giving the other WI owners at least 90 days' notice. The unit operator may assign its unit operatorship to an assignee to whom it disposed of all or a portion of its unit participation, and such assignee shall have the right to become unit operator if it is an affiliate of the unit operator or if the assignee is not an affiliate, if the operating committee approves.

When a unit operator resigns or ceases to be a unit operator, the WI owner with the largest unit participation automatically becomes the interim unit operator, until a replacement unit operator is appointed by the operating committee. The outgoing unit operator will be released and discharged from all duties and obligations of a unit operator once it delivers possession and control of all the unit property to the replacement unit operator.

The unit operator's liability to the other WI owners is limited to any loss, expense, injury, death or damage that arose as a direct result of the unit operator's gross negligence; and the unit operator shall indemnify the other WI owners' for any such losses, expenses, injuries, deaths or damages. Except where the unit operator is to be held solely liable, all liabilities and indemnities shall be borne by the WI owners in the proportions of their respective unit participation. The unit operator's liability does not include consequential losses, indirect losses or loss of profits.

5.4.3.5 *Financial Resources and Taxation*

Article 11 of the model unit operating agreement deals with costs and expenses incurred for unit operations. The unit operator is required to set up and administer a Joint Account. All proper costs and expenses incurred by the unit operator in connection with the unit operations shall be in accordance with the Accounting Procedure. The unit operator may commingle its funds with the moneys received from or for the Joint Account.

The unit operator is required to advance and pay all costs and expenses incurred for the Joint Account, and then charge such costs and expenses to the other WI owners in proportion to their respective unit participation.

Pursuant to the unit operating agreement, the unit operator shall submit a forecast of proposed expenditures to the Operating Committee for approval. The forecast shall include a detailed and specific description of expenditures therein, and an approval of a forecast shall be deemed to constitute approval of all proper expenditures, except capital cost expenditure in excess of the single expenditure limit in the Accounting Procedure.

From the effective date, the unit operator has a lien and charge, which has first priority, with respect to the unit participation of each WI owner in the unit facilities and such WI owners' share of unitized substances.[102] The unit operator shall be reimbursed by each WI owner within three months following the date any payment is due, otherwise, the unit operator shall bill each other owner a pro rata share of such unpaid amount, and each such owner shall be subrogated to the unit operator right as the holder of a lien and charge.

According to section 806 of the model unit operating agreement, each WI owner pays all taxes, rentals and royalties applicable to that owner's WI in the respective tracts. Taxes on unit facilities are paid for from the Joint Account.

5.4.3.6 *Governing Law*

The model Unitization Agreements are governed by the laws of Alberta and Canada.[103]

102 In *Cansearch Resources Ltd. v. Regent Resources Ltd., 2017 ABQB 535 (CanLII)*, the Court of Queen's Bench in Alberta held that an operator's lien is a consensual or contractual lien that is subject to Section 35 of the Personal Property Security Act, RSA 2000, c P-7 (which provides for the "first in time" priority rule) and priority of such lien will depend on when the lien was perfected either through registration in the Personal Property Registry or possession. Perfection of an operator's lien by possession requires the operator to prove that the applicable property was being held as collateral. In other words, the unit operating agreement would need to explicitly provide that the applicable property is being held by the unit operator as a collateral, which is not the case in the model unit operating agreement. See Nigel Bankes, 'An Operator of Gas Processing Facilities Does Not Have a Possessory Lien Under the Possessory Liens Act' (20 September 2017) ABlawg <http://ablawg.ca/wp-content/uploads/2017/09/Blog_NB_Possessory_Lien.pdf>.

103 PJVA Unit Agreement, s. 1513; PJVA Unit Operating Agreement, s. 1817.

5.4.3.7 Dispute Resolution

Exhibit J of the model unit operating agreement provides for resolution of disputes. WI owners to the unit operating agreement are first required to attempt, in good faith, to resolve any dispute through consultation and negotiation. Where such attempts are not successful and any time during negotiations, the WI owners may proceed to mediation. The owners are required to agree on a mediator within ten days of receipt of the notice to pursue mediation, otherwise any owner may submit a request to the Canadian Foundation for Dispute Resolution to select a mediator within two days.

Mediation should commence within 20 days of the selection of the mediator. The mediation will continue until the dispute is resolved, or an owner serves notice that it wishes to terminate the mediation, or the mediator makes a written determination that the dispute cannot be resolved through mediation, or 60 days have passed since the original notice was received. All owners bear their own costs associated with the mediation.

Where a dispute has not been resolved, the owners may proceed to arbitration. Owners may decide if all disputes or only specified disputes will be resolved by arbitration. Arbitration proceedings shall be held in Calgary, Alberta, and shall be governed by the Commercial Arbitration Rules of the Canadian Foundation for Dispute Resolution. Any party may represent the interest of another party.

While the owners attempt to resolve the dispute, limitation periods respecting commencement of an action will be stayed. An owner may seek an interim or provisional relief to protect its interest.

Pursuant to the Oil and Gas Conservation Act, where there is a dispute relating to production allocation, the unit operator shall sell the production with respect to which the dispute has arisen, pay any costs and expenses payable with respect to the tract, and pay the balance of the proceeds to the minister, who will hold the monies in trust pending an order of the Court of Queen's Bench or until a settlement has been reached by the owners.[104]

5.5 Conclusion

Alberta is the only jurisdiction in Canada that has not made provision for compulsory unitization, which would authorize the AER to make a unitization order on its own motion or in response to an application.[105] In the absence of compulsory unitization legislation, owners have complete freedom in deciding whether or not to enter into a unit. It is well established that voluntary unitization may be a prolonged and difficult matter, particularly where it is necessary to secure the signatures of a large number of operators and royalty owners.[106] The delay in establishing a unit means a costly deferral of revenue to owners and the inefficient development of oil

104 OGCA, s. 86.

105 See *supra* note 34. See also Cecilia Low, *supra* note 10 at 822.

106 Richard M Meyers, 'The Necessity of Unitization' (1961) 33(1) Miss LJ 7, 8.

and gas resources.[107] Although voluntary unitization is a valuable instrument, its weaknesses resulting largely from unsigned interests has made the need for compulsory unitization and the requirement for unitization before production apparent to the legislatures of numerous jurisdictions.[108]

The Alberta government has been pressed to include compulsory unitization provisions in its legislation, and such provisions were drafted and passed, but have not been brought into force; they remain part of the Oil and Gas Conservation Amendment Act.[109] The government maintained that leaving the power to make unitization orders in industry's hand would encourage voluntary unitization, which has not necessarily been the case.[110]

The need for compulsory unitization in Alberta was brought to the fore in *Butte Energy Inc.*[111] In this case, Butte Energy Inc. applied to the regulator under section 79(4) of the Oil and Gas Conservation Act and section 5.190 of the Oil and Gas Conservation Regulations to establish a holding on three-quarters of Section 35 and increase well density on its lands. Glencoe Resources Ltd., the unit operator of Chigwell Viking Units surrounding Section 35, filed an objection. Section 35, which was on the edge of the pool, was not included in the Chigwell Viking Units because Glencoe was unable to convince the owner of Section 35 to include the lands in the unit agreement. In the end, Glencoe excluded the Section 35 lands from the unit and obtained an approval for enhanced oil recovery (EOR) by miscible displacement using CO_2. Butte, the lessee of Section 35, owned wells that had been benefiting from Glencoe's CO_2 flood. Butte's application, if successful, would have permitted Butte to drill additional wells on Section 35, which would have resulted in Butte further benefiting from Glencoe's CO_2 flood.

Although the regulator denied Butte's application on the grounds that it would not result in orderly and efficient development and was not in the public interest, Nigel Bankes highlighted two compelling reasons in this case for compulsory unitization.[112] First was the waste occasioned from venting of CO_2 by Butte. The CO_2 was purchased by Glencoe for its EOR program and, in the usual course, an operator engaging in a CO_2 miscible flood EOR would have an incentive to capture and reuse the CO_2. Second was Butte's application which would enable it to further benefit from Glencoe's EOR program in which it was not a participant. In addition, there was some evidence that Butte's actions had caused irreparable damage to Glencoe's EOR scheme. The waste and drainage problems could have been

107 Richard M Meyers, 'The Necessity of Unitization' (1961) 33(1) Miss LJ 7, 8.

108 Richard Meyers, *supra* note 107 at 14.

109 R.S.A. 2000 (Supp.), c. 24.

110 David H Breen, *Alberta's Petroleum Industry and the Conservation Board* (University of Alberta Press 1993) 501, 502.

111 Decision 2013 ABERCB 005: Butte Energy Inc., Application for Special Well Spacing, Chigwell Field.

112 Nigel Bankes, 'Time to Proclaim the Compulsory Unitization Provisions of the *Oil and Gas Conservation Act*' (2 May 2013) online (blog): *Ablawg* <https://ablawg.ca/2013/05/02/time-to-proclaim-the-compulsory-unitization-provisions-of-the-oil-and-gas-conservation-act/>

avoided by a compulsory unitization order. As also noted by Nigel Bankes, compulsory unitization will be required if Alberta is to fully meet the stated purposes of the Oil and Gas Conservation Act, reduce industry footprint, and increase recovery rates for conventional reservoirs.[113]

Key Findings of This Chapter

1. Unitization may be voluntary or compulsory in all jurisdictions in Canada except in Alberta, where there is no compulsory unitization.
2. Federally, unitization orders may be made either to prevent waste (upon the application of the chief conservation officer) or to ensure efficiency and economical production of oil and gas resources (upon the application of 65% or more of the WI owners).
3. The use of standard forms of Unitization Agreements.
4. Despite the existence of compulsory unitization federally, the author did not find evidence of the Canadian Regulator invoking unitization of oil and gas tracts.

113 Nigel Bankes, 'Adjudicating on Waterflood Enhanced Recovery Schemes: Is It Time for Compulsory Unitization in Alberta?' (1 February 2009) online (blog): ABlawg <https://ablawg.ca/wp-content/uploads/2009/10/blog_nb_huntoil_ercb_feb2009.pdf>.

6 Ghana

Thomas Kojo Stephens

6.1 Introduction

The Republic of Ghana, located in West Africa, has four sedimentary basins: the Tano-Cape Three Points Basin (western),[1] Saltpond/Central Basin (central),[2] Accra-Keta Basin (eastern),[3] and the inland/onshore Voltaian Basin,[4] which stretches from southern to northern Ghana, covering about 40% of the country's landmass. The Accra Keta Basin is the only offshore basin yet to be the site of oil production. The Tano-Cape Three Points Basin is the most explored, followed by Saltpond, Accra/Keta, and the inland Voltaian Basin.

Ghana made a very small-scale discovery in 1970 with subsequent start of production in 1978 which was shut down in 1985 due to low productivity. This field was reactivated in 2000 and continued to produce in small quantities but is currently being decommissioned. It was the large-scale commercial discovery in 2007 in the Tano-Cape Three Points Basin that heralded Ghana as an oil-producing country. The unitization of parts of the West Cape Three Points Block and Deepwater Tano constituted Ghana's first and, since then, only unitization in its petroleum industry.

This chapter will focus on the unitization of the Jubilee Field and the attempted unitization of the Sankofa-Afina Fields as a case study for unitization in Ghana generally.

6.2 The Unitization of Parts of Both the West Cape Three Points and Deepwater Tano Blocks (The Jubilee Field)

The government of Ghana and its national oil company, Ghana National Petroleum Corporation (GNPC) on one hand, and Kosmos Energy Ghana Limited and EO Group on the other, executed a petroleum agreement dated 22 July 2004 in respect of the West Cape Three Points (WCTP) Block offshore Ghana.

1 Cretaceous Sedimentary Basin.
2 Paleozoic Basin.
3 Cretaceous Sedimentary Basin.
4 Paleozoic Basin.

DOI: 10.4324/9781003491293-8

Again, the government of Ghana and GNPC on one hand, and Tullow Ghana Limited, Sabre Oil and Gas Limited, and Kosmos Energy Ghana HC on the other, entered into another petroleum agreement dated 10 March 2006 in respect of the Deepwater Tano (DT) Contract area.

The Mahogany 1 (M-1) Exploration well drilled by Kosmos in the West Cape Three Points Block resulted in a commercial discovery of oil. Tullow Ghana Limited also made a commercial discovery when it drilled the Hyedua 1 (H-1) well in its Deepwater Tano contract area. The two wells were drilled about 5 km apart. Appraisal wells confirmed the Mahogany-Hyedua as one continuous structure extending across the two oil blocks in deep waters offshore. Appraisal wells confirmed oil and gas reserves in commercial quantities straddling the two blocks (West Cape Three Points and DeepwaterTano)[5] in the cretaceous zone with ideal hydrocarbon trap conditions. The discovery straddled the two contract areas, intersecting large continuous accumulations of sweet crude.[6] This was confirmed by industry experts as one of the largest finds of crude oil reserves in Africa in recent times. Kosmos affirmed in its filings with the US Securities and Exchange Commission (SEC) that it is "the largest find offshore West Africa in the last decade."[7]

According to section 4(7) of the then governing law, the Petroleum (Exploration and Production) Law, 1984 (PNDCL 84)[8]:

> where a petroleum field extends beyond the boundaries of an area covered by a petroleum agreement or any other authority granted or recognized under this law, the Secretary [Minister] may determine that such petroleum field shall be developed as a single unit and may give appropriate directions to the Corporation or the Contractor or any other person concerned.

Since the discoveries were in the same reservoir, by a letter dated 25 November 2008 from Ghana's Minister for Energy, the parties were directed to unitize the Fields.[9]

A pre-unit agreement was agreed to between the contractor groups in the WCTP and DT Block in late February 2008 to govern operations pending negotiation of a

5 Kosmos Energy, 'United States Securities and Exchange Commission Form 10-K, Annual Report Pursuant to Section 13 OR 15(d) of the Securities and Exchange Act of 1934 for the fiscal year ended December 31, 2015' (Kosmos Energy 2015) 14.

6 Tullow Oil, 'Jubilee Field' (Tullow 2021) <https://www.tullowoil.com/ouroperations/africa/ghana/jubilee-field/> accessed 26 October 2021.

7 Kosmos Energy, 'United States Securities and Exchange Commission, Amendment No 1 to Form S-1 Registration Statement under The Securities Act of 1933: Kosmos Energy Ltd' (United States Securities and Exchange Commission, 3 March 2011) 74 <www.sec.gov/Archives/edgar/data/1509991/000104746911001716/a2201620zs-1a.htm> accessed 29 April 2020.

8 The Laws of Ghana had different suffixes depending on the epoch in which the law was made. In the process of the revision of the laws, it was deemed desirable to have them revised so as to have them all bear the same suffix ("Act"), and the revision was completed in 2004 and came into force in 2007.

9 See s 4(7) of *Petroleum Act*.

comprehensive unitization and unit operating agreement (UUOA).[10] The pre-unit agreement established principal terms and conditions regarding the unitization and development of the field. It also spelt out the roles and responsibilities of the parties, and a Joint Operating Committee composed of a representative of each party holding a unit interest was formed.[11] Parties were required to use all reasonable endeavours to agree and enter into a fully formed unitization operating agreement (UOA) which would, among others, embody the principles set out in the pre-unitization agreement.[12] This entering into a UUOA was to be done as reasonably practicable following the pre-unit agreement's effective date, and the fully formed UUOA was to be entered into prior to submission of the development plan.[13] Prior to the execution of the UUOA, a passmark vote was required to amend the unit area to incorporate extensions of the unitized field confirmed by further drilling and/or gathering or interpretation of additional well or seismic data.[14] After the execution of the UUOA, amendment of the unit area required the unanimous consent of the parties.[15] It was further prescribed that in preparing and negotiating the UUOA, the parties would use as a base the AIPN 2006 Model Form International Unitization and Unit Operating Agreement.[16] Any dispute was to be settled by arbitration in accordance with the joint operating agreement[17] in respect of the WCTP.[18] The pre-unit agreement was to terminate on the date of the execution of the definitive, fully formed UUOA.[19]

A more comprehensive UUOA – which would govern each party's respective rights and duties in the Jubilee Unit – was entered into by the parties on 13 July 2009[20] and became effective on 16 July 2009. The field was christened "Jubilee Field" in commemoration of the country's jubilee year independence celebration. Commenting on these series of events in its SEC filings, Kosmos noted:

> The Jubilee Field straddles the boundary between the West Cape Three Points ("WCTP" petroleum contract) and the Deepwater Tano (DT) petroleum contract offshore Ghana. Consistent with the Ghana Exploration and Production Law of 1984 (PNDCL 84) (the "Ghanaian petroleum law") the WCTP petroleum contract and the DT petroleum contract as required by Ghana's Ministry of Petroleum (formerly Ghana's Ministry of Energy and Petroleum), in order to optimize resource recovery in this field, we entered

10 Kosmos Energy, 'Kosmos Energy 2011 Annual Report' (Kosmos 2012) <http://www.kosmosenergy.com/annualreport/2011/Kosmos-Energy-2011-Annual-Report.pdf> 37 accessed 28 October 2021.

11 Clause 3.1.

12 Clause 2.1.

13 Clause 2.1.

14 Clause 2.5.

15 Clause 2.5.

16 Clause 6.0 – *UOA*.

17 Article 18.2.

18 Clause 23.0 – *Dispute Resolution*.

19 Clause 24.0 – *Termination*.

20 Kosmos (n 6) 29.

into the Unitization and Unit Operating Agreement (UUOA) in July 2009 with the Ghana National Petroleum Corporation ("GNPC") and the other block partners of each of these two blocks. The UUOA governs the interests in and development of the Jubilee Field and created the Jubilee Unit from portions of the WCTP petroleum contract and the DT petroleum contract areas.[21]

According to the pre-unit agreement, the initial Jubilee Field unit area was deemed to consist of 35% of an area from the WCTP Block and 65% of an area from the DT Block.[22] However, the tract participations were allocated 50% for the WCTP Block and 50% for the DT Block pending the results of the Mahogany-2 well.[23] The parties agreed that interests in the Jubilee Unit would be initially shared equally, that is, with tract participations of 50% for each block.[24] "Tract participation" is defined under the UUOA as follows:

> Each Tract's undivided allocation of unit substances . . . and the undivided share of the rights and obligations of the Parties under this Agreement or the Joint Operating Agreements to the extent that such transfer covers all or a portion of the Unit Interval, other than an encumbrance or a transfer of the transferring Party's Entitlement and its rights to any credits, refunds or payments in this Agreement, and excluding any direct or indirect charge in control of a part.[25]

The percentage of such contributed interests was then subject to a process of redetermination once sufficient development work had been completed in the unit. Tullow Ghana was the unit operator with Kosmos, being the technical operator for the development of the field.[26] A technical operator is defined under the UUOA as "a party designated from time to time pursuant to Article 7[27] to conduct technical Operations, in such capacity and not in its capacity as a Party." Kosmos explains this distinction in its filing with the SEC thus: "The Technical Operator plans and executes the development of the unit whereas the Unit Operator manages the day-to-day production operations of the unit."[28]

21 Kosmos (n 5) 21.
22 Kosmos (n 10) 37.
23 Ibid.
24 Kosmos Energy, Securities and Exchange Commission, 'Jubilee Field Unitization' <https://www.sec.gov/Archives/edgar/data/1509991/000104746912001964/R11.htm> (Securities and Exchange Commission, 31 December 2011).
25 Ghana Petroleum Commission, 'Tullow Ghana Limited – Jubilee Unitization Agreement' (Tullow 2021) 11 <http://www.petrocom.gov.gh/L&C_folder/Pet_register/jubilee/Part%201.pdf> accessed 26 October 2021.
26 Article 7.1 – *Designation of Unit Operator and Technical Operator.*
27 Article 7 – *Unit Operator.*
28 Kosmos (n 7) 2.

The UUOA thus brought the "the collective interest holders in each of the WCTP and DT Blocks"[29] (GNPC, Tullow, Kosmos, Anadarko West Cape Three Points Company, Sabre Oil and Gas Holdings Limited, and the EO Group Limited) into one. Thus, the Recitals of the Agreement stated:

> WHEREAS, Tullow, Kosmos, Anadarko, Sabre and EO Group or their predecessors-in-interest entered into a Petroleum Agreement with the Government (represented by the Minister) and GNPC dated July 22, 2004 covering certain areas located in the West Cape Three Points (WCTP) Block Contract area offshore Ghana;
>
> WHEREAS, Tullow Kosmos, Anadarko and Sabre or their predecessors-in-interest entered into a petroleum agreement with the Government (represented by the Minister) and GNPC dated March 10, 2006 covering certain areas located in the Deepwater Tano (DWT) Contract area offshore Ghana
>
> WHEREAS, a letter has been received from the Minister dated November 25th 2008 determining that the field encompassed by the Unit Interval extends across the boundary between the Contract Areas and that such field shall be developed and exploited as a single unit pursuant to unitization and engineering principles and practices and is in accordance with accepted international petroleum industry practices and the Laws/Regulations and instructing the Parties to negotiate and enter into a unitization and unit operating agreement setting forth the terms of the unitization;
>
> WHEREAS, the parties and the government have agreed that the terms of this Agreement relating to unitization satisfy any requirements of the Laws/Regulations with respect to unitization; and
>
> WHEREAS the parties desire to define their respective rights and obligations with respect to their development and operation at the Unit Interval on a unitized basis . . .[30]

The scope of the UUOA was the development and operation of the interval area,[31] production of unit substances, handling and transportation thereof up to the applicable delivery period, and if agreed unanimously between the parties, to a point downstream.[32] It also covered the principles in accordance with which each party was entitled to have delivered to it and to take unit substances, or any proceeds of sale.[33] It further covered the acquisition, construction, operation, use, ownership, maintenance, repair and removal of floating and fixed facilities,[34] regulation of

29 Article 7 – *Unit Operator*.
30 Ghana Petroleum Commission (n 14).
31 Article 3.1(A)(1).
32 Article 3.1(A)(2).
33 Article 3.1(A)(3).
34 Article 3.1(A)(4).

non-unit operations affecting the unit area,[35] regulation of associated agreements,[36] and development of information and promotional marketing material relating to crude oil from the unit interval.[37] Further, it covered decommissioning of unit facilities[38] and all other activities in connection with any of the foregoing.[39] The effect of the unitization, as aptly noted, was that all rights and interests of the parties in so far as they related to the unit interval, unit substances and the conduct of unit operations, were deemed unitized.

Under the UUOA, Tullow held 34.70%, Kosmos 23.49%, Anadarko 23.49%, GNPC 13.75%, Sabre 2.81%, and EO Group 1.75%. Tullow's acquisition of the EO Group in 2011 increased its interest in the field to 36.45%.[40] As Kosmos noted in its filings with the SEC:

> These interest percentages are subject to redetermination of the working interests in the Jubilee Field pursuant to the terms of the UUOA . . . The unit partners' respective interests in the Jubilee Unit are subject to redetermination and our interests in such unit may decrease as a result.[41]

Thus, pursuant to the terms of the Jubilee UUOA, the tract participations were subject to redetermination.[42] "Redetermination" is defined under the UUOA as

> the process established . . . for the review and possible revision of the Tract Participations, Unit Interests and Paying Interests . . . as applicable including any such review and revision involving a referral to an Independent Expert. The term "Redetermination" shall include both the revision of Tract Participations, Unit Interests, and Paying Interests and where applicable . . . the reapportionment of each Party's rights to Unit Substances and obligations for Unit Account costs.[43]

The initial redetermination process was completed on 14 October 2011, and any party with an interest of more than 10% participating interest in the field could call for a second redetermination. After the initial redetermination process, the tract participation was determined as 54.366660% for the WCTP Block and 45.63340% for the DT Block instead of the original 50% each for the two blocks. Tullow's

35 Article 3.1(A)(5).
36 Article 3.1(A)(6).
37 Article 3.1(A)(7).
38 Article 3.1(A)(8).
39 Article 3.1(A)(9).
40 Ministry of Finance and Economic Planning (Ghana Extractives Transparency Initiative – GHEITI), 'Final Report on the Aggregation/Reconciliation of Oil and Gas Sector Payments and Receipts: 2010–2011' (GHEITI, February 2013) 35 <https://eiti.org/files/documents/2010–2011_ghana_eiti_report_oil-gas.pdf> accessed 28 October 2021.
41 United States Securities and Exchange Commission (n 8) 86.
42 Article 5.4 – Redetermination of Tract Participations.
43 1.140 of the *Definition* Section.

interest decreased slightly from 36.42% to 35.48%, whilst Kosmos' unit interest was increased from 23.50868% (which was its percentage interest after Tullow acquired the interest of the EO Group) to 24.07710%. Ghana's interest reduced from 13.75% to 13.64%.

The Jubilee Field[44] is approximately 37 miles (60 km) offshore Ghana and 81 miles (130 km) west-southwest of the port city of Takoradi, in water depths of approximately 1,100–1,700 m. Production commenced on 28 November 2010[45] in a record time of 3½ years after discovery but was officially inaugurated on 15 December 2010 by President John Atta Mills. As aptly noted by Kosmos, production from the field began in November 2010, just 42 months after initial discovery, a record for deep-water development at that water depth in West Africa.[46] Crude oil thereafter began to flow into the FPSO Kwame Nkrumah MV21 – the floating, production, storage and offloading/offtake vessel – for processing.

The Jubilee Field is operated by Tullow Oil and is estimated to hold up to 1.8 billion barrels of crude. The oil has low sulphur content and is easy to refine. It is light, sweet crude[47] which is world-class quality and much sought after in the international market.[48]

The successful unitization and fast track of the Jubilee Field was mainly due to the fact that it was not in dispute that the discoveries overlapped each other and formed part of the same reservoir. There was agreement between the parties as to this state of circumstances. Further, despite the national oil company's relative lack of familiarity with unitization, things progressed smoothly and quickly because there was a recognition that this was the way to go and thus a determination to move in a concerted manner. Ghana currently produces crude from three fields, Jubilee, TEN, and Sankofa Gye Nyame (SGN). For the year 2023, a total of 32 liftings – amounting to 30,403,546 barrels – were made from the Jubilee Field by the parties.[49]

44 It straddles two contract areas, that is, Deepwater Tano and West Cape Three Points contract areas, and was unitized and approved for development in 2009.

45 Anadarko Petroleum, 'Anadarko Announces First Oil at the Jubilee Field Offshore Ghana' (Anadarko 2010) <www.anadarko.com/Investor/Pages/NewsReleases/NewsReleases.aspx?relea se-id=1507873> accessed 25 May 2020.

46 United States Securities and Exchange Commission (n 8) 3.

47 The lighter the crude, the more valuable it is as more products can be obtained from it. Crude with higher than average sulphur content is known as "sour," whilst crude with low levels is known as "sweet." "Sour" crude – crude contaminated with sulphur and other impurities – has less value than "sweet" crude.

48 Tullow Oil Plc, 'Jubilee Development – The Story So Far' (Tullow Oil Plc, June 2010) 2, <www.tullowoil.com/ghana/files/jubilee_esia_brochure.pdf> accessed 18 November 2020.

49 Public Interest and Accountability Committee, 'Annual Report on Management of Petroleum Revenues for Year 2023' 30.

6.3 Governing Law on Unitization Within Ghana

In 2016, Ghana enacted the Petroleum (Exploration and Production) Act, 2016 (Act 919) which repealed the Petroleum (Exploration and Production) Act, 1984 (PNDCL 84). Section 34 of the Act states:

> Where *an accumulation of petroleum extends beyond the boundaries of one contract area into one or more other contract areas*, the Minister in consultation with the Commission may, for the purpose of ensuring optimum recovery of petroleum from the accumulation of petroleum, direct the relevant contractors, to enter an agreement to develop and produce the accumulation of petroleum as a single unit [emphasis added].

Thus, the litmus test for determining whether unitization must occur is whether the relevant petroleum reservoir crosses into the boundaries of another contract area. This position is not different from what pertained under the repealed Petroleum (Exploration and Production) Act, 1984 (PNDCL 84), which stated that

> where a petroleum field extends beyond the boundaries of an area covered by a petroleum agreement or any other authority granted or recognized under this law, the Secretary may determine that such petroleum fields shall be developed as a single unit and may give appropriate directions to the Corporation or the Contractor or any other person concerned.

Thus, though the wording in the two pieces of legislation is different, the import is the same.

Further, Regulation 50 of the Petroleum (Exploration and Production) (General) Regulations, 2018 (L.I. 2359) gives effect to section 34 of the Petroleum Act by prescribing the modalities of the unitization agreement. It states:

(1) A unitisation and coordination agreement under subsection (1) of Section 34 of the Act shall be governed and construed by the laws of the Republic.
(2) A unitisation and coordination agreement under the Act shall be entered into in accordance with a model agreement provided by the Minister.
(3) A unitisation or coordination agreement and any amendment to the unitisation or coordination agreement shall be submitted to the Minister for approval.
(4) The relevant contractors shall submit to the Minister a draft unitisation and unit operating agreement or an agreement to coordinate and develop separate petroleum accumulations based on the model agreement described in sub-regulation (1) within six months after the finalisation of appraisal of the petroleum accumulation.

6.4 The Sankofa-Afina Unitization Issue (ENI and Springfield Saga)[50]

Years after the Jubilee unitization, the issue of unitizing two fields came up again but in vastly different circumstances in respect of the Afina discovery by Springfield, and the Sankofa Field operated by ENI.

In 2020, Ghana's Ministry of Energy directed that the Afina Field, held by an indigenous Ghanaian company, Springfield Exploration and Production Ltd., be unitized with the Sankofa Field of Italian major, ENI, on the basis that the same Cenomanian channel straddled both the OCTP Block (ENI) and WCTP 2 Block (Springfield). ENI opposed the unitization of the two fields on the basis that Springfield had not sufficiently tested its discovery to show that it was in dynamic communication with ENI's Sankofa.[51] Despairing that the parties would reach an agreement, the Ministry of Energy issued a directive that imposed unitization on the parties. Springfield was in favour of this directive whilst ENI challenged it.

6.4.1 The Sankofa Field and Afina Fields Directive to Unitize

ENI Ghana Exploration and Production Ltd.[52] and Vitol Upstream Ghana Ltd.,[53] per a petroleum agreement with an effective date of 5 May 2008, were granted a license over the contract area known as the Offshore Cape Three Points (OCTP) Area with ENI being the operator and having 44.44% interest, Vitol, 35.36% interest, and GNPC with a combined carried and participating interest of 20%. The field, known as the Sankofa Field, began production in July 2017 through the FPSO John Agyekum Kufuor.

Springfield Exploration and Production Ltd., GNPC and its exploration company, Explorco, per a petroleum agreement with an effective date of 26 July 2016, were granted a license to a contract area known as the West Cape Three Points Block 2 (WCTP 2). Springfield is the operator of the Afina Field, which is within WCTP 2, with an interest of 84%, with GNPC and Explorco holding the remaining interest.

In March 2018, after acquiring 3D seismic data and conducting analysis on that data, Springfield wrote to the Minister for Energy that per its analysis, the Sankofa Cenomanian Reservoir of ENI and Vitol extended into its WCTP 2 contract area. It requested the minister to direct the parties in both fields, to commence unitization discussions.

50 An expanded version of this section onwards can also be seen in the 2020 Annual Report of the Ghana Chamber of Bulk Oil Distributors (CBOD).

51 As noted by Ed Reed in 'ENI Calls for Afina Proof on Unitization Push' *Energy Voice* (13 November 2020) <https://www.energyvoice.com/oilandgas/africa/ep-africa/278992/eni-afina-sankofa-unitisation/> accessed 7 June 2021, ENI's stance is that it would want more subsurface analysis in order to demonstrate the fields were straddling the license.

52 ENI is a company registered under the laws of Ghana in accordance with Section 70 of the *Petroleum (Exploration and Production) Act*, 2016, and a subsidiary of the Italian multinational company, ENI International.

53 Vitol Upstream Ghana Ltd. is similarly incorporated in Ghana and a subsidiary of the multinational company, Vitol, an energy and commodities company.

In May 2018, the minister invited Springfield to make a presentation to the ministry and GNPC (with the national oil company a partner in both the OCTP and WCTP 2 Blocks and thus with information on both blocks). GNPC was tasked with independently evaluating Springfield's claim and presenting a report. GNPC presented this report in support of Springfield's claim in July 2018, and consequently the minister wrote to ENI informing of Springfield's claim and requesting a response.

In August 2018, ENI responded disputing Springfield's claim and asserting that per the data available to them (ENI and Vitol), there was no evidence of straddling. Consequently, the ministry advised Springfield to drill its prospect to further prove its claim. Springfield spudded its first well, the Afina-1x well in WCTP 2, in October 2019.[54] The well is 60 km offshore and in close proximity to the Jubilee Field and Greater Pecan Development areas. Drilling was completed in November 2019 using the Stena Forth drillship. The acreage was relinquished by Kosmos Ghana, following the carveout of Jubilee in 2011.[55] Commenting on the Afina discovery, *Wood Mackenzie* stated, "If confirmed, Afina could be a defining moment for both Springfield and Ghana. It marks the first time an independent African energy company has stepped out into a sole deep-water exploration venture."[56] It further noted, "The ingredients are certainly there – existing infrastructure, and relatively favourable fiscal terms. Flanked closely by its more illustrious IOC explorers and developers, Springfield will certainly require a strong partner, and so a farm-down would be a logical next step, if Afina is big enough to attract interest."[57]

By a letter dated 27 January 2020, Springfield wrote to the Ministry of Energy and informed it of its post-drilling analysis. It asserted that the Afina-1x Cenomanian Reservoir and the Sankofa Cenomanian Reservoir were the same and requested that the ministry direct the parties to WCTP 2 and OCTP, to unitize the two fields and produce them as one unit.[58] The ministry, however, requested the Petroleum Commission to undertake an independent assessment of the post-drilling data of Springfield's Afina-1x well for the purposes of fully satisfying all stakeholders that the accumulation actually straddled each other.

By a letter dated 9 April 2020,[59] the Ministry of Energy informed the parties that the Petroleum Commission had confirmed that the petroleum accumulations of the two oil blocks were the same. It noted,

> Further reference is made to the Petroleum Commission's letter dated 2nd April 2020, also in respect of the above subject matter, where the Commission recommended that, after engaging both ENI and Springfield and conducting

54 Springfield Energy, 'Ghanaian Energy Company Springfield Group Spuds First Well', *Springfield* (9 October 2019) <https://www.springfieldgroup.com/ghanaian-energy-company-springfield-group-spuds-first-well/> accessed 9 June 2021.

55 "Springfield Strikes Oil in Ghana – But How Much?" *Wood Mackenzie* (November 2019) 2.

56 "Springfield Strikes Oil in Ghana – But How Much?" *Wood Mackenzie* (November 2019) 2.

57 "Springfield Strikes Oil in Ghana – But How Much?" *Wood Mackenzie* (November 2019) 2.

58 Paragraph 23.

59 Reference Number SLR/KA 118/255/05.

> independent assessment of the parties' position, the Afina 1x Cenomanian discovery and the Sankofa Cenomanian accumulation were one and same.[60]

The minister also noted in the said letter that

> It is worthy of note that prior to requesting the Commission to review Springfield's claim, the Ministry had, consequent to Springfield's earlier letter dated 20th March 2018, on this same subject matter, requested GNPC to furnish it with an independent opinion on the veracity or otherwise of Springfield's claim.

It went on to state: "GNPC by a letter dated 5th June 2018, with an accompanying technical report, opined that based on interpretation of seismic data, the Sankofa Field extended into the WCTP-2 Contract area." The minister went on to note that

> based on this opinion, and to ensure that there was ample evidence to justify unitization, the Ministry advised Springfield to drill their side of the reservoir to confirm the seismic data interpretations . . . Per the post-drill data and analysis, the Afina-1x Cenomanian reservoir has identical reservoir and fluid properties as the Sankofa Cenomanian reservoir, thus proving further evidence that the two reservoirs are one and the same.

The minister went on to rebut ENI's claim that declaration of unitization was premature. The minister noted:

> The Commission noted that ENI, in responding to Springfield's claim, indicated that it was premature for Springfield to be talking about unitization since, per publicly available information, Springfield had not appraised and tested their discovery. The Commission in disagreeing with this position, indicated that the unitization of the Jubilee Field was triggered by geological interpretations, seismic amplitude signature and pressure data from wells in Kosmos and Tullow Ghana's respective acreages. They further stated that testing of the respective wells was a post-unitization event.

The minister therefore, among others, directed that Springfield, ENI, and Vitol begin the process of unitizing the two fields, Afina and Sankofa, and accordingly, furnish the ministry with a draft UUOA within 120 days from the date of the letter.[61] The minister noted that this directive was in accordance with section 34 of the Petroleum (Exploration and Production) Act, 2016 (Act 919)[62] and was to "ensure efficient production of the reservoir, to maximize economic recovery of petroleum

60 Letter from the Minister for Energy, John Peter Amewu, to Springfield and ENI, dated 9 April 2020.

61 The minister also requested the parties to exchange relevant data to establish the structural extent and distribution of the petroleum between the contract areas.

62 Section 34 is titled, *Co-ordination with Petroleum Activities and Unitization.*

from the two Contract Areas, to avoid unnecessary competitive drilling which might destroy the reservoir, [and] above all, in the national interest." Further to this, the minister noted that "you are reminded that pursuant to Regulation 50(6) of L.I. 2359, I am to stipulate the terms and conditions of the unitization, if you fail to comply with this directive."[63]

6.4.2 Springfield's Position

Springfield's position was that its WCTP and ENI and Vitol's OCTP shared a common boundary. Springfield noted in a letter dated 20 March 2018 to the then Minister for Energy, Hon. Boakye Kyeremateng Agyarko, that "as our technical report clearly indicates, the Sankofa Production Area is part of a common reservoir complex straddling the two license areas (OCTP and WCTP 2)."

Springfield's case was that it came to its attention that the accumulation of petroleum in ENI and Vitol's Sankofa Cenomanian Reservoir extended beyond and into Springfield's WCTP 2 contract area where its petroleum within its area was accumulated. Springfield noted that these facts became known to it after it conducted some geophysical and geological analysis of its data including seismic attribute analysis and structural analysis.[64]

It was Springfield's position that the effect therefore of its finding that ENI and Vitol's accumulation extended into its reservoir was that any exploration and production activities carried out in ENI and Vitol's production area would automatically affect petroleum accumulations in its contract area, and vice versa.[65] It noted in the aforementioned letter that:

> we understand from our technical studies that failure to treat the broader Sankofa Reservoir complexes in the license areas as a unit area for the purposes of joint development and unitized operations between the Sankofa production area and the Sankofa extension in WCTP 2 will result in sub-optimal development of the resource base.

Making the argument along the lines of the preservation of the reservoir as well as the interest of the government of Ghana, it noted;

> If both operators of OCTP and WCTP 2 continue to independently develop the Field based on the rule of capture, it would lead to accelerated loss of reservoir pressure and drive mechanism, a major reduction in the maximum ultimate recovery of the common reservoir and a competitive drilling and production practice by both operators. This would further lead to a consequent waste of capital investment and erosion of economic value and returns.

63 Regulation 50 is titled, *Co-ordination of Petroleum Activities and Unitization.*

64 Paragraph 9.

65 Paragraph 12.

> Furthermore, such excessive wells and unnecessary infrastructure would represent a duplication of costs, such increased costs to ultimately be recovered as Cost Oil from the production revenue of the common reservoir. This "economic waste" of higher costs and uncoordinated drilling and infrastructure will ultimately lead to the physical waste of oil or gas as the field will be abandoned earlier than is the norm as it will cease to be commercially profitable in its later stages. This potential economic and physical waste will also have a direct and adverse economic impact on the Government of Ghana's revenues and minimize the gas production. The increased cost oil to be recovered because of duplication in drilling and infrastructure costs will significantly reduce the Government's share of revenues from production of the common reservoir. Furthermore, the reduction in ultimate recoveries from the common reservoir because of early abandonment due to uncoordinated drilling that reduces commercial profitability will have a negative impact on the Government's projected revenues.

Making arguments in specific reference to the impact on its operations, it noted:

> Specifically, we understand from public domain information that the OCTP development is based on the assumption that the oil reservoirs are in an Oil-Down – To (ODT) situation meaning that no oil-water-contact (OWC) could be found. According to ENI's plan disclosed at the time of first oil, the water injection well for the development are located close to the WCTP 2 boundary. The location of water injection wells so close to the WCTP 2 boundary could sweep oil in WCTP 2 reservoirs without any control and can seriously compromise Springfield's efforts to recover oil from its part of the joint pool and may even damage the reservoirs affecting the oil recovery. The planned water injectors may adversely affect the sweep efficiency and hence the ultimate recovery of the WCTP 2 part of the Sankofa East oil field.

It was Springfield's case that although its data confirmed that ENI and Vitol's Sankofa Cenomanian Reservoir extended into its contract area, it decided, for the avoidance of doubt, to engage the services of an independent expert to determine whether or not its findings that ENI and Vitol's reservoir extended into its contract area, was correct.[66] It noted that it thus engaged the services of an expert in the industry, ERC Equipoise, to verify its findings. Springfield noted in the said letter dated 20 March 2018 that

> WCTP shares an Eastern boundary with Offshore Cape Three Points (OCTP), a block licensed to and operated by ENI Ghana Exploration & Production Ltd. ("ENI"). From our extensive geological and geophysical studies, including seismic attribute analysis of the WCTP2 contract area, we have

66 Paragraph 13.

> discovered that the Sankofa production area contained in the OCTP license area extends into WCTP2. This has been proven by extensive work carried out by Springfield's in-house geoscientists and verified by ERC Equipoise (a leading United Kingdom Oil and Gas Reservoir Evaluation Firm and an independent third party expert on the subject matter).[67]

Springfield asserted that the independent expert confirmed its findings that Vitol and ENI's Sankofa Cenomanian Reservoir indeed extended into its contract area and that any activity undertaken in ENI and Vitol's reservoir would affect Springfield's right and petroleum deposits in the WCTP 2.[68]

Thus, in the said letter of 20 March 2018, Springfield requested that the ministry exercise its statutory mandate to direct the parties to "commence unitization discussions immediately with regards to the Sankofa production area in OCTP and the Sankofa extension in WCTP 2 and to enter into a unitization agreement within a defined and reasonable time."[69]

The ministry requested that GNPC independently assess Springfield's claim. GNPC, upon concluding its investigations, confirmed Springfield's position that the deposits of ENI and Vitol extended into its contract area.[70] Springfield argued that it was to establish beyond any shadow of doubt that the deposits in ENI and Vitol's Sankofa Field actually extended into and included petroleum deposits in Springfield's area, that the ministry advised in August 2018 that a well be drilled within its contract area,[71] which it did[72] by successfully drilling the Afina-1x well in the WTCP-2 Block. It was Springfield's position that it indeed drilled this well to, among others, confirm whether or not the petroleum accumulation in the Sankofa Cenomanian Reservoir straddled the contract areas of the parties.[73] Springfield's position was that the post-drilling data confirmed that ENI and Sankofa's accumulation indeed extended into Springfield's contract area and that the two fields were one and the same.[74]

Springfield contended – including in a letter dated 10 June 2020 to ENI – that ENI had rebuffed all efforts to commence unitization efforts.

6.4.3 ENI's Position

It was ENI's position that there had not been enough data to establish the veracity of the claim that there was some communication between Sankfoa and Afina, nor

67 Letter to the Minister for Energy, Hon. Boakye Kyerematen Agyarko, dated 20 March 2018, Page 1.
68 Paragraph 14.
69 Page 2 of letter, Paragraph 17 of Statement of Claim.
70 Paragraph 17.
71 Paragraph 19.
72 Paragraph 20.
73 Paragraph 20.
74 Paragraph 21.

to ascertain definitively that the discovered resources were producible.[75] It noted that without that, it was difficult to accept the unitization deal as presented by the Ministry of Energy on behalf of the government.[76] It contended that Springfield's Afina discovery had not been sufficiently tested to show that it shared a reservoir with the Sankofa Field.

ENI noted in its letter dated 22 June 2020 to the Minister for Energy that "the law and industry best practice require as a fundamental pre-requisite that a thorough technical assessment be carried out in order to determine the appropriate solution for the development of the resources and optimum recovery of petroleum."[77] It then stated its position equivocally, stating, "without demonstrable evidence of the extension of the petroleum accumulations across the two contract areas and that unitization would ensure optimum recovery of petroleum from any such accumulation, we are unable to commit to the implementation of the Directives."[78]

ENI went on to make reference to section 34(1) of the Petroleum Act, 2016,[79] which notes that the minister may direct contractors to enter into a UUOA where an accumulation of petroleum extends beyond the boundaries of one contract area and for the purpose of ensuring optimum recovery of petroleum from the accumulation. It argued that

> the law therefore requires that there must necessarily be a comprehensive assessment of the petroleum accumulation to establish and confirm the extension of an accumulation across any shared contract area boundary in a manner that would ensure the optimum recovery of petroleum prior to determining the appropriate course of action and setting out the relevant timetable.[80]

ENI further contended that the law, under section 34(3) of the Petroleum Act, 2016, considers alternatives to unitization that may be more appropriate where accumulations are in proximity. It contended that in this case, however, there is not sufficient evidence to demonstrate that a unitization approach will deliver optimum recovery of petroleum. It emphasized its position that, "based on the data available to us, the existence of hydrocarbon communication between the Afina discovery and the Sankofa Field has not yet been duly established and a proper evaluation, by all parties, is required."[81]

75 Iain Esau and Barry Morgan, 'ENI Hits Back at Ghana for Imposing Unitization Deal on Sankofa and Afina Fields' <https://www.upstreamonline.com/production/eni-hits-back-at-ghana-for-imposing-unitisation-deal-on-sankofa-and-afina-fields/2-1-913911> Upstream Energy Explored, 18 November 2020.

76 Ibid.

77 Page 1.

78 Page 1.

79 Section 34 – *Coordination of Petroleum Activities and Unitization.*

80 Page 1 of letter from ENI to the Ministry of Energy dated 22 June 2020.

81 Page 2.

Further making arguments as to why the decision to unitize had not crystallized, it noted that, with regard to the timetable indicated in the Directives, Regulation 50(4) of the Petroleum (Exploration and Production)(General) Regulations, 2018 (L.I. 2359)[82] provides that relevant contractors are to submit a draft UUOA to the minister within six months of the finalization of the appraisal of the petroleum accumulation. Regulation 50(4) states:

> The relevant contractors shall submit to the Minister a draft unitization and unit operating agreement or an agreement to coordinate and develop separate petroleum accumulations based on the model agreement described in sub-regulation (1) within six months after the finalization of appraisal of the petroleum accumulation.[83]

ENI thus contended that it was necessary to first appraise the hydrocarbon accumulations, and only when this appraisal was finalized would it be possible to determine the appropriate course of action and set out the relevant timetable. ENI argued that, consequently, the statutory timeline of six months according to Regulation 50(4) began only after the finalization of the appraisal of the petroleum accumulation. It was thus their submission that the proposed timeline requiring the parties to submit a draft Unitization Agreement within 120 days from the date of the Directives was practically impossible to commit to and was also inconsistent with Regulation 50(4).

ENI further noted that, appraisal was defined under section 95 of the Petroleum Act, 2016, as

> operations or activities carried out following a discovery of petroleum for the purpose of delineating the accumulations of petroleum to which that discovery relates in terms of thickness and lateral extent and estimating the quantity of recoverable petroleum and all operations or activities to resolve all uncertainties required for determination of commerciality of a discovery.[84]

ENI asserted that the appraisal process "must be conducted in accordance with the law and best industry practice."[85]

ENI in essence noted over the months that unitization is appropriate where

> a hydrocarbon accumulation straddles a contract boundary area; hydrocarbons from one contract area can migrate into another contract area; hydrocarbons are commercially producible on both sides of the contract boundary

82 Regulation 50 is titled, *Coordination of Petroleum Activities and Unitization.*

83 Page 2 of letter from ENI signed by Roberto Daniele, managing director to Hon. John Peter Amewu, dated 22 June 2020, with reference number RD/MD/2020/06/751.

84 Section 95 is titled, *Interpretation.*

85 Page 2 of letter from ENI signed by Roberto Daniele, managing director to Hon. John Peter Amewu, dated 22 June 2020, with reference number RD/MD/2020/06/751.

area; and the hydrocarbon accumulation can be developed as one unit for an optimum petroleum recovery and operational efficiency.[86]

ENI noted its commitment to supporting the government of Ghana to maximizing hydrocarbon recovery, and to progress the matter starting with the exchange of raw data with Springfield on a like-for-like basis but with the purpose of evaluating the existence of hydrocarbon communication between the Afina discovery and the Sankofa Field. It indicated that it had informed Springfield very clearly of its position and its willingness to progress with technical evaluations for the purpose which it stated.

In its concluding remarks, ENI noted that the contents of Springfield's letter of 10 June 2020 were inaccurate and inflammatory. It unreservedly refuted any allegations of obstructive or irregular conduct made against it. It further stated that it had shared with Springfield a data exchange agreement that was consistent with law and which agreement did not require any party to exchange data without first obtaining any necessary approvals, followed international best practice, was entirely appropriate for the process, and offered equivalent contractual protections to the WCTP 2 form of confidentiality agreement which Springfield contended it was obliged to use.

As the Public Interest and Accountability Committee[87] aptly noted in its 2020 Annual Report, ENI's basis for objecting to the unitization were basically that there was insufficient data to ascertain whether:

- The Afina discovery drilled in 2019, and the Sankofa Cenomanian oil field discovered in 2012 and in production for about four years, were straddling each other.
- The Afina discovery had been sufficiently tested or appraised to demonstrate that it was in dynamic communication with the Sankofa Field.
- Unitization would ensure efficient reservoir exploitation, avoid unnecessary, costly and competitive drilling (rule of capture), and maximize economic recovery of the reserves.
- Unitization or any other form of coordinated development would be appropriate in accordance with the laws of Ghana.[88]

ENI rejected claims that it was deliberately trying to prevent unitization, or even worse, sabotage the process. Giuseppe Valenti, managing director of ENI Ghana, noted that ENI had submitted to the Ministry of Energy its analysis of the two

86 'ENI Says Working to Find Acceptable Solution to Unitization Stalemate' *Ghana Business News* (5 June 2021) <https://www.ghanabusinessnews.com/2021/06/05/eni-says-working-to-find-acceptable-solution-to-unitisation-stalemate/> accessed 11 June 2021.

87 This is a statutory committee with the mandate to, inter alia, monitor the use of petroleum revenue by the government to ensure that it is in consonance with the law.

88 '2020 Public Interest and Accountability Annual Report' 15 <https://www.piacghana.org/portal/files/downloads/piac_reports/piac_2020_annual_report.pdf> accessed 8 June 2021.

fields, and believed that cooperation and data sharing would help find a commercially viable solution. He noted that "we are confident that the analysis and resulting report will allow the parties to progress discussions toward an agreeable, commercial solution of the matter."[89] He further noted that ENI Ghana was only requesting an appropriate shared work program and evaluation process to assess the elements or factors that would necessitate a unitization.[90] He noted that "ENI will need an appraisal program of the Afina area including (but not limited to) production and interference tests in order to understand the potential benefit of a unitization of the Sankofa and Afina discovery."[91]

Springfield issued a statement disputing the above.

6.4.4 Springfield's Response to ENI and Vitol's Assertions

On 5 June 2021, Springfield issued a press release in which it stated that it sought to correct inaccurate statements in respect of the unitization, which statements had been attributed to ENI, ACEP,[92] PIAC[93] and IES.[94] In respect of the unitization process, it noted a number of things.

It noted that it had been stated in some publications that "unitization needs to follow an appropriate, shared work programme and evaluation process to assess the elements before taking decisions."[95] Springfield contended that this was erroneous and not the position of the law. It stated that, "per the laws of Ghana, the sole requirement for the unitization of fields is when an accumulation of petroleum extends from the boundaries of one contract area into another." Springfield contended that this had been established and that "any further activity or work programme beyond proving that the fields straddle is a post-unitization activity that would be carried out as part of the unit operations."

It further noted that it has been erroneously stated that "the unitization process for Afina and Sankofa Field would entail an appraisal programme of the Afina area including (but not limited to) production and inference tests." It asserted that

> a key objective of appraisal activities is to delineate fields and know how far they extend. Thus, appraising a field would apply to the entire petroleum accumulation and not just a portion of it. With the Afina and Sankofa Fields already established as a single unit, the drilling of Afina-1 fulfilled the

89 'ENI Ghana Ready for Unitization with Springfield If. . .' *Norvan Reports* (3 June 2021) <https://www.norvanreports.com/eni-ghana-ready-for-unitization-with-springfield-only-if/> accessed 8 June 2021.

90 Ibid.

91 Ibid.

92 Africa Centre for Energy Policy.

93 Public Interest and Accountability Committee.

94 Institute for Energy Studies.

95 Press Statement Issued by Springfield Energy.

appraisal objective as it proved that the Sankofa Fields extended further into the Springfield operated area.[96]

It noted that though Afina-1 is an exploratory well for Springfield, due to contractual obligations and the fact that it was the first well drilled in the WCTP 2 area, it could be deemed an appraisal well as well in the grand scheme of appraising the Sankofa hydrocarbon accumulation. Springfield asserted that it drew a parallel with the Hyedua well drilled by Tullow as an exploration well for the Deepwater Tano Contract area, which was later reclassified as an appraisal well for the purposes of unitizing the Jubilee Field. It thus concluded that

> in this regard, the Afina 1X well can either be an exploration well or an appraisal well, depending on the context – it is an exploration well in the context of the WCTP 2 contract area, and an appraisal well in the context of the unitized field with Sankofa.[97]

Springfield went on to note in respect of costs and liabilities that it had been stated in some publications that "each party must first pay its share of the costs of producing hydrocarbons from the unitized field in order to have a right to the oil produced and proceeds from the production."[98] It rebutted this as a misrepresentation of the process. It noted that the field had been in production for almost four years already. It stated that past production from the unitized field had to be re-allocated to the parties in accordance with their respective interests in the unitized field. It went on to note that, as per industry practice, a reconciliation of past costs as well as revenue from production had to be conducted in order for a determination to be made as to the entitlement of the parties to past revenue and costs. It asserted that after this reconciliation, if the cost was higher than the revenues, then there would be an amount for it to pay and vice versa. It noted that thereafter, that is, after such reconciliation, Springfield would bear its pro rata share of future costs and be entitled to its share of oil produced in line with industry standard practice. It contended:

> This is in line with the international convention on unitization that where there is pre-unitization expenditure and/or pre-unitization production in the Unit Area (whether by one or both Contract Groups), the Unitization and Unit Operating Agreement (UUOA) would seek to re-allocate and balance such costs and production from the unit area to the contractor groups in accordance with their respective shares of the unit. This set-off mechanism is clearly contemplated in the 2020 Model UUOA issued by the Association of International Petroleum Negotiators (AIPN).[99]

96 Ibid.
97 Ibid.
98 Ibid.
99 Ibid.

6.4.5 Different Perspectives

Some foreign publications portrayed these events in a negative light in respect of Ghana, basically arguing that the government of Ghana was forcing the unitization on ENI in a situation where it was neither legally nor geologically required or warranted. Thus, there were such headings as "Ghana Forces ENI to merge its Sankofa Field with a Domestic Discovery," "ENI Faces Forced Unitization of West Africa Fields," "Ulterior Motive Behind Energy Minister Amewu's Push for ENI and Springfield's Shotgun Wedding," "ExxonMobil, Aker Energy and ENI Fed up with Accra," "Ghana's Political Meddling Could Derail its Oil Boom"[100] and the like.[101] Viktor Katona, for instance, commenting on these developments in Ghana's upstream petroleum industry, stated:

> As is often the case with projects that exceed general expectations, the Ghanaian government might be overexerting itself in making the nascent oil industry serve its interests . . . Accra's assertive view of how it would prefer its offshore crude production to develop has another deficiency. The Energy Ministry wants ENI to operate the prospective Sankofa-Afina field, however, it should be Springfield that gets the largest stake as Afina's nominal reserves are higher, despite its commercial nature remaining questionable. Mirroring a 54.5–45.5% split between Afina and Sankofa, ENI would receive only 20.2% of the future joint project, Vitol would be left with 16.2% whilst Springfield would get 44.7%. Interestingly, the Ghanaian authorities have set up a May 2022 deadline to finalize the unitization deal so despite the indisposition of ENI and Vitol the outcome is already foreordained for them. Ghana ought to be very careful in how it treats the Sankofa/Afina issue because it carries enormous reputational risks for future offshore projects.[102]

100 Viktor Katona, 'Ghana's Political Meddling Could Derail Its Oil Boom' *OilPrice.com* (17 January 2021) <https://business24.com.gh/2021/06/07/springfield-ep-is-committed-to-unitisation-process/?> accessed 8 June 2021.

101 Ekow Dontoh and Yinka Ibukun, 'Ghana Forces ENI to Merge Its Sankofa Field with a Domestic Discovery' *World Oil* (11 December 2020) <https://www.worldoil.com/news/2020/11/12/ghana-forces-eni-to-merge-its-sankofa-field-with-a-domestic-discovery> accessed 8 June 2021.

Ekow Dontoh and Yinka Ibukun, 'ENI Faces Forced Unitization of West Africa Fields' *Bloomberg* (12 December 2020) <https://www.rigzone.com/news/wire/eni_faces_forced_unitization_of_west_africa_fields-12-nov-2020-163837-article/> accessed 8 June 2021.

'Ulterior Motive Behind Energy Minister Amewu's Push for ENI and Springfield's Shotgun Wedding' *Africa Intelligence* (7 December 2020) <https://www.africaintelligence.com/oil – gas_corporate-strategy/2020/12/07/ulterior-motive-behind-energy-minister-amewu-s-push-for-eni-and-springfield-s-shotgun-wedding,109625622-art> accessed 8 June 2021.

'ExxonMobil, Aker Energy and ENI Fed Up with Accra', *Africa Intelligence* (7 June 2021) 1.

Viktor Katona, 'Ghana's Political Meddling Could Derail Its Oil Boom' *OilPrice.com* (17 January 2021) <https://business24.com.gh/2021/06/07/springfield-ep-is-committed-to-unitisation-process/?> accessed 25 June 2021.

102 Katona (n 100).

James Gavin noted that Ghana's imposition of a unitization deal on the parties "highlights the government's impatience at delays in developing hydrocarbon resources but may also reveal an element of resource nationalism as the state throws its weight behind a homegrown company."[103]

The Institute for Energy Studies (IES) in Ghana made a spirited charge for the quick unitization of the two fields on the basis that the benefits to the country would be immense. According to the IES, from a study it had conducted, the unitization would lead to maximum economic benefits of some $8.4 billion to the State as opposed to the $2.065 billion to be derived if the unitization was not done.[104] IES asserted that benefits to the State in the incidence of unitization would be in the form of significant reduction in operational and capital costs of the unitized fields, as well as increases in royalties, taxes, additional oil entitlement (AOE), levies and fees.[105]

Mark Agyemang, the technical director of the Public Interest and Accountability Committee, opined that the parties ought to have come to the negotiation table and appointed an independent assessor to reassess the two fields and present the data to the parties. Agyemang noted:

> In my opinion, I think that there should have been an independent assessor. It should not have been government carrying out the assessment. They should have appointed an independent assessor, who will make the data available to all parties, especially ENI.[106]

The Public Interest and Accountability Committee, commenting on this ongoing matter in its 2020 Annual Report, noting the effect of the minister's directive if complied with, noted; "A successful outcome of government's directive on this would register the very first unitization agreement between an international oil company (IOC) and a Ghanaian operator, and could usher in a new era of meaningful local participation in Ghana's upstream petroleum sector."[107]

The African Centre for Energy Policy (ACEP) noted: "The negative press associated with these issues has the potential to undermine the progress made over the years to encourage investments into Ghana's upstream petroleum sector."[108] It further noted that the situation is worsened by the current global context of the energy transition, which is engineering a shift away from fossil fuel to alternative

103 James Gavin, 'Ghana Unitization Order Puts ENI in a Bind' *African Energy Newsletter* (3 December 2020).

104 Norvan (n 89).

105 Ibid.

106 'ENI, Springfield Impasse . . . PIAC Calls for Independent Reassessment of Fields' *Public Interest and Accountability Committee* (31 May 2021) <https://www.piacghana.org/portal/12/13/495/eni-springfield-impasse-%E2%80%A6piac-calls-for-independent-reassessment-of-fields> accessed 8 June 2021.

107 PIAC (n 88) 15.

108 'ACEP's Comments on the ENI-Springfield Unitization Tussle and ExxonMobil's Exit from Ghana' 1 Africa Centre for Energy Policy (3 June 2021) <https://cdn.modernghana.com/images/content/report_content/642021113833-0eu2xkjwwr-aceps-comments-on-the-eni-springfield-unitisation-tussle-and-exxonmobils-exit-from-ghana.pdf> accessed 9 June 2021.

energy sources.[109] It opined that the shift is shrinking available capital for investments in new exploration activities in the oil industry and generating extreme competition for the limited money available for upstream activities.[110] It thus noted that attracting investment therefore, required an assuring, positive, and less risky political environment. It went on to state that "ACEP's statement on these developments is a cautionary call on government and stakeholders to act right and preserve the investment climate of the industry."[111] ACEP contextualized the issues thus:

> The reports from GNPC and ENI point to contentions about the conditions precedent for unitizing the two fields. GNPC, on the one hand, summarily, is of the view that the existing seismic data and oil properties of the Afina discovery within the same Cenomanian Channel as SGN is enough proof of straddling. On the other hand, ENI holds the opinion that further studies are required to establish commerciality and dynamic communication.[112]

ACEP concluded thus:

> ACEP cautions without judgment that:
>
> - Unitization is an age-old industry practice with established technical parameters and conditions necessary for joint development and production of adjacent fields, often necessitated by straddling or proximity. In most cases, the commercial benefits accruing to both parties ensure a smooth unitization process without state intervention. However, where the state's intervention becomes necessary, it is required that the state is transparent in the application of the principles, laws, and science of unitization. Unfortunately, the government's silence amid raging media war is unhealthy for creating a competitive and assuring environment to the investor community. Government must inform the public on the basis of

109 'ACEP's Comments on the ENI-Springfield Unitization Tussle and ExxonMobil's Exit from Ghana' 1 Africa Centre for Energy Policy (3 June 2021) <https://cdn.modernghana.com/images/content/report_content/642021113833-0eu2xkjwwr-aceps-comments-on-the-eni-springfield-unitisation-tussle-and-exxonmobils-exit-from-ghana.pdf> accessed 9 June 2021.

110 'ACEP's Comments on the ENI-Springfield Unitization Tussle and ExxonMobil's Exit from Ghana' 1 Africa Centre for Energy Policy (3 June 2021) <https://cdn.modernghana.com/images/content/report_content/642021113833-0eu2xkjwwr-aceps-comments-on-the-eni-springfield-unitisation-tussle-and-exxonmobils-exit-from-ghana.pdf> accessed 9 June 2021.

111 'ACEP's Comments on the ENI-Springfield Unitization Tussle and ExxonMobil's Exit from Ghana' 1 Africa Centre for Energy Policy (3 June 2021) <https://cdn.modernghana.com/images/content/report_content/642021113833-0eu2xkjwwr-aceps-comments-on-the-eni-springfield-unitisation-tussle-and-exxonmobils-exit-from-ghana.pdf> accessed 9 June 2021.

112 'ACEP's Comments on the ENI-Springfield Unitization Tussle and ExxonMobil's Exit from Ghana' 1 Africa Centre for Energy Policy (3 June 2021) <https://cdn.modernghana.com/images/content/report_content/642021113833-0eu2xkjwwr-aceps-comments-on-the-eni-springfield-unitisation-tussle-and-exxonmobils-exit-from-ghana.pdf> accessed 9 June 2021.

its unitization directive in an effort to diffuse the local and international controversies on the matter.

- The position of GNPC and ENI also contest Ghana's Petroleum (Exploration and Production) Law's provisions on unitization and the regulations developed to operationalize it. Therefore, ACEP suggests the immediate interpretation of the provisions on unitization by the Attorney General to guide the government's position.
- GNPC is an interested party, and, by law, a partner to every investor in the sector. That position requires that GNPC maintains credibility and trust with its partners. Government must recognize the commercial position of GNPC and not use them to settle contentious issues. In this particular unitization tussle, GNPC should not have been assumed as the independent arbiter. The Petroleum Commission or an independent party appointed by ENI and Springfield would have been better suited in this case.

6.4.6 Legal Process and Outcome

On 10 July 2020, Springfield filed a suit at the Commercial Court, Accra, titled *Springfield Exploration and Production Ltd. v. ENI Ghana Exploration and Production Ltd. and Vitol Upstream Ghana Ltd.* directed at ENI and Vitol to inter alia comply with the Minister for Energy's directive to enter into a Unitization Agreement.

On 25 June 2021, the Court ordered ENI to pay 30% of its revenue generated from the sale of its crude from the Sankofa Field into an escrow account pending the final determination of the matter.[113] The order took immediate effect. The Court noted that this order would protect the interests of Springfield while allowing ENI and Vitol to continue operating and cover costs.[114] While Springfield welcomed it as "a vindication" of its position, ENI noted in a statement issued that "we fully expect to take the appropriate steps necessary in order to protect our operations in the country, including appealing against this ruling."[115]

On 4 December 2020, ENI and Vitol sent a Notice of Dispute[116] to the Republic of Ghana, via the Minister for Energy. By letter dated 29 January 2021, ENI and Vitol provided GNPC with a Dispute Notice[117] pursuant to Article 24.1 of their

113 Alessandro Bianchi, 'Court Rules 30% of ENI Ghana Oilfield Revenue to Go Into Escrow' *Reuters* (28 June 2021) <https://www.reuters.com/business/energy/court-rules-30-eni-ghana-oilfield-revenue-go-into-escrow-2021-06-25/> accessed 1 July 2021.

114 Ibid.

115 Ibid.

116 GV/MD/2020/12/1593.

117 Letter addressed to Dr. Kofi Koduah Sarpong, CEO, GNPC, Reference Number GV/MD/2021/01/100, and signed by Giuseppe Valenti, managing director, ENI Ghana E & P Ltd, and James Thorburn, country manager, Vitol Upstream Ghana Ltd.

petroleum agreement[118] in respect of the Offshore Cape Three Points Area. They laid out their claim as follows:

> 2. In reliance on GNPC's "technical report" and "independent opinion" dated 5th June 2018, which ENI and Vitol have not received but which are referred to in the MoE's letter of 9th April 2020, and the GNPC Report, the Republic of Ghana, acting through the MoE, has sought to impose terms and conditions for the unitization of the Afina Discovery in the West Cape Three Points Block 2 Area and the Sankofa Field in the Offshore Cape Three Points Area ("the purported unitization".)
>
> 3. The Republic of Ghana, acting through the MoE, has by virtue of the purported unitization breached the Petroleum Agreement . . .
>
> 4. By virtue of producing the "technical report" and "independent opinion" dated 5th June 2018 and the GNPC Report, GNPC has enabled the MoE's unlawful conduct in relation to the purported unitization. In doing so, GNPC has also breached the Petroleum Agreement. Accordingly, we hereby serve you with this written notice of dispute regarding the purported unitization, pursuant to Article 24.1 of the Petroleum Agreement ("the notice").[119]

They noted in conclusion that

> This notice triggers a 30 day consultation and negotiation period under Article 24.1 during which we should be pleased to meet with you. We invite your proposals in this regard. If the Dispute is not resolved within that period, we reserve our right to proceed to refer the Dispute to arbitration in accordance with Article 24 of the Petroleum Agreement without further notice to you.[120]

118 Article 24 – *Consultation, Arbitration, Independent Expert and Settlement of Third Party Disputes*

24.1 Subject to the prior fulfilment of any procedures specified in this Agreement to resolve disputes arising hereunder, any dispute arising between the State and GNPC or either of them on one hand and Contractor on the other hand in relation to or in connection with or arising out of this Agreement, shall be resolved by consultation and negotiation among senior personnel authorized by each. In the event that no agreement is reached within thirty (30) days after the date when the State and/or GNPC on the one hand and the Contractor on the other hand notifies the other that a dispute exists within the meaning of this Article or such longer period specifically agreed to by the parties or provided elsewhere in this Agreement, any party shall have the right subject to Article 24.9 [determination by a sole expert] to have such dispute settled exclusively through international arbitration under the auspices of the International Chamber of Commerce (the "ICC") and adopting the Rules of Arbitration of the International Chamber of Commerce (the "ICC Rules") in force on the date on which the proceedings are instituted, which ICC Rules are deemed incorporated by reference into this Article 24, save as otherwise provided herein."

119 Letter (n 117) 1.

120 Ibid, 2.

ENI in the said letter stressed a desire to avoid the matter going to arbitration. It noted that, "we have been seeking and continue to seek to avoid the need for formal arbitration proceedings through amicable discussions with the MoE."[121]

On 9 April 2021, ENI and Vitol met with the president of Ghana, Akufo-Addo, and noted that they had no objection in principle to any potential unitization as long as it followed a consensual process, was in accordance with Ghanaian law, and recognized international oil and gas best practice.[122]

ENI and Vitol, referencing this meeting with the president, subsequently noted in a letter to the Minister for Energy, dated 12 April 2021, that notwithstanding their willingness to engage in this process, they were obliged to take steps to preserve their legal rights in respect to Springfield's continued pursuit of its legal action in relation to the "purported unitization"[123] as well as the expiry of the limitation period of six months (on 14 April 2020) of the right to apply for judicial review of the minister's directive of 14 October,[124] while reserving the right to progress with international arbitration under the petroleum agreement.[125] They noted that Springfield was now seeking to rely upon the minister's letter imposing terms and conditions for unitization to support an application for a court order to freeze their accounts.[126] They noted that they would process the available data related to the Afina discovery received from the Petroleum Commission and deliver the outcome of the analysis by the end of April 2021. They concluded by noting that they were confident that an intervention by the minister could "steer the process and contribute to solve amicably the matter in dispute."[127]

Thus, in June 2021, ENI and Vitol noted that they were working with the Ministry of Energy, Petroleum Commission and GNPC, to find a mutually acceptable solution in order to enable the country to capitalize on the Afina discovery. Giuseppe Valenti, managing director of ENI Ghana, noted that "in principle, we are not opposed to unitization, but this needs to follow an appropriate, shared work programme and evaluation process to assess the elements listed above before taking decisions in the interest of all parties."[128]

Feeling pressured to enter into a unitization agreement they deemed as unjustified, by a Statement of Claim dated 16 February 2022, ENI Ghana and Vitol pursuant to Article 3 of the 1976 United Nations Commission on International

121 Ibid, 1.

122 See letter dated 12 April 2021 with Reference Number GV/MD/2021/04/398, from ENI and Vitol, to the Minister for Energy, Matthew Opoku Prempeh, and copied to Nana Asante Bediatuo, Executive Secretary to the President, and Dr. K.K. Sarpong, Ghana National Petroleum Corporation.

123 Ibid.

124 Ibid.

125 Ibid.

126 Ibid.

127 Ibid.

128 'ENI Says Working to Find Acceptable Solution to Unitization Stalemate' *Ghana Business News* (5 June 2021) <https://www.ghanabusinessnews.com/2021/06/05/eni-says-working-to-find-acceptable-solution-to-unitisation-stalemate/> accessed 11 June 2021.

Trade Law Rules brought an action before the Stockholm Chamber of Commerce (SCC) against Ghana and GNPC through the law firm Herbert Smith Freehills LLP, in a suit titled *In the Matter of an UNCITRAL Arbitration between ENI Ghana of Ghana; Ghana National Petroleum Corporation*, seeking inter alia "that the Respondents take no further action to implement the purported unitization of the Sankofa Field and Afina Discovery."[129] By a Statement of Defence dated 7 September 2022, the Respondents responded asserting inter alia that "All of Claimants' claims are denied with prejudice in their entirety."[130] The Claimants filed a Reply to this Statement of Defence.

On 8 July 2024, the Tribunal issued its final award where it concluded that the unitization directives were wrong and unlawful. It declared, inter alia, that the Republic of Ghana breached the petroleum agreement by issuing the unitization directives in the circumstances in which they were issued.[131] The conditions that had to exist to give ground for the minister to exercise its discretion under section 34 of the Petroleum (Exploration and Production) Act to trigger unitization was not established, that is, "a single accumulation of petroleum straddling two or more contract areas."[132]

Further, the Tribunal concluded that the unitization measures taken by the ministry were not implemented in a manner that was consistent with the applicable legal framework in several respects, namely, the statutory unitization trigger was not established, the imposition of the unitization terms was unlawful and the determination of the tract participation was arbitrary.[133]

6.5 Conclusion

There had been the concern that Ghana needed to be very careful about how it went about this matter so as not to adversely affect its industry. Ghana currently has only two oil producers – Tullow (Jubilee and TEN Field) and ENI (Sankofa). It is the case that there has been stagnation in Ghana's industry, further hampered by COVID-19. Thus, as Katona notes, the output volumes are unlikely to increase significantly as there seems to be no other project in the pipeline. He rightly notes

129 Statement of Claim – In the Matter of an Arbitration under the 1976 Arbitration Rules of the United Nations Commission on International Trade Law (UNCITRAL): Stockholm Chamber of Commerce Arbitration U2021/114 Between ENI Ghana Exploration and Production Limited; Vitol Upstream Ghana Limited (Claimants) and The Republic of Ghana; Ghana National Petroleum Corporation (Respondents).

130 Statement of Defence dated 7th September 2022 – Government of Ghana and GNPC.

131 In the Matter of an Arbitration under the 1976 Arbitration Rules of the United Nations Commission on International Trade Law (UNCITRAL): ENI Ghana Exploration and Production Limited and Vitol Upstream Ghana Limited (The Claimants) v. The Republic of Ghana and Ghana National Petroleum Corporation (The Respondents) – Final Award, Paragraph 489.

It further declared that each party bear its own costs and ordered the Republic of Ghana to pay to ENI and Vitol EUR189,900 for the costs of the Tribunal and SCC, and dismissed all other requests for relief.

132 Ibid, Paragraph 361.

133 Ibid, Paragraph 359.

that the Pecan Field, operated by Aker, might be the one to supplement Ghana's production portfolio, but delays in its development will postpone the commissioning of this field, even more so the fact that Aker now wants to split it in two separate phases for the field's Northern and Southern part.[134] Any output additions over the course of 2021–2025 will thus come from Tullow's Greater Jubilee Production ramp-up and not new projects.[135]

It is instructive to note that the Jubilee Field unitization was pulled off successfully and the field was brought to production in record time as opposed to the difficulties encountered with respect to the Afina-Sankofa precisely because that recognition as to unitization being triggered was absent in the latter case.

Key Findings of This Chapter

1. Unitization is easy to achieve when it is well established to all parties involved that the conditions necessary for it to occur are present.
2. An appraisal is deemed a key prerequisite for a determination as to whether there should be unitization.
3. There must necessarily be a comprehensive assessment of the petroleum accumulation to establish and confirm the extension of an accumulation across any shared contract area boundary.
4. Unitization is appropriate where "a hydrocarbon accumulation straddles a contract boundary area; hydrocarbons are commercially producible on both sides of the contract boundary area; and the hydrocarbon accumulation can be developed as one unit for an optimum petroleum recovery and operational efficiency."[136]
5. There must be a genuine commitment by all parties involved to adhere to procedural and substantive requirements for a unitization to be successfully executed.

134 Katona (n 100).
135 Ibid.
136 Ghana Business News (n 86).

7 Mexico

Dario G. Lamanna

7.1 Introduction

The discovery of the Zama oilfield in 2017 by a consortium comprised by Talos Energy (Operator), Wintershall DEA and Premier Oil (former Sierra Oil & Gas) has put the concept of unitization of hydrocarbon operationshigh on the agenda in Mexico. Other potential shared deposits have been discovered, but the Mexican government has not confirmed them yet. Unitization of hydrocarbon fields could potentially help Mexico achieve higher efficiency in its oil and gas exploration and extraction, among others.

As a result of the discovery, the topic of unitization became important and relevant and hastened the approval of the laws and regulations concerning this concept. Therefore, now Mexico has regulation and legislative provisions regarding the matter.

For an oil or gas field to be unitized in Mexico, there must be an opinion by the National Hydrocarbons Commission that applicable criteria have been met, and then an administrative decision by SENER (the Ministry of Energy of Mexico) is required. For such determination, technical and legal basis must be met. Prior to that, there must be a SENER instruction to unitize a field.

After the unitization of a field is determined, the assignees or contractors of adjacent unitized fields are to enter into an unitization agreement, aiming at reaching the most efficient manner to exploit the shared reservoir.

In Mexico, once the unitization of an oilfield or reservoir has been declared by the relevant authority, the companies involved in each area must sign a unitization contract or agreement. The agreement can be entered into between companies within the same country, or between the governments of various countries if a field spans an international border.

7.2 Principles of Regulation of the Unitization Process

Mexico has opted for making the assignees or contractors of a specific area that is potentially shared, in charge of giving notice to Mexican government (it is worth noting that PEMEX; a state-owned company, plays a major role in Mexican hydrocarbons operation, and therefore, this is not entirely left on private actors). The

DOI: 10.4324/9781003491293-9

determination of unitization is an executive branch decision, and if determined, is up to the correspondent assignees or contractors to reach specific terms for an agreement, taking into consideration the information and conditions minimally required by SENER. The unitization, in all cases, is to be determined by SENER.

There is no one right way to regulate unitizations in accordance with the mandatory guidelines[1] published in 2018 and other applicable regulations, which lay out the following principles:

1. Energy security, namely, the uninterrupted availability of energy at an affordable price (IEA)[2]
2. Platform sustainability
3. Market diversification.

Therefore, to unitize a field, not only geological and technical considerations are relevant, but also political and economic ones.

There are several steps that can be taken and efforts that could be made in order to find the necessary components and propose a series of minimum conditions that favor efficient agreements between parties. The authority has the capacity to make a mandatory unitization agreement model, but has failed to do so.

As the International Association of Energy Negotiators (AIEN) has drafted a model unitization contract, this could potentially fix such omission by the Mexican government, and the AIPN model could be used as a standard for the industry in Mexico. The 2020 model contains minimum provisions such as the determination of the operator of the deposit, the obligations and responsibilities of the parties, the disposition of production, tax aspects, the calculation of the royalties, treatment of costs and investments, working programs and budgets, accounting procedure, dispute resolution, and other basic provisions. It is a model, not a standard, and unites the best practices of the international industry. Nevertheless, it must be adapted to the specific case (parties, project, obligations, etc.) and adjusted to local legislation. The model has a series of annexes to the contract, among which are the Accounting Procedure, the Production Lifting Procedure, the Authorization of Expenses Procedure (AFEs), Use of Existing Facilities, and many others.

7.3 Regulatory and Legal Framework

The main regulatory bodies in Mexico in terms of unitization are the aforementioned SENER (Mexican version of an energy ministry), which is responsible for declaring the unitization, the National Hydrocarbons Commission (Comision Nacional de Hidrocarburos [CNH]), the Ministry of Finance and Public Credit (Secretaria

1 "Lineamientos que establecen el procedimiento para instruir la unificación de yacimientos compartidos y aprobar los términos y condiciones del acuerdo de unificación", published in the Official Gazette (DOF) on 15 March 2018.

2 <https://www.iea.org/topics/energy-security> (20 January 2023; 08:50).

de Hacienda y Credito Publico [SHCP]), the Ministry of Economy (Secretaria de Economia [SE]), and the National Agency for Industrial Safety and Environmental Protection in the Hydrocarbons Sector (Agencia Nacional de Seguridad Industrial y Protecion al Medio Ambiente del Sector Hydrocarburos [ASEA]).

The Mexican legal framework addresses unitization through various different legal instruments. The Hydrocarbons Law[3] and its Regulation provide the general criteria of cataloguing and carrying out the unitization process in Mexican land and waters. Other state provisions include the guidelines for the unitization of fields or deposits issued by the SENER as a recommendation for presenting a notification about a shared field; and the administrative guidelines of the CNH aimed at regulating the unitization protocol. In addition, there are international agreements which govern the process of managing fields crossing international boundaries (like the one signed with the United States).

Article 42 of the Hydrocarbons Law[4] provides that it is up to the SENER to conduct the unitization of oilfields or deposits based on an expert opinion on the subject issued by the CNH. This applies to national and, in terms of international agreements, to transboundary oilfields. In addition, the Hydrocarbons Law contains three more articles that regulate issues related to transboundary oilfields (Articles 1, 3, and 17). Chapter VI, Articles 62 to 64 of the Regulation of the Hydrocarbons Law[5] establish the minimum requirements, characteristics, and mechanisms that must be met by the entitlement holders and contractors so that the authority can determine the possible existence of a shared oilfield or deposit, and conduct the unitization of the latter; in particular, the entitlement holder or contractor must notify the SENER and the CNH of the discovery of a shared oilfield or deposit within 60 business days after its discovery. The SENER must decide upon the economic terms, and to this end, it must notify the SHCP and the Mexican Petroleum Fund (FMP) of the unitization.

National shared oilfields, unlike the transboundary ones, are accumulations of natural hydrocarbons in the subsoil, contained in porous or fractured rock, and located inside the borders of the Republic of Mexico and which exceed the coordinates of a single granting instrument. In this case, it is up to the SENER to conduct the unitization of the oilfields, based on an expert opinion of the CNH. Once the unitization has been declared, a unitization agreement must be signed by the contractors or entitlement holders.

In the bidding guidelines and the model agreement annexed thereto, of each of the rounds carried out by the CNH (Rounds 1, 2, and 3), there is a detailed description of the procedure of unitization of shared oilfields or reservoirs, ensuring strict adherence to the regulatory provisions in force. In particular, Clause 9 of the Contracts of Shared Production approved for every round, which are to be

3 Ley de Hidrocarburos, published on the Official Gazette (DOF) on 11 August 2014, and Last Reform Published in the Official Gazette (DOF) on 20 May 2021.

4 Published in the Official Gazette (DOF) on 11 August 2014.

5 Published in the Official Gazette (DOF) on 31 October 2014.

signed by all of the contractors, establishes the obligation of the contractor to notify the SENER and the CNH within a maximum of 60 business days after gathering all of the elements necessary to infer the existence of a shared oilfield or reservoir. The said notification must contain at least (1) supporting technical analysis, which can determine the possible existence of the shared reservoir; (2) the general characteristics of the said shared reservoir; (3) geological, geophysical, and other studies used to determine the possible existence of the shared reservoir, including the information obtained during the drilling of the wells, which determined that the reservoir in question exceeds the limits of the contract area; (4) a proposal of a working program of oil activities to be carried out prior to the execution of the unitization agreement between the contractor and the parties entitled to the area into which the field extends; and (5) the additional information that the contractor may consider necessary. Once the notification had been received, the procedure that the authorities must follow in order to declare the shared reservoir was established in the same model agreement. The model agreement also establishes the scenario of unitization of fields that have not been yet assigned or contracted.

In the CNH Guidelines,[6] which regulate the procedure for the presentation, approval and supervision of the fulfillment of the exploration and development plans for the extraction of hydrocarbons, as well as any modifications, Article 3, Section XXXIII of the Guidelines defines unitization in the following manner:

> Actions with regard to a Field, Reservoir or installations, which are shared or are susceptible to sharing, instructed by the Secretariat, with prior expert opinion from the Commission, in order to make the procedures of Exploration and Extraction more efficient, with the expenses made and the benefits obtained distributed among the participating Oil Operators, in the corresponding proportions.

At the beginning of 2017 the SENER issued a document called "Guide to the Unitization of Oilfields and Reservoirs" (translation by the author). The purpose of this guide was to present the recommendations of the SENER regarding the submission of the notification about the possible existence of a shared oilfield or reservoir referred to in Article 62 of the Regulation of the Hydrocarbons Law, as well as all of the documentation that the entitlement holders or contractors shall submit with the notification and the procedure for the unitization of shared oilfields or reservoirs in accordance with the principles of economy, competitiveness, efficiency, legality, and the best practices of the industry, necessary for the greater exploitation of hydrocarbons in situ. This guide served as a basis for the issuance of the new Guidelines of the SENER in March of 2018, mentioned above. The draft version of these new SENER Guidelines was published by the COFEMER on 17 October 2017, having received comments and suggestions from various actors of the industry, among them PEMEX and Amexhi.

6 Published in the Official Gazette (DOF) on 13 November 2015.

In March of 2018 the SENER published the Guidelines,[7] which aimed at establishing the procedure for conducting the unitization of national shared reservoirs and approve the terms and conditions of the agreement of unitization. The objective of these new SENER Guidelines is to establish the procedure for the unitization of national shared reservoirs, through the following activities: (1) approval of the draft unitization agreement; (2) conduct of the unitization of national shared reservoirs; (3) approval of the terms and conditions of the unitization agreement; and (4) determination of the terms and conditions of the unitization agreement when the parties are not able to reach said agreement. From their side, the entitlement holders and/or contractors will have 120 business days to file their proposal of the unitization agreement, which must at least include the following information: (1) the list of entitlements and/or contracts for the exploration and extraction concerned; (2) rights and obligations of the parties; (3) identification of the volume and distribution of the hydrocarbons to be produced; (4) administrative, accounting, and commercial procedures; (5) dispute resolution procedures; (6) period of validity of entitlement, that it is the same term of the principal PSA or any other associated agreement; and (7) identification, duties, and obligations of the operator. Nevertheless, as mentioned, the new guidelines did not provide an approved model unitization agreement or contract, as had been done with other processes such as farm-outs.[8]

The agreement shall have effect from the effective date and shall continue in effect until the earliest of the following: (1) the expiration, termination or revocation of the principal contract (PSA); (2) all parties have become defaulting parties; (3) the abandonment of one contract; (4) the withdrawal of all of the parties; or (5) the prior written agreement of all of the parties.

While Mexico continues to carry out its new energy model, it is of key importance to provide clarity and certainty to the industry through clear and well-formulated rules. The mechanisms that have already been adopted are the basis for the creation of a robust regulatory framework, which could provide the necessary clarity to the government, as well as to the companies and investors. However, specific criteria for the analysis of energy security and market implications of the potential unitization of fields is still missing.

In this sense, Zama is not a unique or isolated case in the oil and gas sector. However, it will be the first of many that will leave a mark and become a precedent in the sector.

7.3.1 Transboundary Unitizations

In contrast to national fields, transboundary oilfields are reservoirs the position and geological nature of which are within national jurisdiction and have physical continuity outside of it (Article 1 HL, 2014). The said article amplifies the concept,

7 Published in the Official Gazette (DOF) on 15 March 2018.

8 "Liniamientos para la Unificacion de Yacimientos Compartidos", by Dario G. Lamanna, published in Energia a Debate Magazine, #86, Year 15, June 2018, Mexico City.

considering as transboundary all reservoirs and oilfields outside national jurisdiction, shared with other countries in accordance with the treaties to which Mexico is a party, or under the provisions of the UN Convention on the Law of the Sea (in force as of 16 November 1994, signed by 168 countries, ratified by 60, including Belize and Guatemala, as well as Mexico, but not by the United States of America).

The Agreement between the United States of America and the Mexican United States concerning Transboundary Hydrocarbon Reservoirs in the Gulf of Mexico, signed in Los Cabos on 20 February 2012,[9] in its turn, regulates the terms and conditions and the cooperation between the two countries regarding the joint exploration and exploitation of the geological structures of hydrocarbons and reservoirs that extend across the defined delimitation line, the entirety of which are located beyond 9 nm from the coastline. Once the executive authorities of both countries have jointly confirmed the existence of a transboundary reservoir, the agreement establishes the steps, requirements, and mechanisms necessary for the respective contractors or licensees to celebrate a unitization agreement, which in turn needs to be approved by the executive authorities of both countries in order to enter into force.

7.4 Fiscal Regime

In addition to the payment of the regular taxes such as income tax and VAT, the parties must pay the compensations and royalties to the state through the FMP, in accordance with the Hydrocarbons Revenue Law,[10] including exploration phase fees, basic royalty, and a profit percentage, depending on each exploration and production model contract. Regulations also stipulate limitation to deductions for the calculation of profit percentages, as well as different percentages for the deduction of investments regarding income tax. Therefore, specific taxation of hydrocarbons activities lead to a negative impact on the activities and investments to be carried out by the parties, as costs increase in comparison to other activities.

The treaties to avoid double taxation executed by Mexico with several foreign countries avoid the additional tax burden to which taxpayers carrying out operations abroad may be subject when the same income causes the tax twice; the first from the country from which it comes, said income "country of source", and the second in the "country of residence" of the taxpayer which, commonly in a large part of the countries, taxes its residents with the criterion of "worldwide income", that is, for all the income that is obtained inside or outside its territory.

7.5 Environmental and Social Aspects

In this type of contract, it is important to clearly identify the socio-environmental risks associated with the operation of shared fields and delimit the responsibilities of each party.

9 Published in the Official Gazette (DOF) on 18 July 2014.

10 Published in the Official Gazette on 11 August 2014 and last reform published on 9 December 2019.

For this, it is important that both parties agree in the contract regarding the preparation and compliance with the permits required in the industry. Among the main environmental permits are the approval and validity of the Environmental Impact Study (EIA), the Social Impact Assessment (EVIS), the Certificate of Non-existence of Archaeological Remains (CIRA) in the case of terrestrial areas, permit for the discharge of industrial/domestic wastewater, and some others, which are issued by different organizations and ministries including the Ministry of Energy and Mines (MEM), Ministry of Agriculture (MINAG), Ministry of the Environment (MINAM), National Service of Natural Areas Protected by the State (SERNASTETP), and others.

It is also important that the contract specify the social aspects that impact the operation, such as the effects and compensation to land owners, easements, rights of way, and so on.

It should be noted that current legislation includes compensation and indemnification for use and occupation of the land, as well as consultation and participation processes including the communities affected by the activities.

7.6 Local Content

While PEMEX as a state-owned company is the legal preferent company to conduct exploration and extraction activities, private companies (such as Talos Energy) are to be contracted. When it comes to the Zama Oilfield Exploration and Extraction, an agreement was executed between Talos Energy and CNH,[11] by which, an obligation to use local content of 13% in the exploration phase and from 25% to 35% in the development phase was established, while the national oil company PEMEX has a percentage in its adjacent area (Uchukil[12]) equal to 20%. There is no legal mechanism that permits a contractual rebalance of these different local content commitments, even though local content commitments can be met in other activities in the contractual area.

7.7 Dispute Resolution

In accordance with the Hydrocarbons Law and the contract, the parties may agree to resolve any general dispute that might arise between them through an international arbitration procedure under the standard rules of UNCITRAL (currently established in contracts, but not mandatory by law, and therefore other rules could be agreed upon).

7.8 Dispute Between PEMEX and Talos Energy in the Zama Oilfield

A dispute between the national oil company PEMEX and the American company Talos Energy occurred regarding the location of the greater part of the Zama deposit

11 Contrato CNH-R01-L01-A7/2015.

12 Asignación No. AE-0152-Uchukil.

and the right to be appointed operator in the field. This dispute caused a delay in the negotiation process between the parties. Talos Energy alleged that it made the discovery, and PEMEX affirmed that the greater part of the discovered reservoir is located in its area and gave assurances that it can start production earlier than Talos. Control of the oilfield was ultimately granted to PEMEX by Mexican authorities, and PEMEX was appointed as operator.

7.9 Conclusion

The Zama oilfield unitization process was the first case of a shared oilfield between a public and a private company in Mexico. Its existence prompted regulatory challenges, and the discovery of the Zama oilfield in July 2017 by Talos Energy in 2015 put the concept of unitization on the agenda in Mexico.

The Hydrocarbons Law, its Regulation, the contract, the CNH and SENER Guidelines, as well as the agreements and treaties mentioned above, describe the process of declaring the unitization of shared oilfields or reservoirs, establishing the obligation to notify the authorities about the discovery, which in its turn must determine and declare the unitization of the said oilfields or reservoirs for the joint and efficient exploitation of the existing hydrocarbons by the operators of both of the blocks involved, through the signing of a unitization agreement. As already mentioned, the new SENER Guidelines from March 2018 did not approve an official model contract, as it had been done in other cases by the Mexican authorities. It is, therefore, highly recommended that the SENER-CNH develop a model unitization agreement, which could be used by contractors and entitlement holders, using as a basis the premises of an international model, for example the 2006 AIPN model, in order to accelerate and maximize the negotiation process between the entitlement holders and/or contractors of the adjacent areas. Even though these guidelines were an important step forward, legal uncertainty still exists, which calls for the need to carry out a full revision of all existing regulations aimed at giving more security and clarity to the involved parties.

8 Unitisation in the Nigerian Oil and Gas Industry

Damilola S. Olawuyi and Olujobi Olusola Joshua

8.1 Introduction

The chapter explores the practical gaps and challenges that unitisation in the Nigerian oil and gas industry is facing and analyses legal innovations for addressing such challenges. Nigeria practices the domanial theory of ownership like many other countries, where absolute ownership and control of extractive resources is vested in the federal government.[1] Similar to the system in the United States, which is largely at the exclusive preserve of each state, no individual, legal entities or private ownership of extractive resources exists. Rights, interests and assignments are acquired by way of licences and leases under the Nigerian Petroleum Industry Act 2021, unlike the practice in the United Kingdom. The upstream sector has a unique and distinct regulatory body called the Nigerian Upstream Petroleum Regulatory Commission (hereinafter the Commission). The Nigerian Midstream and Downstream Petroleum Regulatory Authority regulates the midstream and downstream petroleum sector.

Since the discovery of oil in viable quantities in Nigeria in 1956 in Oloibiri, Bayelsa State, the Nigerian economy has largely relied on crude oil for revenue. Petroleum accounts for one-third of the country's gross domestic product, 76% of the federal government's revenues and 95% of the country's foreign exchange earnings. Nigeria is ranked the tenth largest crude oil producer globally and the largest crude oil producer in Africa, with 3% global crude oil production input. The country is ranked ninth among countries with abundant gas reserves globally.

Astronomical growth in investment in the Nigerian oil and gas industry over the last few decades necessitates the need for unitisation agreements for the recovery of hydrocarbons by the contracting parties which have become commonplace and could become even more frequent in the future. The newly passed Petroleum Industry Act 2021, which is the primary legal regime regulating the sector, harmonises the various legislations regulating the industry to entrench transparency and accountability in the sector. Since the country's discovery and production of crude

1 O J Olujobi, *Nigerian Petroleum, Energy and Gas Resources Law (Legal Theories, Cases & Practice) Petroleum Industry Act 2021 & Climate Change Act 2021* (Princeton & Associate Publishing Limited, Ikeja, Lagos, 2022) 28.

DOI: 10.4324/9781003491293-10

oil, no detailed law has been enacted for the sector's fiscal, regulatory, administration, governance and control.[2]

Unitisation is an investment tool by which reservoirs for oil and gas are exploited as a unit by one operator called the unit operator, and the parties utilise mutual production facilities under an agreement called a unitisation agreement, despite different contractual terms and licence terms. The rationale is to achieve significant recovery of the hydrocarbon reservoir, to combat waste, inefficiency, maladministration and duplication of efforts by constructing additional oil infrastructure by the contracting parties, thereby occasioning a decline in oil revenue to the grantors of the leases and the parties. The significance of unitisation is that it thwarts disputes between the contracting parties which could impair the efficient, successful exploitation and production of crude oil. Pooling comprises working interests for diverse adjoining tracts in a drilling spacing unit where a drilling spacing unit is the least area set up by the pertinent statutory institution to drill a well.

The statutory rationale for the unitisation in Nigeria is provided under section 80 of the Petroleum Industry Act 2021,[3] which obliges a licensee or lessee to inform the commission swiftly of any petroleum reservoir which runs or spreads outside the borders of its licence or lease area. To guarantee the best recovery of oil from a petroleum reservoir, the Commission may necessitate all petroleum activities concerning viable discovery to be done by the licensee or lessee on the grounds of a unitised development of the viable discovery if the petroleum reservoir is contained in an area where a licence or lease covers or expands outside the borderlines of such acreage into a location where another licence or lease is connected with which was awarded to a different licensee or lease with a declaration of viable discovery by at least one licensee or lessee.

The Commission, after notification, may order the licensee or lessee to participate in a unit agreement to evolve the petroleum reservoir as a unit within a specified duration as stipulated by the Commission at a minimum of two years. The unit agreement must have been endorsed by the Commission based on the conditions stipulated by the contracting parties and conformity with the regulations formulated by the Commission and the best global petroleum industry practices.

A unit agreement comprises credible scientific, operational and economic considerations, how the parties to the licences, joint hydrocarbon reservoir or frontier, will mutually assess the reservoir, and the formulation of a mutual field development blueprint or strategy. Preliminary unit interests of the contracting parties, the nomination of an "operator" for management of the unit activities such as formulation of the work plan and financial plan, the structure of the operating team to analyse and endorse all unitisation actions such as records of each licensee with

2 O J Olujobi and S I Oshobugie, 'Strategies, Legal and Regulatory Measures for Combatting Illicit Mining Operations in Nigeria: A Comprehensive Legal Perspective, Resources Policy' (2024) <https://www.scopus.com/sourceid/110031> <https://authors.elsevier.com/tracking/article/details.do?aid=104459&jid=JRPO&surname=OLUJOBI> accessed 12 December 2023.

3 Specifically, subsection 80(1)(a) and (b); (3); (4); (5)(a), (b), and (c); (6); (7)(a) and (b); (8); and (9).

confidentiality obligations with the third parties, scientific analyses that will govern the scope of the field acreage and aggregate of oil and gas in each block, statutory compliance, bargaining of unitisation agreement, duration, termination event provisions, and the decision of a licensee not to participate in the development upon the signature of a unitisation agreement.

Where the licensee or lessee fails to reach an agreement two months after the prescribed duration by the Commission, the Commission shall appoint a consultant whose fees shall be paid by the parties. The parties are obliged to jointly nominate a consultant to formulate terms and conditions that are fair and equitable to the parties and government which shall become a binding instrument after the endorsement of the Commission. Unitisation may be intentional or obligatory. Unitisation is intentional where the parties are expected to agree amongst themselves to enter into a unitisation while it is obligatory where the law makes express provisions for it.

The five sections of this chapter unpack the key legal and institutional frameworks on unitisation in Nigeria. After this introduction, section 8.2 provides a short overview of oil and gas regulation and supervision in Nigeria. Section 8.3 discusses the legal framework of unitisation in Nigeria with a focus on extant legislation, rules, and guidelines. Section 8.4 discusses the main legal challenges that inhibit the effective implementation of unitisation schemes in Nigeria and explores legal innovations for addressing the identified gaps. Section 8.5 sets out the conclusions.

8.2 Legal Framework on Oil and Gas Resources in Nigeria

To ensure the efficient, safe, orderly and environmentally responsible development of unitised fields in Nigeria, many laws, regulations and guidelines have been put in place. The legal framework on unitisation in Nigeria sets out the obligations and main requirements of unitisation contracts, the rules for the non-contracted areas, obligations relating to royalties and tax, environmental compliance, local content and stakeholder engagement, among many other rules.

The Ministry of Petroleum and Energy Resources develops and oversees the oil and natural gas policy in Nigeria. The federal government enacted several legislations to regulate these mineral resources, as the country largely depends on them as significant sources of revenue. The principal legislation about oil and gas exploration and production in Nigeria is listed in the following sections.

8.2.1 The 1999 Constitution of the Federal Republic of Nigeria (as Amended)

This is the most significant oil and gas legislation in Nigeria. It confers an exclusive right on the federal government to own, control, and regulate the activities of minerals, mineral oil and by-products. Section 44(3) of the Constitution states the following:

> Notwithstanding the preceding provisions of this section, the entire property inland of all minerals, mineral oils and natural gas in, under or upon any land in Nigeria in, under or upon territorial waters and the economic zones

> of Nigeria shall vest in the government of the federation and shall rest in the government of the federation and shall be managed in such a manner as may be prescribed by the National Assembly.

The impact of this provision is that no person may undertake any activity to explore or produce oil and gas without a valid licence or authorisation by the federal government.[4] Such authorisation would be by the grant of a Petroleum Exploration Licence or Petroleum Prospecting Licence.

8.2.2 The Petroleum Industry Act 2021

On August 16, 2021, President Muhammadu Buhari gave assent to the Act that has been under legislative process since the administration of late President Umaru Musa Yar'adua. The Act offers legal, governance, administrative, regulatory and fiscal frameworks for the petroleum industry in Nigeria. The Act creates a new regulatory agency for the petroleum industry, the Nigerian Upstream Petroleum Regulatory Commission, to regulate the upstream sector and the Nigeria Midstream and Downstream Petroleum Authority to regulate both the midstream and the downstream sectors.[5] It establishes and incorporates the Nigerian National Petroleum Company Limited to replace the Nigerian National Petroleum Corporation (NNPC) with the ownership vested in the federal government. It provides for the introduction of the Petroleum Host Communities Development and Host Communities Development Trust Fund to promote sustainable social and economic development for the host communities due to the petroleum operations being carried out in the areas. It introduces the Petroleum Industry Fiscal Framework.[6] Section 1 confers the ownership and control of all petroleum within Nigeria and its territorial waters, continental shelf and exclusive economic zone (EEZ) on the federal government. Section 310 of the Act repeals about ten laws regulating the sector before enacting the Petroleum Industry Act 2021 to consolidate those laws into a single Act.[7]

The Petroleum Industry Act 2021 substitutes the petroleum profit tax with the hydrocarbon tax, which applies to crude oil, condensates and natural gas liquid products of associated gas. It is levied on the profits of companies operating in the upstream petroleum sector. It is a shift from the old regime where upstream petroleum companies pay petroleum profit tax. Hydrocarbon tax applies to individuals who are engaged in and profit from upstream petroleum activities. It is charged at the rate of 30% for any accounting period of a company from the profit made

4 Sections 70, 71 and 72 Petroleum Industry Act 2021.

5 D O E Borha and O J Olujobi, *An Examination of the Petroleum Industry Act 2021: Prospects, Challenges, and the Way Forward* (Taylor & Francis, F1000Research 2023) 12:551, <https://doi.org/10.5256/f1000research.153263.r197203>.

6 O J Olujobi and others, 'The Legal Framework for Combating Gas Flaring in Nigeria's Oil and Gas Industry: Can It Promote Sustainable Energy Security?' (2022) 14(13) Sustainability 7626.

7 O J Olujobi and others, 'COVID-19 Pandemic: The Impacts of Crude Oil Price Shock on Nigeria's Economy, Legal and Policy Options' (2022) 14(18) Sustainability 11166.

on crude oil for Petroleum Mining Licences regarding onshore and shallow water areas, and 15% for onshore and shallow water for Petroleum Prospecting Licences for companies engaged in upstream petroleum operations either by way of partnership or joint venture agreement in conformity with their equity interest under the arrangement for upstream petroleum operations.

8.2.3 The Land Use Act 1978

The Act expropriated land ownership by individuals and communities in Nigeria, turning their interests into rights of occupancy only, and vested the right of ownership in the governor of the state. Section 1 of the Land Use Act vests all lands in the territory of each state in the governor of the state, who in turn shall hold such land in trust and administer it for the use and common benefit of all Nigerians. Considering section 1 of the Land Use Act and section 44(3) of the 1999 Constitution, the land is vested in the governors while the mineral resources are vested in Nigeria's federal government.

8.2.4 The Nigerian Minerals and Mining Act 2007

The Act repeals the Minerals and Mining Act and re-enacts it as the Nigerian Mineral and Mining Act, which regulates the exploration and exploitation of minerals in Nigeria. Section 1 of the Act vests the entire mineral resources under or upon any land in the federal government of Nigeria. The Act provides that the territorial waters, EEZs, and all lands in which minerals have been found viable or in commercial quantities shall be acquired by the federal government in conformity with the provisions of the Land Use Act. Section 3 excluded some land from mineral exploration, and exploitation and no mineral title can be granted concerning such land.

8.2.5 The Exclusive Economic Zone Act

Section 2(1) of the Act vests sovereign and exclusive rights regarding the natural resources of the seabed, subsoil and superjacent water of the EEZ in the federal government of Nigeria. The rights of the host states were granted under the EEZ concept enacted after many sessions of the United Nations Conference of the Law of the Sea (UNCLOS) under Articles 55 and 57 which provides an area of the sea, beyond, adjacent to the territorial sea, extending to 3700.65KN (200 nm).

8.2.6 The Environmental Impact Assessment Act[8]

The Act makes it obligatory for environmental impact assessments to be conducted in respect of projects that are likely to have significant effects on the environment. Oil and gas projects must be registered with the Federal Ministry of Environment for an environmental impact assessment. Section 2 of the Act provides for the

8 Cap E12, LFN 2004.

assessment of public or private projects that are likely to substantially affect the ecosystem for prior approval.[9]

8.2.7 Companies Income Tax[10]

The Act makes tax a mandatory payment payable annually based on the evaluation of the profits of the oil and gas firms that are not subject to the provisions of the Petroleum Profits Tax Act (Repealed). Sections 9(1) and 40(1) provide that company income taxes are payable by oil and gas firms incorporated in Nigeria at the rate of 30% of the firm's chargeable profit; that is, 30 kobos are payable for every naira. After paying dividends to shareholders, oil and gas firms are obliged to pay taxes on profits.

8.2.8 The Oil Pipelines Act[11]

The Act confers the power to grant permits to survey routes for oil pipelines and grant licences for the construction, maintenance, and operation of the oil pipelines on the minister of petroleum. Section 9(1)(b) Oil Pipelines Regulations (Under the Oil Pipelines Act), establishes the requirements of environmental emergency plans, and section 26 proscribes non-compliance with a fine of 500,000 naira and/or with imprisonment for a term of six months. Section 17(4) establishes that oil licence grants are subject to regulations concerning public safety, and land and water pollution prevention.

The Nigerian Oil and Gas Industry Content Development Act[12] provides provisions for the administration and regulation of the petroleum sector with regulatory agencies that implement government policies to ensure compliance with the laws. The Harmful Waste (Special Criminal Provisions) Act[13] prohibits depositing, carrying and dumping harmful waste on any land or territorial waters in Nigeria.

The National Oil Spill Detection and Response Agency Establishment Act (as amended) regulates wastes from oil production and exploration and their potential effects on the environment. The National Environmental Standards and Regulations Enforcement Agency Act prohibits the discharge of hazardous substances into the air, land and water.

Nigeria Extractive Industries Transparency Initiative (NEITI) Act[14]: Nigeria signed up with the global Extractive Industries Transparency International on November 7, 2003, and the NEITI Act was passed on May 28, 2007. Section 3 of the Act states the functions to include developing a framework for transparency

9 O J Olujobi, O A Oyewunmi, and A E Oyewunmi, 'Oil Spillage in Nigeria's Upstream Petroleum Sector: Beyond the Legal Frameworks' (2018) 8(1) Int J Energ Econ Policy 220–226.

10 The Companies Income Tax Act (CITA) Cap C21, Laws of the Federation of Nigeria 2004.

11 1969, Cap. 07, LFN, 2004.

12 2010, Cap. N124A, LFN 2004.

13 Cap. H1, LFN 2004 (then a Decree in 1988).

14 2007, Laws of the Federation of Nigeria.

and accountability in the reporting and disclosure, by all extractive industry companies, of revenues due to or paid to the federal government, evaluating without prejudice to any relevant contractual obligations and sovereign obligations the practices of all extractive industry companies and government respectively regarding the acquisition of acreages, budgeting, contracting, materials procurement and production cost file to ensure due process, transparency and accountability.[15]

The Petroleum (Drilling and Production) Regulations restrict the abandonment of existing oil wells without the director of petroleum resources' written permission, but this is poorly enforced in the sector due to corruption.

8.3 Unitisation in the Nigerian Oil and Gas Industry

Before the enactment of the Petroleum Industry Act 2021, the enabling law on unitisation was the Petroleum (Drilling and Production) Regulation 1969 (repealed). Section 47 Unitization Guidelines 2008 formulated by the (defunct) Department of Petroleum Resources (DPR) made in conformity with the authority conferred on the minister of petroleum Resources under section 9 of the (repealed) Petroleum Act.[16] Currently, section 80 of the Petroleum Industry Act 2021[17] regulates unitisation in Nigeria's oil and gas industry to maximise the benefits of oil and gas and to mitigate the resource curse associated with oil in developing oil and gas countries. However, weak implementation and poor awareness of unitisation has been the challenge in Nigeria.[18]

Where the federal government's agency, the Nigerian Upstream Petroleum Regulatory Commission, is satisfied that an oil field straddles a concessional boundary into licensed areas that are owned by one or more licensees and the government considers that it is in national or economic interests to secure optimal recovery to combat waste and unhealthy competitive drilling, it may require a unitisation exercise between licensee and lessees.[19]

To guarantee optimal and best viable recovery from petroleum reservoirs by licensees or lessees, the federal government sets up a variety of institutions to regulate Nigeria's oil and gas sector. The Nigerian Upstream Petroleum Regulatory Commission was set up as the principal institution to regulate the upstream petroleum sector as stated under sections 5, 6, and 7 of the Petroleum Industry Act

15 O A Oyewunmi and O J Olujobi 'Transparency in Nigeria's Oil and Gas Industry: Is Policy Re-Engineering the Way Out?' (2016) 5(4) Int J Energ Econ Policy 630–636.

16 Cap 350, LFN 1990.

17 Specifically, subsection 80(1); (2)(a) and (b); (3); (4); (5); (6); (7)(a) and (b); (8); and (9).

18 O J Olujobi, *COVID-19 Pandemic and Illegal Oil Refineries in Africa: Evidence from the National Oil Wealth in Nigeria, in Socioeconomic Shocks and Africa's Development Agenda Lessons and Policy Directions in a Post-COVID-19 Era Edited By Evans Osabuohien, Gbadebo Odularu, Daniel Ufua, Romanus Osabohien* (Routledge, Taylor Francis 2022) 332 <https://doi.org/10.4324/9781003208358> <https://www.taylorfrancis.com/chapters/edit/10.4324/9781003208358-20/covid-19-pandemic-illegal-oil-refineries-africa-olusola-joshua-olujobi?context=ubx&refId=aaa33c5d-eed5-4750-a8cf-524d9919d46c> accessed 26 September 2022, Chapter 15–19, 231–248.

19 O J Olujobi and A O Oyewunmi 'Annulment of Oil Licences in Nigeria's Upstream Petroleum Sector: A Legal Critique of the Costs and Benefits' (2017) 7(3) Int J Energ Econ Policy 364–369.

2021, which stipulates the statutory functions of the Commission to include the following, among others: to regulate the upstream operations including technical operations and commercial activities, to ensure compliance with all the applicable laws and regulations governing upstream petroleum operations, and to ensure that upstream petroleum operations are carried out in a manner that will minimise waste and achieve optimal government revenues. The Nigerian Midstream and Downstream Petroleum Regulatory Authority was also set up as the principal regulatory body to regulate the midstream and downstream sectors in Nigeria.

In Nigeria, the unitisation process comprises three stages: (1) identification and notification of straddle structure; (2) a pre-unitisation agreement, which is an initial agreement by the contracting parties to commence early unitisation appraisal work while negotiations continue; and (3) a unitisation and unit operating agreement, which is the bedrock of any unitisation. It expresses how straddle fields are to be utilised and describes unit areas' tract involvement and unit operator.

Unitisation reduces the cost of production and optimises the quantity of recoverable hydrocarbon; petroleum reservoirs are exploited optimally via efficient methods to make the most of oil recovery from the unit reservoirs to guarantee fair, equitable grant of oil and gas resources among the parties and all stakeholders.

8.3.1 Hurdles Militating Against Unitisation in Nigeria

One of the challenges to successful unitisation in Nigeria is the perception of non-straddling reserves within a unit. The Petroleum Industry Act 2021 does not explicitly address non-straddling reservoirs, a consideration that is generally addressed in other oil-producing countries such as China, Angola, and Senegal. In these countries, national oil companies often mandate unitisation, particularly for fields developed through joint ventures and production agreements.[20] The aim is to attain field development and to guarantee optimal recovery of oil from the oil field. Other hurdles militating against unitisation in Nigeria are economic considerations, contractual disputes and the failure of some oil and gas companies to utilise alternative dispute resolution mechanisms to resolve their contractual disputes to guarantee amicable and speedy resolution of their commercial or contractual disputes.[21] The processes may be a Herculean task, thereby locking down a lot of oil reserves. Fear of non-reimbursement of cost for oil produced, block cessation, production of an oil field before the unitisation contract and secrecy of petroleum contracts have hampered the precise determination of the reserves at the initial stage of the unitisation exercise,[22] which often occasions corruption.[23]

20 O A Ajayi, *Current Challenge in Unitization: The Nigeria Experience* (Society of Petroleum Engineering SPE International 2010).

21 O J Olujobi and others, 'Commercial Dispute Resolution: Has Arbitration Transformed Nigeria's Legal Landscape?' (2018) IX, Spring, 1(31) J Adv Res Law Econ 204–209.

22 A Ndoma Egba and others, 'Case Study of Unitisation and Joint Development of Straddled Fields in Nigeria', SPE Nigeria Annual International Conference and Exhibition, Lagos 2–4 August 2016, 1–14.

23 O J Olujobi, 'Legal Framework for Combating Corruption in Nigeria -The Upstream Petroleum Sector in Perspective' (2017) VIII 3 (25) J Adv Res Law Econ 956–970.

Another hurdle is the weak enforcement of the legal regime on unitisation in Nigeria's oil and gas industry by the regulatory authorities. Also, where a party has begun production of crude oil before the formal endorsement of the unitisation straddling arrangement, development must continue as stated in the agreement.[24]

Similarly, in terms of the utilisation of distinct tracts of oil for participation in oil and gas, though it is commonly recognised as the conventional industry practice if all parties consent, the hurdle is centred on the utilisation of reasonable conversion issues. In a nation like Nigeria, the mode is to utilise the heating value of the mechanisms for conversion to produce a barrel of oil equivalent.

Oil permit or licence cessation: unitisation often hits a brick wall where the oil licence or permit of one of the parties ceases before the licence of the other party to the arrangement expires. Regulatory institutions are set up to guarantee the persistence of oil operations pending the statutory decommissioning exercise of the unitised field.[25]

8.4 Regulatory Bodies in Nigeria's Oil and Gas Industry

The Nigerian Upstream Petroleum Regulatory Commission (the "Commission") and the Midstream and Downstream Petroleum Regulatory Authority are the primary regulatory authorities responsible for oil and gas operations in Nigeria. The regulatory authorities are established under sections 4 and 29 of the Petroleum Industry Act 2021, replacing the Department of Petroleum Resources which was a department under the Nigerian Federal Ministry of Petroleum Resources. It was formed in 1970. Sections 5, 6 and 7 of the Petroleum Industry Act stipulate the statutory functions of the Commission to include the following, among others: to regulate the upstream operations including technical operations and commercial activities, to ensure compliance with all the applicable laws and regulations governing the upstream petroleum operations, and to ensure that upstream petroleum operations are carried out in a manner that will minimise waste and achieve optimal government revenues.

The Ministry of Petroleum Resources exercises supervisory and oversight functions in the petroleum sector; it is responsible for formulating, implementing and coordinating government policies in the oil and gas industry.

The Nigerian Oil and Gas (Industry Content Development) Act 2010: The Act is designed to leverage Nigeria's oil and gas industry's local content to enhance socio-economic development and the country's economy. However, the lack of political will and commitment to the spirit of Nigeria's local content policy has been a challenge due to the lack of adequate capacity and efficiency of the Nigerian Content Development and Monitoring Board (NCDMB). Section 70 established the Board to implement the Act. The Act provides that Nigerian operators must be given first consideration in awarding oil blocks, oil field licences and all projects where contracts are to be awarded in the sector.

24 O A Ajayi and G Otoh, 'Current Challenges in Unitisation: The Nigerian Experience', 34th Annual SPE International Conference and Exhibition Tinapa, Calabar, Nigeria, 7–31 July 2010.

25 O J Olujobi, E S Olarinde and T E Yebisi, 'The Conundrums of Illicit Crude Oil Refineries in Nigeria and Its Debilitating Effects on Nigeria's Economy: A Legal Approach' (2022) 15(17) Energies 6197.

Previously, there was no law devoted to promoting Nigerian content in the upstream oil and gas industry; only the Petroleum Act of 1969 and the Nigerian National Petroleum Corporation's directives were regulating the sector. This Act will be relevant in combating corruption in the upstream petroleum sector by enhancing the value of Nigerians through the use of home-grown materials, products and services to inspire growth by building indigenous competence in the oil and gas sector.[26] The Nigerian Content Development and Monitoring Board (NCDMB) was established under section 55 of the Nigerian Oil and Gas Industry Content Development (NOGICD) Act to implement the provisions of the Nigerian Content Act to promote the utilisation and development of local capacities for the industrialisation of Nigeria and to carry out the effective implementation of the Act.

8.4.1 The Niger Delta Development Commission (Establishment) Act[27]

The Act established the Niger Delta Development Commission for the development of the Niger Delta areas in Nigeria which are affected due to crude oil exploration activities by multinational companies. The Commission is to formulate policies and guidelines for the development of the Niger Delta areas and prepare master plans and schemes designed to promote the physical development of the Niger Delta areas at the cost of implementing such plans. The provisions in other statutes may restrain or inhibit its enforcement.

8.4.2 The Nigeria Extractive Industries Transparency Initiative Act

Nigeria signed up with the global Extractive Industries Transparency International on November 7, 2003. The Nigeria Extractive Industries Transparency Initiative Act was passed on May 28, 2007. The objective of the Act is to ensure due process, good governance, transparency, accountability and elimination of all forms of corrupt practices in all payments to the federal government from the extractive industries. Oil companies are to disclose everything they pay to the federal government, and the government must disclose everything they receive from the extractive industries operating in Nigeria.[28]

8.4.3 The National Environmental Standard and Regulations Enforcement Agency (NESREA) (Establishment) Act

The federal government established the National Environmental Standard and Regulations Enforcement Agency as an institution to regulate environmental

26 O J Olujobi, E S Olarinde and T E Yebisi, 'The Conundrums of Illicit Crude Oil Refineries in Nigeria and Its Debilitating Effects on Nigeria's Economy: A Legal Approach' (2022) 15(17) Energies 6197, s.106.

27 Cap N86 LFN 2004.

28 O.J. Olujobi and O.S. Irumekhai, 'An Analysis of the Abolition of Premium Motor Spirit (PMS) Subsidies in Nigeria: A Breach of Social Contract or Climate Change Action?' (2024) 5(71) Discover Sustainability <https://doi.org/10.1007/s43621-024-00252-z> <https://link.springer.com/content/pdf/10.1007/s43621-024-00252-z.pdf> accessed 19 September 2024.

standards in Nigeria through the legal framework by regulating the air, and water, to prevent the depletion of ozone layers via the discharge of substances and effluent wastes.[29] Despite the ample power to regulate the environment, its scope is exempt from the oil and gas sector under section 7 of the Act. There is a need to review the law to include oil and gas pollution arising from illegal oil refinery operations and to reflect the sector's current economic reality with maximum penalties for defaulters.[30]

8.4.4 Significant Prerequisites of Model Unit Agreement and Unit Operating Agreement in Nigeria

The following clauses are sine qua non in the model unit agreement and unit operating agreement in Nigeria.

Cooperation and sharing ratio of resources among the parties: Parties retain an undivided interest in the unit infrastructure which is equivalent to its unit involvement and the unit operator shall maintain such interests in good faith for the owners.

Restrictions are another fundamental term in a model unit agreement where the owner may execute oil activities on its territory for the discovery and production of crude oil, other than the unitised constituents if the parties safeguard the unitised area and thwart meddling with the unit activities. One who is exerting this right must reimburse all the owners against all litigations, other legal responsibilities and expenditures that may be occasioned due to the party applying his right. Management of the operations is done by the Operating Committee, which opens the door for the non-unit operators to oversee the unit operator's undertakings. Owners' delegates shall manage and oversee all unit activities, excluding issues unambiguously indicated to be under the absolute scope of the unit operator.

The unit operating agreement often fails to state expressly how the parties should vote, whether under individual first choice or in the best interest of the unit. The unit agreement must state the operator's obligations, rights and powers in the management of the unit infrastructure on behalf of the parties. The operator is an independent service provider who is accountable for the personnel and suppliers used for the unit undertakings but subject to the endorsement of the Operating Committee.

The unit operator's agreement or service is terminated where he becomes bankrupt or insolvent or he is incapable of paying its debts, where he assigns his powers and tasks without the approval of the Operating Committee, he ceases to be an owner and where he resigns he must give a minimum of 90 days' notice in

29 O J Olujobi and others, 'Carbon Emission, Solid Waste Management, and Electricity Generation: A Legal and Empirical Perspective for Renewable Energy in Nigeria' in *International Environmental Agreements: Politics, Law and Economics* (Springer Nature 2022) doi: 10.1007/s10784-021-09558 <https://link.springer.com/article/10.1007%2Fs10784-021-09558-z#cite> accessed 14 November 2022.

30 O.J. Olujobi, 'Nigeria's Climate Change Act 2021: A Pathway to Net-Zero Carbon Emission, Energy Security and Sustainability, Environmental Science and Pollution Research' <https://trebuchet.public.springernature.app/get_content/9526d5b6-f51b-4fad-b8e67fffcfa85461?utm_source=rct_congratemailt&utm_medium=email&utm_campaign=nonoa_20240517&utm_content=10.1007/s11356-024-33347-1> <https://doi.org/10.1007/s11356-024-33347-1> accessed 9 September 2024.

writing, he must keep the records of all the financial resources, taxation and maintenance of joint account for the parties with details of expenditures and overhead incurred in the operations in conformity with the book-keeping practice and must allot the expenditures and overhead to the working interest owners following their percentage contributions to the unit capital. The unit operating agreement must make provisions for dispute resolution via consultation, negotiation, mediation and arbitration. Each party bears the costs.

8.5 Legal Preparedness for Sustainable Unitisation in the Nigerian Oil and Gas Industry

Due to the absence of a comprehensive legal regime on fiscal, regulatory, administration, governance and control on the unitisation in Nigeria's oil and gas industry, it is important to enact detailed guidelines on the sustainability of unitisation in the industry to conform with international oil field practices and procedures.[31] This section identifies key challenges and gaps in Nigeria's legal framework on unitisation that will need further explanation.

The conspicuous gap in Nigeria's Petroleum Industry Act 2021 on unitisation operations is that the Act fails to provide a comprehensive, specific and elaborate legal regime on unitisation despite the country's clear commitment to ensuring optimal utilisation of extractive resources for the benefit of Nigerian citizens. Relatively advanced oil and gas jurisdictions such as the United States and United Kingdom, with many years of experience in unitisation practices, have unambiguous and inclusive national unitisation strategies which Nigeria can gain insight from to reform its legal regime or guidelines on unitisation to achieve significant recovery of a hydrocarbon reservoir to combat waste, inefficiency, maladministration, duplication of efforts, risk reduction between the operators, the host government and third parties to enhance stakeholder engagement and maximise delivery capacity in the unitisation processes by developing a comprehensive action plan and strategy in collaboration with stakeholders in the oil and gas industry. The following are examples of unitisation in Nigeria: Joint Development of Jisike-Izombe, Akri-Oguta Fields 1980, unitisation of Amenam/Kpono, Balea North and Agbami Fields, Niger Delta 2004. Shell Bellema (OML 25) and Chevron Belema North Field (OML55) 2002, Agbami Field 2005, and the Biseni/Samabri unitisation and unit operating agreement, Niger Delta.

8.5.1 Conclusion and Policy Implications

It is now fundamental for Nigeria to enact comprehensive and sophisticated legal regimes or guidelines on unitisation in the oil and gas industry to bring the industry in conformity with the international oil field practices and procedures in other relatively advanced jurisdictions. Enactment of inclusive statutes, strategies,

31 O.J. Olujobi and I.S. Odogbo, 'Strategic Evaluation of the 2021 Nigeria Climate Change Act: Surmounting Challenges, Paving the Way for Success, and Envisioning Future Trajectories' (2024) 10 Social Sciences & Humanities Open, 100928 <https://www.sciencedirect.com/science/article/pii/S2590291124001256?via%3Dihub> accessed 6 May 2024.

guidelines and focal institutions on unitisation in Nigeria will promote an efficient, safe, orderly and ecologically friendly unitisation in the oil and gas industry. Making unitisation obligatory will be required in Nigeria to satisfy the aim of the Petroleum Industry Act 2021 to promote the maximum or best recovery of crude oil from petroleum reservoirs. An inclusive legal framework or strategy on unitisation in the Nigerian oil and gas industry is indispensable to promote the best global petroleum industry practices.

As a contribution to knowledge, the chapter advocates stringent legal frameworks or strategies on unitisation to promote optimal recovery of crude oil and enhance Nigeria's economy. As policy implications, the chapter further advocates the need for stringent execution of Nigeria's oil and gas laws to guarantee sustainability.

Key Findings of This Chapter

1. Absence of comprehensive, sophisticated and specific tailored legal regimes or guidelines on unitisation in the oil and gas industry to bring the industry in conformity with the international oil field practices and procedures in other relatively advanced jurisdictions.
2. Non-mandatory or obligatory provisions on unitisation in Nigeria to satisfy the aim of the Petroleum Industry Act 2021 to promote the maximum or best recovery of crude oil from the petroleum reservoirs.
3. Absence of stringent legal frameworks or strategies on unitisation to promote optimal recovery of crude oil and enhance Nigeria's economy.
4. Absence of stringent implementation of Nigeria's oil and gas laws to guarantee energy security and sustainability.

9 Unitisation in Norway

Rune Omdahl

9.1 Introduction

Geographical delimitation lines are man-made, either by agreement, law or decree. These lines attribute certain rights to the holder of the designated geographical area (the "licensee")[1] – rights that the licensee might want to exploit. Nature is not abiding such artificial boundaries and may transgress these from time to time. Petroleum by nature is fugacious and migrates through the underground without hindrance of virtual boundaries. Consequently, the rights of one licensee may be conflicting with the rights of another licensee. This chapter intends to provide an overview over the legal regulation in Norway of such conflicting interests in the petroleum industry.

In the spring of 1971, Elf struck gas in Block 25/1 in the North Sea. Approximately six years earlier, on 10 March 1965,[2] Norway and the United Kingdom had signed an agreement on the division of the continental shelf between the two countries.[3] The discovery in Block 25/1, later to be named the Frigg Field, was on the Norwegian side of the dividing line – the Norwegian continental shelf (NCS). Later, Total made a discovery on the British side. It turned out that the two discoveries were the same deposit that extended across the dividing line.[4]

In order to find a solution to the exploitation of the common reservoir, the governments of the two countries sat down and discussed an accord to the issues at hand. On 10 May 1976 the Agreement related to the Exploitation of the Frigg Field Reservoir and the Transmission of Gas therefrom to the United Kingdom (the "Frigg Agreement") was signed.

1 I will for simplicity refer to the person, physical or legal, that holds the right to exploit the geographical area in question as a licensee (or licensees).

2 Instruments of ratification were exchanged on 29 June 1965, and the agreement entered into force on that date.

3 Agreement between the Government of the United Kingdom of Great Britain and Northern Ireland and the Government of the Kingdom of Norway relating to the Delimitation of the Continental Shelf between the two Countries, 10 March 1965.

4 Industrial heritage Frigg <https://frigg.industriminne.no/en/2018/08/09/the-unitisation-agreement/> accessed 9 April 2024.

DOI: 10.4324/9781003491293-11

The Frigg Agreement states in sub-Article 1 of Article 1 of Part I (Exploitation of the Frigg Field Reservoir), inter alia, that the "gas in the Frigg Field Reservoir and the hydrocarbons produced with or from the gas (excluding oil underlying the gas and gas and oil in other horizons) . . . shall be exploited as a single unit". The Frigg Agreement continues in sub-Article 2 of Article 1 of Part I (Exploitation of the Frigg Field Reservoir) that

> [e]ach Government shall require those who are its licensees at the date of signature of this Agreement to enter into agreements between themselves and the licensees at that date of the other Government to regulate the exploitation in accordance with this Agreement of Frigg Gas.

Thus, the elements of the first agreement involving unitisation of Norwegian petroleum interests were put in place.

Where a petroleum deposit discovered on the NCS extends across international borders, such deposits shall be unitised to secure the optimal utilisation of the resources.[5] The relevant countries will enter into a "unitisation convention". This unitisation convention will include an obligation for the petroleum companies on both side of the border to agree and enter into a unitisation agreement to be approved by the affected countries government.[6] Cross-border unitisation is not a part of this chapter and is dealt with in other chapters of this book.

The word *unitisation*, in the context of petroleum activities, was first used in the United States back in the 1920s as a contractual response to the "rule of capture".[7] The rule of capture gives the land owner

> the right to produce all of the oil and gas that will flow out of the well on one's land; and this is a property right. And it is limited only by the physical possibility of the adjoining landowner diminishing the oil and gas under one's land by the exercise of the same right of capture.[8]

The rule encourages the land owners to produce as much as possible as fast as possible. This led to waste of resources, oversupply and falling prices. In short, it became a commercial issue.[9] Consequently, the industry sat out to establish

5 In all international agreements Norway has entered into on the limitation of the NCS (with Denmark, UK, Iceland, Greenland/Denmark and Russia) there is included a provision that obligates the parties, where there is a cross-border petroleum deposit, to unitise the reservoirs.

6 See <https://www.regjeringen.no/no/tema/utenrikssaker/folkerett/innsikt_delelinje/olje/avtale_unitisering/id626574/>.

7 "The owner of a tract of land acquires title to the oil and gas which he produces from wells drilled thereon, though it may be proved that part of such oil or gas migrated from adjoining lands". Robert E Hardwicke, 'The Rule of Capture and Its Implications Applied to Oil and Gas', (1935) 13 Tex L Rev 391, 393.

8 *Brown v. Humble Oil Co.*, 126 Tex. 296 at 305, 83 S.W.2d 935 at 940 (1935).

9 For further reading on the "rule of capture" you may seek out Terence Daintith's book, *Finders Keepers? How the Law of Capture Shaped the World Oil Industry* (RFF Press 2010).

agreements to regulate the competing interests by operating the production from the adjacent areas as a single unit separated from the division of the land area above – the unitisation of petroleum reservoirs.[10] Thus, in the United States the term is given a distinct legal meaning as the joint development of one petroleum deposit that straddles geographical areas controlled by different companies.[11]

The term *unitisation* is not used in the Frigg Agreement, which refers to the concept of "exploitation as a single unit", which indicates a concept of unitisation. Neither is the term used in any of the preceding Norwegian legislations on the topic. In Norway the issue of regulating the exploitation of a petroleum deposit that extends across the boundaries of two or more concession areas was addressed in article 32 of the Royal Decree of 9 April 1965 relating to Exploration for and Exploitation of Petroleum in the Seabed and Substrata of the Norwegian Continental Shelf.[12] This provision was later superseded by article 32 of Royal Decree of 8 December 1972, then section 16 of the Petroleum Activities Act of 22 March 1985 and is now to be found in section 4–7 of the Petroleum Activities Act of 29 November 1996 (the "Act").[13]

The Act and its pertaining regulation does not use the term *unitisation* (or *unit*), and there is no clear legal meaning of the term in Norwegian law.[14] This view is also taken by the court[15] in the Breidablikk-case,[16] where it states that the term holds no precise meaning.[17] The industry seems to commonly use the term *unitisation* to describe a situation where one deposit is jointly exploited.[18] The Ministry of Energy, in the Johan Sverdrup decision,[19] states that when a petroleum deposit extends over more than one block with different licensees, an obligation to unitise the petroleum deposit and operate it as one unit arises. The court in the Breidablikk-case uses the term basically to explain the administrative organisation of the activities but seems to understand the term in much as the same way.[20]

10 Henry L Doherty, a self-made businessman in Bartlesville, Oklahoma, later an oil tycoon, is arguably the first who campaigned for unitisation of petroleum fields.

11 *Williams & Meyers Manual of Oil and Gas Terms* (17th edn, Williams & AL 2018).

12 The two Royal Decrees regulates one common deposit.

13 Lov 29. november 1996 nr. 72 om petroleumsvirksomhet.

14 Case TSTAV-2008-67552 at the then Stavanger Tingrett relates to the Åsgard Unit and of a guarantee issued by Statoil ASA, now Equinor ASA, and seems not to discuss the issue.

15 This case was heard by the court of first instance, Rogaland Tingrett, and has been appealed to the Appeal Court. Consequently, the decision is not yet final.

16 Case no. 22-095402TVI-TSRO/TSTA of 30 January 2024 handed down by Sør-Rogaland Tingrett. I will revert to this case on various occasions in the following and will then use the short form the "Breidablikk-case".

17 On page 28 of the Breidablikk-case.

18 See Lasse Hagen, 'Plikt til å samarbeide – samordning etter petroleumsloven' (1987) Marius No. 135 1, 2. (Obligation to cooperate – coordination in accordance to the Petroleum Activities Act). Lasse Hagen may use a wider understanding of the phrase. See Lasse Hagen and others. 'Petroleumsloven med kommentarer' (1989) Tano 205, 206 (Comments to the Petroleum Activities Act 1985).

19 Royal Decree of 18 December 2015 on the apportionment of unit interest in the Johan Sverdrup Field (the "Johan Sverdrup Decision").

20 In its explanation of the term the court uses the word *forekomsten* ("deposit") in the singular indicating one common reservoir; see p. 3 of the Breidablikk-case.

The theme of this chapter is unitisation in Norway, and for this purpose I will discuss the topic from the perspective, in the words of Jaqueline Weaver and David Asmus, that

> the unitized area, usually a reservoir, is treated as a single unit for development purposes. It is as if the separate leases and licences are merged into one single lease or licence, with a single unit operator appointed to manage the development of the field, within the limits of authority granted the unit operator by the unit operating agreement and the management committee composed of all the different lessees or licensees with interest in the unit.[21]

And when using the word *unitisation*, it will be with the unity of the reservoir in its physical state as well as in its legal, organisational state in mind. Consequently, for the rest of this article it can be assumed that the "the most efficient co-ordination of petroleum activities" will be as a unit.

The legal foundation for unitisation in Norway is to be found in section 4–7 of the Act and a short introduction to this provision is provided in section 9.2.

Section 4–7 of the Act establishes a legal obligation on the relevant licensees if certain criteria are fulfilled. These criteria will be discussed in section 9.3.

If the criteria are fulfilled the licensees are obligated to agree on "the most efficient co-ordination of petroleum activities", the obligation and the possible structure and content of a unitisation agreement will be discussed in section 9.5.

There may be a need for the licensees to regulate the relationship between them in the interim between the evaluation of the possibility of a unitisation and the concluded unitisation agreement and an interim agreement, a pre-unitisation agreement, may be put in place. In section 9.4 the pre-unitisation agreement will be addressed briefly.

The end result of the co-ordination discussions is for the licensees to reach an agreement "on the most efficient co-ordination of petroleum activities", within the framework of this chapter, the unitisation agreement. Issues on the unitisation agreement will be addressed in section 9.5.

The administration of the state's resources is delegated to the King in Council[22] acting through the relevant ministries. Presently this is the Ministry of Energy. The ministry administers a set of rules and regulations that requires that the licensees operate within the limits of various decisions, approvals and consents. The ministry's authority includes, inter alia, the right to approve co-ordination agreements and, in the event of the licensees not reaching an agreement, to "determine how such joint petroleum activities shall be conducted, including the apportionment of the deposit." The authority of the ministry will be addressed in section 9.6.

21 Jaqueline Weaver and David F Asmus, 'Unitizing Oil and Gas Fields Around the World: A Comparative Analysis of National Laws and Private Contracts' (22 September 2005) Houston J Intern Law.

22 Cf. first paragraph of section 1–2 of the Act.

9.2 The Legal Basis for Unitisation

The Norwegian state has the proprietary right to subsea petroleum deposits[23] and the exclusive right to resource management.[24] In this context there should be no debate on the ownership of the petroleum extracted from the underground. However, the Norwegian state, as many other states, has elected to let experienced exploration and production companies perform the petroleum activities on the NCS.

To facilitate the licencing system the geographical area of the NCS is divided into smaller geographical areas – blocks. Each block is 15 latitude minutes and 20 longitude minutes in size, unless adjacent land areas, common boundaries with the continental shelf of other states, or other circumstances warrant otherwise.[25] A petroleum licence may cover one or several blocks or parts of blocks[26] and is defined by UTM coordinates, and sometimes also delimited stratigraphically.

Qualified persons (natural or incorporated) can apply for a production licence.[27] Interested parties apply individually or a group of interested parties form a tentative licence group prior to an application.[28] The authority to decide on who shall be granted a particular licence is presently granted to the ministry, and such decision is made notwithstanding any prior agreement between the applicants. Upon granting a production licence the ministry will combine a group of eligible applicants considered to be the most suitable to exploit a given area in a joint venture and appoint one of the licensees to be the operator for the joint venture.

The licensees are obligated to enter into an agreement regulating the relationship between the parties in the joint venture[29]; the agreement concerning petroleum activities, colloquially referred to as the joint operating agreement (JOA).[30]

The production licence entails an exclusive right to survey, exploration drilling and production of petroleum deposits in the areas covered by the licence.

23 The Norwegian state has through the state's direct financial interest (SDFI) a direct share in 36 producing fields on the NCS and in numerous licenses in the exploration phase <https://www.petoro.no/hjem> accessed 20 August 2021. The SDFI was formerly managed by Equinor ASA, but when this company was partly privatised in 2001 and listed in a dual listing on the stock exchange in Oslo and New York, the management of the SDFI was transferred to the then newly established Petoro AS, a corporation formed under the private limited liabilities act, and 100% owned by the state. The Norwegian state continues to hold a majority share in Equinor ASA. The state's current shareholding of 67% is managed by the Ministry of Trade, Industry and Fisheries.

24 Cf. section 1–1 of the Act.

25 See section 3–2 of the Act.

26 See first paragraph of section 3–3 of the Act.

27 Cf. section 3–3 (3) of the Act. There are two types of petroleum licenses: a survey licence and a production licence (PL). The production licence is by far the most relevant license.

28 Cf. section 3–4 of the Act. This form of cooperation is usually formalised through an agreement for area of mutual interest (AMI).

29 Cf. fourth paragraph of section 3–3 of the Act.

30 The agreement concerning petroleum activities consists of three parts, of which the joint operating agreement proper is one part. The other two are the special provisions (containing, inter alia, voting rules) and the accounting agreement.

The production licence will apply to a limited geographical area – the licence area, that may encompass one or more blocks, or part of a block or blocks.

The main principle is that the right holder of a tract of a geographical area is entitled to (1) utilise the tract as it sees fit and (2) acquires the riches derived from such tract. The third paragraph of section 3–3 of the Act stipulates that a "production licence entails an exclusive right to survey, exploration drilling and production of petroleum deposits in areas covered by the licence. The licensee becomes the owner of the petroleum which is produced."

The challenges rise when such rights interfere with the same and competing rights of a neighbour. In such circumstances, the competition may lead to sub-standard solutions and waste of resources. The competing parties may meet and agree contractual solutions, but where "[t]he owner of a tract of land acquires title to the oil and gas which he produces from wells drilled thereon, though it may be proved that part of such oil or gas migrated from adjoining lands",[31] the incentive to cooperate with the neighbours may not be overwhelming.

Consequently, when discoveries are made in adjoining areas and questions may arise on the possible communication of the discoveries, making it one deposit instead of two, and the division of the value of the field emerges, external regulation and pressure may be required to reach a satisfactory solution.

Section 4–7 (Joint Petroleum Activities) of the Act provides a basis for regulating this issue.

Section 4–7 (Joint Petroleum Activities)

> If a petroleum deposit extends over more than one block with different licensees, or onto the continental shelf of another state, efforts shall be made to reach agreement on the most efficient co-ordination of petroleum activities in connection with the petroleum deposit as well as on the apportionment of the petroleum deposit. This shall apply similarly when, in the case of several petroleum deposits, joint petroleum activities would obviously be more efficient.
>
> Agreements on joint exploration drilling shall be submitted to the Ministry. Agreements on joint production, transportation, utilisation and cessation of petroleum activities shall be submitted to the Ministry for approval. If consensus on such agreements is not reached within reasonable time, the Ministry may determine how such joint petroleum activities shall be conducted, including the apportionment of the deposit.[32]

Section 4–7 of the Act does not use the term *unitisation*. In the original Norwegian version, the term *samordnet* is used. The term is not defined in the Act but can

31 Robert E Hardwicke, 'The Rule of Capture and Its Implications as Applied to Oil and Gas', (1935) 13 Tex L Rev 391, 393 (Hardwicke).

32 Translation from <https://www.npd.no/en/regulations/acts/act-29-november-1996-no2.-72-relating-to-petroleum-activities/>.

roughly be translated into English as "co-ordinated".[33] Neither does the provision prescribe that the deposit shall be exploited as a single unit. It is for the parties to find "the most efficient co-ordination of petroleum activities".

Section 4–7 applies in two main situations: when there is one common petroleum deposit (what can be referred to as unitisation) and where "joint petroleum activities would obviously be more efficient".[34] From a legal perspective there is no need to distinguish between these two situations since in either one of these situations the legal obligation on the licensees is the same: to exert "efforts . . . to reach agreement on the most efficient co-ordination of petroleum activities".

That the difference between these two alternatives perhaps is more of form than substance can be exemplified by the Norwegian Offshore Directorate's (NOD) view on the possibility of communication between two discoveries referred to as H and F: on this basis (the NOD) will assert that there is a significant possibility that the H and F is one and the same petroleum deposit. If so, then F must automatically be included in the unit area. It will under any circumstances be considered obviously more efficient that a co-ordinated development of the Grane Unit includes the F structure.[35] Consequently, exploitation as a single unit may take place in both instances.[36]

9.3 Unitisation (Co-ordinated Petroleum Activities)

The unitisation situation is regulated in the first paragraph of section 4–7 of the Act. This provision establishes an obligation on the relevant licensees if certain criteria are in place. The criteria are that (a) there must be one petroleum deposit that (b) extends over more than one block, and there are (c) different licensees in these blocks.[37]

The first criterion is that there is "one petroleum deposit". Section 4–7 of the Act does not itself define "petroleum deposit", but a definition is included in section 1–6(b) of the Act. A petroleum deposit is an accumulation of petroleum in a geological unit, limited by rock characteristics by structural or stratigraphic

33 The English translation on the web site of the Norwegian Offshore Directorate is the term "Joint Petroleum Activities", cf. <https://www.npd.no/en/regulations/acts/act-29-november-1996-no2.-72-relating-to-petroleum-activities/>. The English translations of the Act and pertaining regulations used in this text are all lifted from the unofficial translations provided by the Norwegian Offshore Directorate.

34 In the United States, unitisation is distinguished from "pooling". The term *pooling* describes the process of combining separately owned, small tracts of land into drilling units or spacing units of the land and can be compared to the Norwegian concept of co-ordination of activities related to separate deposits.

35 My rendition of an excerpt from a letter from the then Norwegian Oil Directorate (now: Norwegian Offshore Directorate) of 17 November 1999 as quoted in the Breidablikk-case on p. 39.

36 The discussion on when joint petroleum activities would obviously be more efficient is interesting but will not be pursued in this chapter.

37 Where the reservoir extends into an area on the NCS that is not awarded to any licensing group, the licence group in question may, and usually will, apply for such area outside of the ordinary licensing rounds. If awarded, the licensees of the group will receive it as a separate production licence connected to the original production license.

boundaries, contact surface between petroleum and water in the formation, or a combination of these, so that all the petroleum comprised everywhere is in pressure communication through liquid or gas.[38]

The definition indicates that there is a minimum requirement before the obligation arises. In order to establish an "accumulation of petroleum" there must be a discovery,[39] and most likely also that the discovery may have a commercial value and is considered for further appraisal. The extent of a petroleum deposit is an issue of fact and arguably it can be stated that certain appraisal work must have taken place, so that an impression on the extent of the petroleum deposit can be made, before the obligation is manifest. However, it is not necessary that any activity has taken place on the adjacent area.

Furthermore, "all the petroleum comprised everywhere [shall be] in pressure communication through liquid or gas". The Act or its pertaining regulation does not clarify what qualifies as communication. The preparatory white paper (Ot.prp.nr.72 1982–83) does not offer much in this regard but states that water communication does not establish communication of the reservoir within this definition.

Communication between reservoirs is an issue in the Breidablikk-case. The Breidablikk Field consists of two geological formations, the D formation and the F formation. The adjacent Grane Unit includes the main H formation and a part of the F formation. One of the questions in the case is whether the F formation is in communication with the H formation or not.[40]

The Grane Unit Agreement (GUA) contains an appendix setting out certain evaluation criteria for when communication can be established.

> A Deposit is said to be in Communication with the Unit Reservoir when all of the following three criteria are fulfilled:
>
> a) Such Deposit has Oil-bearing sediments with Net Sand characteristics, which are in direct and continuous hydrocarbon contact with the Unit Reservoir.
> b) Such Deposit belongs to the same hydrocarbon pressure regime as that Unit Reservoir, with which it is in direct and continuous hydrocarbon contact as defined in a) above.
> c) The composition of the hydrocarbons of such Deposit is consistent with the composition of the Unit Reservoir hydrocarbons, with which they are in direct and continuous hydrocarbon contacts as defined in a) above.

38 Cf. section 1–6(b).

39 This indicates that the provision applies after the initial exploration phase. However, first sentence of second paragraph of section 4–7 of the Act refers to "[a]greements on exploration drilling", the Green Paper (NOU 1979:43) states that the provision applies in all phases of the petroleum activity (p. 64) and commentators seems to take the view that the provision also encompasses activities that are not connected to a specific "accumulation of petroleum".

40 If the F structure is in communication with the H structure at Grane, Vår Energi ASA will receive a larger share of the F formation with a possible value between 7 and 10 billion NOK.

There seems to be a common understanding that these criteria coincide with the criteria prescribed by the Act[41] and therefore can form the basis for the evaluation of communication.

Furthermore, the petroleum deposit must straddle two or more blocks. A block is a geographical area on the NCS of a certain form and size.[42] The wording seems to indicate that if the relevant petroleum deposit does not extend beyond the boundaries of a block, then the criterion is not fulfilled. However, the licenses rights as such are not directly connected to the geographical bloc but to the geographical licence area as set out in the production licence, and this area may consist of one or more blocks or part of a block. Consequently, a petroleum deposit may well be within a block but still extend into a different licence area. It seems quite evident that this criterion is fulfilled in such a circumstance. The reference to "block" must not be taken too literally.

The third criterion is that there must be "different licensees". At first glance, this may seem to be a reference to each participant in a licence group indicating that there is no obligation if the same companies are on all sides. However, the Act uses the word *licensee* as a reference to each individual participant in a licence group and as a reference to the licence group as a whole.[43] Consequently, the reference can be read as referring to different licence groups.[44] Where the same companies operate on both sides but with different participating interest, there might be a conflict of interest and section 4–7 should apply. It might be argued that where the two (or more) licence groups consists of the same companies with the same participating interest, no conflict of interest exists and thus no coordination or unitisation is needed. This might be a simplification. Each licence is a separate joint venture and the joint activity among the licences will still need an overreaching agreement.[45]

9.4 Pre-Unitisation Agreement (Cost Sharing Agreement)

To clarify if there is one or more reservoirs may require technical, geological, geophysical and mathematical input to decide and can be a lengthy,[46] cumbersome and costly exercise. The areas in question may be in various states of maturity and there may be extensive work still outstanding before the parties can sit down and negotiate the unitisation agreement proper. In the interim the parties may wish to

41 See p. 51 of the Breidablikk-case.

42 Cf. section 3–2 of the Act.

43 Cf. section 1–6(j) of the Act.

44 The preparatory white paper (Ot.prp.nr.72 1982–83) states on p. 42 that the word refers to each individual licensee. Considering the resources management perspective, that the same companies can participate with different ownership shares and there might be different operators, and that the common understanding is that one must look at totality and not only the companies, it seems safe to disregard this entry.

45 The various initial licensees in the Alvheim Area agreed on an alignment of participating shares and a relatively short licence coordination agreement.

46 But not indefinitely. The second paragraph of section 4–7 states that the negotiations must be concluded "within reasonable time".

perform studies, conduct work and so on. Considering this, before entering into a fully termed unitisation agreement, the parties often decide to enter into a pre-unit agreement (or cost-sharing agreement). The main purpose of a pre-unit agreement is to regulate the exchange of information, who shall perform the preparatory work and how to split the cost for such work.

A pre-unitisation agreement will set out a preliminary unit interest of the parties. This interest is the basis for the division of pre-unit cost. The assumption being that a recalculation of cost shall take place when the final tract participation is decided. There may also be established an interim management committee that may evaluate the suggested work programme and budgets.

Exchange of field information is important so that the parties can establish a common basis for inter alia the division of the resources. However, the JOA has confidentiality rules so that no participant in a license shall inform a third party about, or in other ways make public plans, programs, maps, archive data, reports, technical or scientific data or any other information concerning technical, economic or commercial activities related to the license.[47] Consequently, agreement on the exchange of information is established.

An interim operator may be appointed, but often the operatorship is kept as initial and instead various areas of responsibility are distributed among the existing operators.

9.5 The Unitisation Agreement

If the criteria for unitisation are fulfilled, "efforts shall be made" by the licensees to "reach agreement on the most efficient co-ordination of petroleum activities". There is no legal obligation to reach agreement, but the licensees must make contact and engage in substantive discussion, and some resources must be poured into the negotiation. The exact level of exertion the licensees must make is probably of minor concern since the ministry can intervene if the effort or progress is lacking.

The Act does not directly prescribe the form the "co-ordination of petroleum activities" must take, save for it to the "most efficient". In theory the licensees are free[48] to discuss any solution they deem appropriate. The licensees can elect to align their interests in the relevant licenses, carve out and sell the relevant portion of the license, agree on a "right to produce" for one of the licenses and so on. Section 4–8 (Use of Facilities by Others) with pertaining regulation, the TPA regulation,[49] can also be seen as an extension of section 4–7.[50] The provision authorises the ministry

47 Cf. Article 27.2 of the JOA.

48 The agreement must be approved by the ministry and that the ministry can set conditions for such approval, section 10–18 of the Act, so there is limitations to the contractual freedom of the licensees.

49 FOR-2005-12-20-1625 Regulations relating to the use of facilities use by others.

50 In June 2006 the ministry, following a consultation process with the industry, approved a model agreement to facilitate in the negotiations, the "Terms and Conditions for Third Party Use of Installations" as amended from time to time". There is no obligation for the parties to use the model

to decide that facilities used for petroleum activities, and that are owned or used by a licensee, may be used by others.[51] For the purpose of this chapter it is assumed that the parties will exploit the common deposit as a single unit through a unitisation agreement.

Section 4–7 of the Act does not provide much guidance as to the content of an agreement save for the principled statement that it shall provide for the most efficient co-ordination of petroleum activities and the apportionment of the petroleum deposit in the event of a common petroleum deposit.

A unitisation agreement contains provisions that establish the unit and the licensees' individual rights and obligations, and provisions of a more general character that relates to the operation of the unit. In some jurisdictions the unitisation element is covered by a separate unit agreement, while the latter may be covered in a separate unit operating agreement.[52] The ministry produced in 2006 a model form, "Agreement relating to the Unitisation and Operation of the Unknown Field" (the "Unitisation Agreement").[53] The Unitisation Agreement includes both unitisation elements and unit operating elements. Notwithstanding this, the court in the Breidablikk-case stated that these two parts could be separated and perhaps be individually construed.[54]

The main purpose of the unitisation agreement is that the deposit shall be exploited as one unit. Through the unitisation agreement a new joint venture, the unit, is established[55] for the purpose of jointly performing the petroleum activities

agreement, but it seems that the model, with appropriate changes, is used as a model in most of the agreements on third-party use of facilities (other than pipelines).

51 Section 4-7 applies inter alia to transportation. Transportation is defined in (h) of section 1-6 of the Act as "shipment of petroleum by pipeline as well as the construction, placing, operation and use of a facility for the purpose of transportation". The production licence does not apply to the "construction, placing, operation and use of a facility for the purpose of transportation". Such activity demands a separate permit, a licence to install and to operate facilities, cf. section 4-3 of the Act. In granting such licence the ministry has the authority to post conditions cf. section 28 of the FOR-1997-06-27-653 Regulations to Act relating to petroleum activities (the "Regulation"). In this sense the two provisions, section 4-3 and section 4-7, overlaps. However, the obligation to cooperate after section 4-7 applies also in time prior to the application. Considering the Polarled gas pipeline: Polarled is a 480-km-long pipeline connecting the Aasta Hansteen field in the Norwegian Sea with the Nyhamna gas processing facility at Aukra in Møre and Romsdal in Norway. The construct of the Polarled was a coordinated effort between the Asta Hansten field licensees, Equinor Energy AS, Wintershall DEA Norge AS, OMV (Norge) AS and ConocoPhillips Skandinavia AS, and other interested parties in the area, at that time being Petoro, Shell, Total, and Edison. Ownership shares in the Polarled has subsequently been transferred with the owners at the time of writing being M Vest Energy (5.000%), Petoro AS (SDFI) (11.946%), Equinor Energy AS (37.076%), CapeOmega AS (28.271%), Sval Energi AS (13.255%) and ConocoPhillips Skandinavia AS (4.452%).

52 Se Arvid Frihagen, 'Unitavtaler' (1985) and Bustnesli and others; Oil and Gas activities in Norway; Regulatory and contractual framework (2021).

53 The Association of International Petroleum Negotiators (AIPN) produced a model form unitisation and unit operating agreement in the same year. Although the ministry may have glanced at the AIPN model, there is little indication that it has had any impact on the final form.

54 See p. 30 of the Breidablikk-case.

55 See p. 10 of the Johan Sverdrup Decision.

in question. The unit is separate from the underlying production licenses and the rights and obligations of the licensees under the production licences in question are unitised insofar as they relate to the unit reservoir. Outside the unit reservoir the production licenses continue to be operative, and the unitisation agreement will usually contain a provision stating that the parties' rights and duties that do not relate to the unit area shall not be affected by the agreement.

When establishing the unit, the licensees must agree on their respective participating share in the unit, the unit interest. The unit interest is usually the sum of the respective licensees' participating interest in the relevant production license multiplied with the tract participation.

Tract participation is the part of the unitised deposit that shall be apportioned to the relevant production license included in the unit.[56] Establishing the individual licensees' tract participation may prove challenging, and the Johan Sverdrup Resolution and the Breidablikk-case concerns the division of interest between the involved licensees.

Deciding on the tract participation is not an easy task and there are several methods that can be used. There are in general four main methods used to determine tract participation: stock tank oil originally in place (STOOIP), gross rock volume, reserve estimation and moveable oil originally in place (MOOIP).

STOOIP is the total quantity of petroleum in the petroleum deposit before production commences. This is usually done by using estimates of static geologic data, that is data that will not change with time due to production, measured form core and log data (the volumetric method).[57] This estimation is considered as relatively easy to do and not very contentious.

A variant of STOOIP is MOOIP. This is STOOIP less the estimated petroleum left in the petroleum deposit after abandonment.

Another method is an evaluation of the total volume of rock between a top and base reservoir surface and above a known or postulated hydrocarbon-water contact in a geologic trap, gross rock volume. Gross rock volume is considered an important parameter when determining the magnitude of resource volumes potentially contained in that trap.[58]

The amount of petroleum in the reservoir that can be recovered is sometimes also used to set the tract participations. However, technical recoverable petroleum may not be economical recoverable. What is considered as economical will depend on available technology, reservoir characteristics, the quality of the petroleum, current market price and so on. Hereunder the relevant companies own commercial evaluation of the of the project. Consequently, economical recoverable resources are a moveable target and may be difficult to agree on.

In the Johan Sverdrup Decision, the ministry stated that the starting point when considering the apportionment of a common deposit should be petroleum in place

56 See e.g. p. 35 of the Breidablikk-case.

57 <https://www.e-education.psu.edu/png301/node/607>.

58 <https://www.searchanddiscovery.com/abstracts/html/2013/90166ice/abstracts/james.htm>.

in the areas that contains the deposit in question. In this case STOOIP.[59] All the relevant licensees in Johan Sverdrup agreed to this starting point.

The ministry stated further that this starting point may be modified due to inherent characteristics in the subsoil, such as reservoir quality, zones with uncertain recovery potential, recoverability and so on. Hereunder the uncertainty in all these assumption and estimates. Expectations as to drilling and well expenses may also be taken into consideration. Based on an overall geotechnical and geophysical analysis, the ministry decided to use STOOIP with some adjustment based on reservoir characteristics. It seems that all the licensees accepted these principles but disagreed on its application. The decision by the ministry was appealed. The decision of the ministry was upheld by Royal Decree (the "Johan Sverdrup Resolution").[60] The Johan Sverdrup Resolution confirmed the principles set by the ministry for apportionment of a reservoir. The principles have also been supported by the parties in the Breidablikk-case.[61]

From this tract participation, the interest of each licence group will be derived. The unit interest will determine each licensees' expenditure commitment, entitlement to receive hydrocarbons and voting power.

The unit agreement is entered into at a time when information is relatively limited. As time passes, more information is gathered from the petroleum deposit. This again may indicate that the initial tract participation was not correct and a redetermination of the initial tract participation and unit interest of the licensees in line with the new data obtained may be requested. Such redetermination is considered an important principle because it allows for a more accurate allocation of costs and production between the parties to the unitisation agreement.

Most unitisation agreements will provide for the parties right to call for a redetermination. Redetermination is a technical exercise, subjective in nature since it calls for various interpretations of the new date, where the tract participation may be recalculated. The process is also likely to consume a significant amount of time and money and can often lead to disputes between the parties.

Where redetermination is allowed, the unitisation agreement will provide a set of rules outlining the process by which the parties need to follow. Although the parties might want to solve the redetermination by negotiation there is always the possibility of appointing an expert to solve the issue. The expert will be an independent company with technical knowledge of geology and geophysics. The parties will be allowed to submit their technical interpretation of the distribution of the unit reservoir, but at the end the decision is for the expert. The expert's decision will, absent fraud or manifest error, be final and binding and apply until the next redetermination, if any.

59 See the penultimate paragraph on page 13 of the letter from the ministry to the licence partners dated 1 July 2015.

60 Royal Decree dated 18 December 2015.

61 The issue in the Breidablikk-case was that the ministry deviated from these principles and based their decision on a concrete interpretation of the GUA and the questions was inter alia if the GUA was relevant for the apportionment decision and if it was interpreted correctly.

Due to the complexity and cost of a redetermination, provisions may be included in the unit agreement that requires that a requesting party indicates a probability that redetermination will change the tract participation, or that if the interest of the requesting party is not changed with at least an agreed threshold, such party must pay all the cost and expenses related to the redetermination. The number of redeterminations and when a redetermination can be called may differ based on the estimated life of field. In some instances, no redetermination clause is included, and the tract participation is fixed for the duration of the unit.

Unitisation agreements on the NCS has historically been based on the provisions of the JOA and the unit agreement has the same basis in so far as relates to the operational provisions.

The unit agreement establishes an operational framework for the unit, and the terms and conditions are for all practical purposes non-negotiable.[62]

The primary organisational body is the management committee. The voting rules of the management committee is based on three elements; the issue to be resolved (there are some special applications), the number of licensees in the unit and the unit interest of each licensee. The main voting rule is that a majority of both participants and working interest is required for a binding resolution, but certain decisions require unanimity.

The parties' primary liability among themselves is on a pro rata basis, secondarily jointly and severally liable for all obligations arising by virtue of the joint venture's activities. This division of liability does not affect dealings with third parties, which will be at law.

The unit agreement also sets up the framework for the day-to-day activities performed by the operator; procedures for meetings, appointment and removal of the operator;[63] the operator's authority, work programmes and budgets, procurement, payments, and corporate governance; rules on changes in status such as development, withdrawal, decommissioning, and assignment and withdrawal; entitlements such as right to asset and lifting of petroleum; and legal provisions such as liability and confidentiality.

The final unitisation agreement is subject to the approval by the ministry.[64]

9.6 The Authority of the Ministry

The petroleum resources in the subsoil belongs to the state, and these resources shall be managed in a long-term perspective for the benefit of the Norwegian society as

62 Amendments, changes to or exemptions from the agreement must be approved by the ministry prior to implementation.

63 The operator is the company that on behalf of the licensees manage the day-to-day activities. The operator is appointed or approved by the ministry, cf. second paragraph of section 3–7 of the Act.

64 Agreements on joint production, transportation, utilisation and cessation of petroleum activities shall approved by the ministry. Agreements on joint exploration drilling shall be submitted to the ministry for information. Cf. second paragraph of section 4–7 of the Act.

a whole.[65] The participants in the Norwegian petroleum industry are obligated to ensure that the activities are organised and performed so that as much as possible of the petroleum in place in each individual petroleum deposit will be produced.[66] The main obligors are the licensees on the NCS, but the ministry is given the authority to supervise the activities and are granted extensive rights to ensure the effective and proper performance of the petroleum activities.

The ministry's use of the authority can be challenged by the interested parties as an administrative complaint to the King in Council (that will decide on the matter through a Royal Decree), or in a court of law. The courts can test the legality of the administrative decision including the facts and interpretation of the facts also where such facts include complex evaluations.[67] Decisions as to whether something is fair, reasonable, appropriate and so on is to a certain degree outside the court's area of competence. However, the court can always test if the administration acts within the limits of its authorisation, has a correct understanding of the facts and has applied the law correctly to the facts in evidence and is not arbitrary or a misuse of power.[68]

Section 4–7 intends for the affected licensees to reach a negotiated settlement "within reasonable time". This is not a very specific timeline, but it allows for individual considerations depended on the complexity of the negotiations. It also provides the administration with the necessary leeway to decide when to use their discretionary power.

In 2015, after prolonged negotiations for a period of more than two years without reaching a final solution on the apportionment of the petroleum deposit Johan Sverdrup,[69] the ministry decided that the time was up and that it would intervene.[70] The ministry's decision when to use their authority is within their discretion to decide and cannot be overruled by a court of law.

The ministry is, according to section 1–6(b) of the Act, authorised "[i]n cases of doubt [to] determine what shall be regarded as a petroleum deposit". It is argued by commentators[71] that such a decision cannot be challenged in a court of law.

Whether there is one or more petroleum deposits may be complicated but is a question of fact, and the courts deals with facts.[72] The question on the courts ability to decide on complicated facts in regard to communication was considered by

65 Second paragraph of section 1–2 of the Act.

66 Section 4–1 of the Act.

67 See e.g., Supreme Court case quoted in Rt 1995 1499 (1505) and 2009 105 (112).

68 See e.g., Henriette N Tøssebro, 'Læren om begrenset domstolskontroll' (2019) in Henriette N Tøssebro (ed) *Ugyldighet forvaltningsretten* (Universitetsforlaget 2019).

69 Det norske did not consent to the proposal submitted by the other participants on the ground of the apportionment of the resources.

70 See letter from the ministry to the licence partners dated 1 July 2015. The administrative decision was challenged by Det norske and the King in Council upheld the ministry's decision by Royal Decree dated 18 December 2015. The ministry's authority to intervene was not challenged.

71 See e.g. Hammer and others, *Petroleumsloven* (Universitetsforlaget 2009) 314.

72 The states accepted on principle that the issue on communication is a question of fact that can be evaluated by the courts of law, see p. 18 of the Breidablikk-case.

the court in the Breidablikk-case. The court ruled that the issue on communication was too complicated for the court to decide on and that the use of experts, either as witnesses or judges, would not remit the courts challenges.[73]

It is uncontroversial that the factual issue is complicated and may require specialist knowledge, but this is usually not a limitation on the courts that deals with complex facts on a frequent basis. Neither is it in itself a limitation that the decision may require difficult choices. Questions as to the validity of the facts, the understanding of the facts and the application of the facts should all be permitted before a court of law. The question on the courts ability to decide on complicated facts in regard to communication was considered by the court in the Breidablikk-case.

Section 4–7 authorises the ministry when necessary to "determine how such joint petroleum activities shall be conducted, including the apportionment of the deposit". There are various solutions of co-operation that can be elected to ensure "the most efficient co-ordination of petroleum activities". What form of cooperation that ministry may decide on in lieu of an agreement between the partners is probably within the sole discretion of the ministry. The same arguably applies where the ministry decides on the choice of technology[74] or how the facilities shall be designed. What from a conservation point of view is considered "most efficient" must be within the discretion of the ministry to decide.

Apportionment of the petroleum is, as discussed above, based on principles laid down in the Johan Sverdrup Decision such as petroleum in place, inherent characteristics in the subsoil, drilling and well expenses, and so on. The issue on apportionment may be an impasse in the negotiations but there is nothing that states that a tract participation cannot be interim[75] or that it cannot be changed later,[76] so the issue in itself is not a hindrance for a coordinated petroleum activity. This is less so where a decision on coordinated activities has been made. In these cases, the tract participation is more of a commercial issue between the licensees than a public administrative issue. The issue on the ministry's authority to decide on the apportionment of the reservoir in question lingered in the background in the Breidablikk-case, but the court resolved the issue based on the interpretation of the unit agreement in question.

Section 4–7 of the Act together with section 1–6(b) of the Act provides the authorities with a wide discretionary power. The limits of the authority of the

73 The court argued, inter alia, that a decision on the issue of delimitation of a petroleum deposit may be of significance e.g. when deciding on a coordinated development or not. Considering that section 4–7 does not distinguish between on deposit and where it otherwise would obviously be more efficient to coordinate the point seem moot. Neither has the issue any direct impact on resource management since the ministry decided that there was no communication but the field in question should still be developed as part of the Breidablikk Unit.

74 Arguably the ministry can impose the use of e.g. fishbone technology instead of conventional drilling if considered more efficient, but probably not impose a new technology just to test it.

75 See p. 2 in the Johan Sverdrup Decision where the ministry refers to an interim decision on the apportionment of interests.

76 Redetermination provisions are included in many unit agreements and although being expensive and challenging never been considered as something that cannot be done.

ministry and the courts authority to try the decision taken by the ministry when utilising the authority are still up for debate, notwithstanding recent administrative decisions and court decision.

Key Findings of This Chapter

On the NCS coordinated petroleum activity is compulsory where a petroleum deposit straddles one or more license areas or where such coordinated activities is would obviously be more efficient. The parties are at liberty to decide among themselves "on the most efficient co-ordination of petroleum activities", which may be a unitisation, and to enter into the appropriate agreements. Should the parties elect to enter into a unitisation agreement a model unitisation agreement has been produced by the government. The use of the model agreement is as such not compulsory but will in most cases form the basis for the finally agreed document. If the parties are not able to reach agreement or are in disagreement on elements to be include in such an agreement, the government through the Ministry of Energy can intervene and decide on the contented issues. The ministry's decision can be appealed to the King in Council, whose decision again can be tested in a court of law.

10 Unitization in the United Kingdom

Tolulope O Taiwo

10.1 Introduction

Countries rich in oil and gas seek to maximize their potential and the revenue generated from this industry. A common method of achieving this is to split areas of land marked for oil and gas exploration and/or production into multiple blocks, with these blocks conferred as separate licences. The licence is the only method of conferring rights to explore and/or produce oil and gas in the UK.[1]

Where there is a shared reservoir across multiple licence areas, the licensees of the separate blocks have two options. The first option is to rely on the legal principle of the 'rule of capture' as relates to the extraction of hydrocarbons.[2] The second option, which is the focus of this book and this chapter, is that the licensees may voluntarily decide or be mandated by the State to jointly develop the shared reservoir. Unitization is one of the most common methods of joint development of a common/shared reservoir.[3] It would be national or intra-country unitization where the common reservoir is within one country's borders. The more extensive form of unitization is cross-border unitization, where resources straddle the border of multiple countries. In both forms of unitization, the relevant parties would form a 'unit' to jointly develop the resources.

Unitization is often defined as the coordinated operation of a common oil or gas reservoir by multiple parties with rights in different contract/licence areas (or State borders) underlying the joint reservoir.[4] The concept of unitization

1 United Kingdom Petroleum Act 1998, Part 1, Section 2; North Sea Transition Authority, 'Licensing Consents' <https://www.nstauthority.co.uk/licensing-consents/overview/> accessed 28 August 2022.

2 This is a legal principle permitting the extraction of hydrocarbons from one licence area even if such hydrocarbons may have migrated from another licence area. This principle has been discussed in the introductory chapters of this book.

See also Rod Chooramun, 'Unitisation: The Oil and Gas Industry's Solution to One of Geology's Many Conundrums' Notes from the Field – An English Law Perspective on the Oil & Gas Market (Andrew Skurth, August 2014) <https://www.andrewskurth.com/insights-1133.html> accessed 10 February 2016.

3 Danielle Beggs and Justyna Bremen, 'Unitisation and Unitisation Agreements' in Geoffrey Picton-Turbervill (ed), *Oil and Gas: A Practical Handbook* (Globe Law and Business 2009) 57.

4 Jacqueline Lang Weaver and others, 'International Unitization of Oil and Gas Fields: The Legal Framework of International Law, National Laws, and Private Contracts' (Association of International Petroleum Negotiators) (2007) 5(2) Oil and Gas Energy Law (OGEL) 1.

DOI: 10.4324/9781003491293-12

developed in the United States but has been adopted in other jurisdictions, the UK included.[5]

The United States and Canada[6] are unique from the rest of the world in that they recognize the right of private ownership of oil and gas resources.[7] In the UK, all rights to oil and gas are vested in the Crown, with the North Sea Transition Authority (NSTA; formerly known as the Oil & Gas Authority [OGA] until March 2022[8]) empowered to grant licences for the exploration and production of petroleum.[9]

10.2 Objective of Unitization

Prior to an assessment of the legal framework relating to unitization in the UK, it is useful to first consider the objective of unitization as this assists in understanding the rationale guiding the framework.

Where there is a shared reservoir across multiple licence areas or borders, the various companies with separate licences or contracts would drill aggressively, so as to capture as much resources as possible. As well as there being an unnecessary duplication of efforts, aggressive drilling could lead to a company capturing more oil or gas than it is entitled to, and could also cause environmental damage. Additionally, aggressive drilling may mean that the reservoir is not exploited in the most efficient method. Ultimately, this could reduce the volume of oil or gas ultimately recoverable from the shared reservoir.[10]

5 See Rod Chooramun, 'Unitisation – The Oil and Gas Industry's Solution to One of Geology's Many Conundrums' Notes From the Field – An English Law Perspective on the Oil & Gas Market (Andrew Skurth, August 2014) <https://www.andrewskurth.com/insights-1133.html> accessed 1 May 2021; Peter Roberts, *Joint Operating Agreements: A Practical Guide* (3rd edn, Globe Business Publishing 2015) 317–328.

6 The extent of private ownership in Canada is not as significant as in the United States.

7 Yet, even in both countries, the majority of oil and gas reserves are government owned. See Ernest E Smith and others, *Materials on International Petroleum Transactions* (Rocky Mountain Mineral Law Foundation 2010) 30.

8 This change of name reflects the evolving role of the OGA in the UK's energy transition story and the pursuit of net zero by 2050. Department for Business, Energy & Industrial Strategy, North Sea Transition Deal: One Year On' (March 2022) <https://assets.publishing.service.gov.uk/government/uploads/system/uploads/attachment_data/file/1061986/north-sea-transition-deal-one-year-on.pdf> accessed 28 August 2022.

It is useful to note that some publications by the OGA prior to March 2022 continue to have OGA in the header and text even where the website address has been updated to reflect NSTA. This will be seen in relevant references in this chapter.

9 'The North Sea Transition Authority can grant licences that confer exclusive rights to 'search and bore for and get' petroleum'. United Kingdom Petroleum Act 1998, Part 1, Section 2; North Sea Transition Authority, 'Licensing Consents' <https://www.nstauthority.co.uk/licensing-consents/overview/> accessed 28 August 2022.

10 Danielle Beggs and Justyna Bremen, 'Unitisation and Unitisation Agreements' in Geoffrey Picton-Turbervill (ed), *Oil and Gas: A Practical Handbook* (Globe Law and Business 2009) 57; Ernest E Smith and others, *Materials on International Petroleum Transactions* (Rocky Mountain Mineral Law Foundation 2010) 627.

The primary objective of unitization is to secure the maximum recovery of oil and/or gas from a shared reservoir, as well as the avoidance of unnecessary competitive drilling. Both objectives are consistent with the UK's previous maximum economic recovery (MER) strategy, pursued through the then OGA.[11] The MER agenda is principally in the interest of the State, as maximum recovery ensures maximum financial rewards for the State, be it via taxes or other fiscal payments agreed with licensees. The benefit to licensees is implicit in that economic wastage and the unnecessary duplication of efforts are avoided. More importantly, all licensees receive production according to agreed unit interests, rather than on the basis of who captures the most resources. Despite these benefits, licensees may not always favour unitization, on the basis of its inherent complexities and costs. This raises the question of whether licensees operating in the UK are under an obligation to unitize where there is a shared reservoir.

The next section addresses this question in its consideration of the legal framework relating to voluntary and mandatory unitization.

10.3 Legal Framework for Voluntary and Mandatory Unitization

Prior to 2016, the secretary of state had oversight over the UK oil and gas licensing regime. However, this role was transferred to the NSTA in 2016. The Energy Act 2016 sets the legislative framework formally establishing the NSTA as a government company.[12] This Act also confers the NSTA with regulatory powers over exploration and development activities in the UK oil and gas sector.[13]

The NSTA, empowered by the Petroleum Act 1998,[14] has oversight for the UK licensing regime and grants licences conferring exclusive rights for companies to explore and produce petroleum.[15] Each of these licences is governed by corresponding model clauses[16] which empower the NSTA to provide authorization for

11 In February 2021, the OGA released a new strategy which amended its maximum economic recovery (MER) strategy. This new strategy sets a net zero carbon by 2050, highlighting that the pursuit of MER should not conflict with the net zero target. Oil & Gas Authority, 'The OGA Strategy' <https://www.ogauthority.co.uk/regulatory-framework/the-oga-strategy/> accessed 2 June 2021; Oil & Gas Authority, 'The OGA Strategy' <https://www.nstauthority.co.uk/media/7105/the-oga-strategy.pdf> accessed 28 August 2022; Oil & Gas Authority, 'The Maximising Economic Recovery Strategy for the UK' <https://www.nstauthority.co.uk/media/1022/mer_uk_strategy.pdf> accessed 28 August 2022.

12 North Sea Transition Authority, 'Legislative Content' <https://www.nstauthority.co.uk/regulatory-framework/legislative-context/> accessed 28 August 2022.

13 Ibid.

14 Petroleum Act 1998 <https://www.legislation.gov.uk/ukpga/1998/17/contents> accessed 28 June 2021.

15 United Kingdom Petroleum Act 1998, Part 1, Section 2; North Sea Transition Authority, 'Licensing Consents' <https://www.nstauthority.co.uk/licensing-consents/overview/> accessed 28 August 2022; Oil & Gas Authority, 'Requirements for the Planning of and Consent to UKCS Field Developments' (October 2018, updated October 2019) 1, 4 <https://www.nstauthority.co.uk/media/6099/fdp_guidance_requirements-document-oct_update-2019v2.pdf> accessed 28 August 2022. North Sea Transition Authority, 'Field Determinations' <https://www.nstauthority.co.uk/regulatory-information/exploration-and-production/development/field-determinations/>

16 Model Clauses set out the detailed regulatory provisions to which the licence is subject.

certain activities. For production licences, licensees must seek authorization from the NSTA prior to the development of oil and gas facilities or the production of petroleum.[17] This authorization request is known as a 'Development and Production Consent'.[18] It is the receipt of this consent from the NSTA that indicates that the authorization phase is complete.[19] However, as part of the criteria for securing this consent and to proceed with a development, licensees are required to submit a 'Field Development Plan' (FDP) to the NSTA.[20] The Development and Production Consent effectively approves the FDP for implementation. In determining whether to approve a FDP, the NSTA will consider, amongst other issues, whether such plan will allow the MER of petroleum from the concerned field.[21]

Also, where a field determination[22] extends into a neighbouring licence, the NSTA may require that licensees enter into a unitization and unit operating agreement (UUOA) prior to submitting a FDP.[23] In such instances, licensees will not receive the NSTA's consent to the FDP until the UUOA has been approved.[24] This

17 North Sea Transition Authority, 'Field Determination' <https://www.nstauthority.co.uk/regulatory-information/exploration-and-production/development/field-determinations/> accessed 28 December 2023; Oil and Gas Authority, 'Guidance Notes for Onshore Field Development Plans, Fdp Addendums and Cessation of Production' (August 2016) <https://assets.publishing.service.gov.uk/government/uploads/system/uploads/attachment_data/file/549118/OnshoreFDPGuidanceAug2016.pdf> accessed 9 May 2021; Oil & Gas Authority, 'Requirements for the Planning of and Consent to UKCS Field Developments' (October 2018, updated October 2019) 1, 4 <https://www.nstauthority.co.uk/media/6099/fdp_guidance_requirements-document-oct_update-2019v2.pdf> accessed 28 August 2022.

18 North Sea Transition Authority, 'Field Determination' <https://www.nstauthority.co.uk/regulatory-information/exploration-and-production/development/field-determinations/> accessed 28 December 2023; Oil and Gas Authority, 'Guidance Notes for Onshore Field Development Plans, Fdp Addendums and Cessation of Production' (August 2016) <https://assets.publishing.service.gov.uk/government/uploads/system/uploads/attachment_data/file/549118/OnshoreFDPGuidanceAug2016.pdf> accessed 9 May 2021; Oil & Gas Authority, 'Requirements for the Planning of and Consent to UKCS Field Developments' (October 2018, updated October 2019) 1, 4 <https://www.nstauthority.co.uk/media/6099/fdp_guidance_requirements-document-oct_update-2019v2.pdf> accessed 28 August 2022.

19 Oil & Gas Authority, 'Requirements for the Planning of and Consent to UKCS Field Developments' (October 2018, updated October 2019) 1, 17, 22 <https://www.nstauthority.co.uk/media/6099/fdp_guidance_requirements-document-oct_update-2019v2.pdf> accessed 28 August 2022.

20 Ibid., 4. 'The FDP Is the Pre-requisite for the OGA's Development and Production Considerations and Should Provide a Description of the Technical and Economic Information on Which the Development Is Based.'

21 Oil & Gas Authority, 'Requirements for the Planning of and Consent to UKCS Field Developments' (October 2018, updated October 2019) 1, 4, 8 <https://www.nstauthority.co.uk/media/6099/fdp_guidance_requirements-document-oct_update-2019v2.pdf> accessed 28 August 2022.

22 A field determination assists licensees of a concerned block and those licensees in adjacent blocks to understand what makes up the field, for the purpose of development and taxation. North Sea Transition Authority <https://www.nstauthority.co.uk/exploration-production/development/field-determinations> accessed 28 August 2022.

23 Oil & Gas Authority, 'Requirements for the Planning of and Consent to UKCS Field Developments' (October 2018, updated October 2019) 1, 11, 19 <https://www.nstauthority.co.uk/media/6099/fdp_guidance_requirements-document-oct_update-2019v2.pdf> accessed 28 August 2022.

24 Oil & Gas Authority, 'Requirements for the Planning of and Consent to UKCS Field Developments' (October 2018, updated October 2019) 1, 11, 19 <https://www.nstauthority.co.uk/media/6099/fdp_guidance_requirements-document-oct_update-2019v2.pdf> accessed 28 August 2022.

process does not fall squarely within voluntary or mandatory unitization. It is not voluntary because in the absence of the requirement from the NSTA to enter into a UUOA, the licensees may not have favoured unitization. Similarly, it cannot be described as mandatory unitization in the strict sense since the licensees may have determined independently and voluntarily that unitization is the most efficient form of exploiting the reservoir, even without the requirement by the NSTA. Yet, because licensees may be denied consent to a FDP if they do not submit a UUOA where prescribed by the NSTA, the consent phase of the FDP is in itself a signal directing licensees to unitize.

Furthermore, the NSTA will need to be satisfied that the unitization plan is consistent with MER, whilst also avoiding unnecessary competitive drilling (two conditions).[25] These two conditions are cited to be in the national interest for unitization in the Petroleum (Production) (Seaward Areas) Regulations 1988 and the Petroleum (Production) (Landward Areas) Regulations 1995.[26]

For the avoidance of delay in the authorization of the FDP, the recommendation is for neighbouring licensees with a shared reservoir to voluntarily agree to a unitized development early enough and propose this to the NSTA.[27] A recent example of this is the decision of neighbouring licensees in the Marigold Field (UK central North Sea) to agree to develop the field through unitized operations so as to allow optimal field development.[28] The licensees are Anasuria Hibiscus UK, Ithaca Oil and Gas, and Caldera Petroleum UK Ltd.[29] These licensees entered a unitization

25 Oil and Gas Authority, 'Guidance Notes for Onshore Field Development Plans, Fdp Addendums and Cessation of Production' (August 2016) <https://assets.publishing.service.gov.uk/government/uploads/system/uploads/attachment_data/file/549118/OnshoreFDPGuidanceAug2016.pdf> accessed 9 May 2021; Oil & Gas Authority, 'Requirements for the Planning of and Consent to UKCS Field Developments' (October 2018, updated October 2019) 1, 11, 19 <https://www.nstauthority.co.uk/media/6099/fdp_guidance_requirements-document-oct_update-2019v2.pdf> accessed 28 August 2022.

26 The Petroleum (Production) (Seaward Areas) Regulations 1988, Model Clauses for Production Licences in Seaward Areas, Schedule 4, Clause 28.1 <https://www.legislation.gov.uk/uksi/1988/1213/schedule/4/made>; The Petroleum (Production) (Landward Areas) Regulations 1995, Model Clauses for Petroleum Exploration and Development Licences in Landward Areas, Schedule 3, Clause 25.1 <https://www.legislation.gov.uk/uksi/1995/1436/schedule/3/made> accessed 4 July 2021.

27 Oil and Gas Authority, 'Guidance Notes for Onshore Field Development Plans, Fdp Addendums and Cessation of Production' (August 2016) <https://assets.publishing.service.gov.uk/government/uploads/system/uploads/attachment_data/file/549118/OnshoreFDPGuidanceAug2016.pdf> accessed 9 May 2021; Oil & Gas Authority, 'Requirements for the Planning of and Consent to UKCS Field Developments' (October 2018, updated October 2019) 1, 11, 19 <https://www.nstauthority.co.uk/media/6099/fdp_guidance_requirements-document-oct_update-2019v2.pdf> accessed 28 August 2022.

28 Alex Procyk, 'Marigold Field to Undergo Joint Development' (Oil & Gas Journal, 19 September 2023) <https://www.ogj.com/exploration-development/article/14299160/marigold-field-to-undergo-joint-development> accessed 29 December 2023.

29 The unit interests of the parties is as follows: 'AHUK holds 87.5% interest in license P198 Block 15/13a, which contains Marigold West field, with Caldera holding the remaining 12.5%. Ithaca holds 100% in license P2158 Block 15/18b, adjacent to Marigold West field and containing Marigold East field. Pursuant to the UUOA, the respective unit participations in the unitized Marigold field (Marigold West and Marigold East) will be AHUK (61.25%), Caldera (8.75%),

and unit operating agreement for the joint development of the Marigold Field and are expected to submit a FDP in 2024.[30]

However, where licensees have not or do not reach an agreement to unitize operations, the NSTA, under the model clauses[31] of the licence, has the power to compel a unitization between licensees.[32] The exercise of this power would bring about a mandatory/forced unitization. This power is not a soft measure, but rather a strict enforcement under the model clauses. The justifications for exercising this power are that the NSTA deems it to be in the national interest, so as to ensure the MER of petroleum and the avoidance of unnecessary competitive drilling.[33]

One might question what the NSTA's position would be where a proposed development plan can achieve MER without unitization. The NSTA's guidance indicates that should licensees choose not to unitize and instead propose a different commercial agreement, 'it may be appropriate to define two or more Development Areas within the Field Determination to document different ownerships in the different parts of the field'.[34] Additionally, although this author has no known recorded examples, a report by Weaver notes that where economic wastage is not occurring, the position appears to be that 'the UK will allow the rule of capture to apply between licensees rather than to tolerate delayed field development'.[35] Similarly, albeit undocumented, this author was made aware[36] of an instance in the UK continental shelf (UKCS) in the 1990s where an oil company paid a fee to a

---

and Ithaca (30.00%)'. Alex Procyk, 'Marigold Field to Undergo Joint Development' (Oil & Gas Journal, 19 September 2023) <https://www.ogj.com/exploration-development/article/14299160/marigold-field-to-undergo-joint-development> accessed 29 December 2023.

30 Offshore, 'Unitization Deal Clears Path for North Sea Marigold, Sunflower Developments' (20 September 2023) <https://www.offshore-mag.com/field-development/article/14299208/unitization-deal-clears-path-for-north-sea-marigold-sunflower-developments>; Alex Procyk, 'Marigold Field to Undergo Joint Development' (Oil & Gas Journal, 19 September 2023) <https://www.ogj.com/exploration-development/article/14299160/marigold-field-to-undergo-joint-development> accessed 29 December 2023.

31 The Petroleum (Production) (Seaward Areas) Regulations 1988, Model Clauses for Production Licences in Seaward Areas, Schedule 4, Clause 28.1 <https://www.legislation.gov.uk/uksi/1988/1213/schedule/4/made>; The Petroleum (Production) (Landward Areas) Regulations 1995, Model Clauses for Petroleum Exploration and Development Licences in Landward Areas, Schedule 3, Clause 25.1 <https://www.legislation.gov.uk/uksi/1995/1436/schedule/3/made> accessed 4 July 2021.

32 Oil & Gas Authority, 'Requirements for the Planning of and Consent to UKCS Field Developments' (October 2018, updated October 2019) 1, 19 <https://www.nstauthority.co.uk/media/6099/fdp_guidance_requirements-document-oct_update-2019v2.pdf> accessed 28 August 2022.

33 Oil & Gas Authority, 'Requirements for the Planning of and Consent to UKCS Field Developments' (October 2018, updated October 2019) 1, 19 <https://www.nstauthority.co.uk/media/6099/fdp_guidance_requirements-document-oct_update-2019v2.pdf> accessed 28 August 2022.

34 Oil & Gas Authority, 'Requirements for the Planning of and Consent to UKCS Field Developments' (October 2018, updated October 2019) 1, 19 <https://www.nstauthority.co.uk/media/6099/fdp_guidance_requirements-document-oct_update-2019v2.pdf> accessed 28 August 2022.

35 Jacqueline Lang Weaver and others, 'International Unitization of Oil and Gas Fields: The Legal Framework of International Law, National Laws, and Private Contracts' (Association of International Petroleum Negotiators) (2007) 5(2) Oil Gas Energy Law (OGEL) 1, 32, 33.

36 This was brought to the author's attention by a colleague who was an employee in the legal department of the oil company and had proposed the payment of the fee.

neighbouring block holder not to drill a prospect which extended about 15% into their block. This enabled the oil company to extract the said 15% of gas without the secretary of state requiring unitization. It was further added that the secretary of state approved the well in knowledge of the circumstances.[37]

It can therefore be taken that, the need to develop the field, so far as MER can be achieved, would override the need to ensure the fair and equitable recovery of production from a common reservoir. From a regulatory perspective, the NSTA's primary interests in forcing unitization is MER and the avoidance of competitive drilling which may be damaging to the geological structure of the field. Where these two interests can be achieved in the absence of unitization, the justification of 'national interest' is removed and the NSTA will not force unitization on licensees.

The discussion in the next section turns to a consideration of cross-border unitization.

10.4 Cross-Border Unitization

Cross-border unitization involves a situation where a common reservoir underlies the boundary between two or more countries and the countries reach an agreement to jointly develop the reservoir.[38] It is of course possible for each country to exploit the reservoir independently, but this would lead to the violation of the other country's resource right.[39] As expected, this scenario would both be legally and politically unfavourable. Therefore, the more efficient route is for the countries concerned to jointly develop the straddling reservoir. These arrangements are typically (albeit not exclusively) in the form of cross-border unitization agreements. National unitization has its complexities and challenges; these challenges are significantly increased in cross-border unitizations due to the multiplicity of countries, regulations and laws involved.[40]

To effect any cross-border unitization, the framework in the UK (as with other countries) is multi-level. The transboundary agreement between the UK and the other concerned country/countries with the common reservoir is the first and perhaps most crucial agreement. The second level agreement can be described as the conditional approval to development between the licensee and the State; and finally, the contractual agreement between licensees on both sides of the border/borders, in the form of the UUOA.

In relation to straddling reservoirs involving the UK, the guidance from the NSTA is that licensees on the side of the UK seek 'early and specific guidance

37 This was brought to the author's attention by a colleague who was an employee in the legal department of the oil company and had proposed the payment of the fee.

38 North Sea Transition Authority, 'Transboundary Fields' <https://www.nstauthority.co.uk/exploration-production/development/transboundary-fields/> accessed 28 August 2022.

39 See Ana E Bastida and others, 'Cross-Border Unitization and Joint Development Agreements: An International Law Perspective' (2007) 29 Houston J Intern L 355–422.

40 For a discussion on some of these challenges, see Daniel Fjærtoft and others, 'Unitization of Petroleum Fields in the Barents Sea: Towards a Common Understanding?' (2018) 9 Arctic Rev Law Pol 72, 75 <https://pdfs.semanticscholar.org/6e45/8e6f167870ca793596c53624d5da91ad692b.pdf> accessed 20 June 2021.

from the NSTA during the screening stage for any development proposal that may have transboundary implications'.[41] As no two transboundary arrangements are the same, it is critical that licensees collaborate with the NSTA. It is at this stage that licensees together with the NSTA can consider relevant transboundary treaties or agreements with the other country or countries where the reservoir straddles the boundary. Similarly, the licensees or contractors of the other concerned country or countries would also consider the relevant treaty and collaborate with the licensing authority in their respective States. Some of the transboundary agreements involving the UK are discussed below.

10.5 UK Cross-Border Agreements

Where there is a relevant treaty concerning transboundary reservoirs between the UK and another State (or indeed States), the treaty would provide the framework for the joint development arrangement. In the event that there is no applicable treaty, the UK (upon the discovery of a shared reservoir by its licensees) would need to reach a formal agreement with the States concerned for the joint exploitation of the reservoir. The benefit of having a transboundary agreement in place is that it saves a lot of time, and a UUOA can be agreed as soon as is reasonably possible. Countries with a history of transboundary reservoirs often enter into a form of transboundary agreement with neighbouring countries, such that if and when straddling resources are discovered, a framework for joint development is already in place.[42]

The UK is party to a number of cross-border unitization agreements, with a total of 31 Transboundary Treaties and Agreements on Fields, Pipelines and Delimitations currently listed on the NSTA's website.[43] The list of countries involved in these agreements can be accessed on the website of the NSTA.[44] The earliest is the UK Norway Delimitation Treaty 1965,[45] which contained the first of its kind

41 North Sea Transition Authority, 'Transboundary Fields' <https://www.nstauthority.co.uk/exploration-production/development/transboundary-fields/> accessed 29 December 2023.

42 North Sea Transition Authority, 'Transboundary Fields' <https://www.nstauthority.co.uk/exploration-production/development/transboundary-fields/> accessed 29 December 2023.

43 North Sea Transition Authority, 'Transboundary Fields' <https://www.nstauthority.co.uk/exploration-production/development/transboundary-fields/> accessed 29 December 2023. The NSTA notes that the online list of the 31 agreements may not cover all the treaties and agreements available. In an email response to this author dated 26 July 2021, the OGA (the change of name to NSTA had not taken place at the time of the email) noted that there are two further treaties: 1976 Frigg Field Unitisation Treaty and 1973 Ekofisk Agreement. The total number of transboundary treaties is therefore 33. The OGA indicated that these two treaties will be updated on their website in due course. However, as at 29 December 2023, the online list remained at 31.

44 North Sea Transition Authority, 'Transboundary Fields' <https://www.nstauthority.co.uk/exploration-production/development/transboundary-fields/> accessed 28 August 2022.

45 Agreement Between the Government of the United Kingdom of Great Britain and Northern Ireland and the Government of the Kingdom of Norway Relating to the Delimitation of the Continental Shelf Between the Two Countries. Signed at London, On 10 March 1965.

international commitment to jointly cooperate over straddling resources, in its Article 4 set out below.[46] It provides:

> If any single geological petroleum structure or petroleum field, or any single geological structure or field of any other mineral deposit, including sand or gravel, extends across the dividing line and the part of such structure or field which is situated on one side of the dividing line is exploitable, wholly or in part, from the other side of the dividing line, *the Contracting Parties shall, in consultation with the licensees, if any, seek to reach agreement as to the manner in which the structure or field shall be most effectively exploited and the manner in which the proceeds de-riving therefrom shall be apportioned*.[47]

Fjærtoft correctly notes that although Article 4 does not state the procedure or form of joint agreement, unitization has become the preferred option for exploiting cross-border petroleum.[48] To date, the UK and Norway have been involved in several cross-border unitization agreements.[49] Given that the respective licensees of the two countries were not party to the unitization treaties, the obligations therein were passed onto licensees by way of a conditional approval to development between the licensees and their respective States.[50] In the UK, oil and gas licences are actually in the form of a deed such that the licensee is bound to fulfil the licence conditions even where the licence is not in use at a particular point.[51] Where licensees in Norway and the UK first discover a straddling resource, the

46 United Nations, *Handbook on the Delimitation of Maritime Boundaries* (United Nations Division for Ocean Affairs and the Law of the Sea 2000) <https://www.un.org/depts/los/doalos_publications/publicationstexts/Handbook%20on%20the%20delimitation%20of%20maritime%20boundaries_Eng.pdf> 1, 38 accessed 26 June 2021.

47 Agreement Between the Government of the United Kingdom of Great Britain and Northern Ireland and the Government of the Kingdom of Norway Relating to the Delimitation of the Continental Shelf Between the Two Countries. Signed at London, On 10 March 1965. Article 4 (emphasis added).

48 Daniel Fjærtoft and others, 'Unitization of Petroleum Fields in the Barents Sea: Towards a Common Understanding?' (2018) 9 Arctic Rev Law Pol 72, 76 <https://pdfs.semanticscholar.org/6e45/8e6f167870ca793596c53624d5da91ad692b.pdf> accessed 20 June 2021.

49 Examples include: Agreement of 10 May 1976, as amended by the Agreement of 25 August 1998 and the Exchange of Notes dated 21 June 2001 relating to the exploitation of the Frigg Field Reservoir and the transmission of gas therefrom to the United Kingdom; and the use of the installations and pipelines for the exploitation and transmission of Hydrocarbons (also known as the Frigg agreement), Agreement of 16 October 1979, as amended by the Exchange of Notes dated 24 March 1995, relating to the exploitation of the Statfjord Field Reservoirs and the offtake of petroleum therefrom (also known as the Statfjord agreement), Agreement of 16 October 1979 and Supplementary Agreements of 22 October 1981 and 22 June 1983, as amended by the Exchange of Notes dated 9 August 1999, relating to the exploitation of the Murchison Field Reservoir and the offtake of petroleum therefrom (also known as the Murchison Field) <https://assets.publishing.service.gov.uk/government/uploads/system/uploads/attachment_data/file/243184/7206.pdf> accessed 7 July 2021.

50 Jacqueline Lang Weaver and others, 'International Unitization of Oil and Gas Fields: The Legal Framework of International Law, National Laws, and Private Contracts' (Association of International Petroleum Negotiators) (2007) 5(2) Oil Gas Energy Law (OGEL) 1, 115.

51 United Kingdom Petroleum Act 1998, Part 1, Section 2; North Sea Transition Authority, 'Licensing Consents' <https://www.nstauthority.co.uk/licensing-consents/overview/> accessed 28 August 2022.

first step is to notify the respective licensing authorities in their home country, here the Norwegian Petroleum Directorate (NPD) and the NSTA, in respective of the proportion of the field lying in Norway and the UKCS.[52]

Another important unitization treaty signed by the UK is the UK-Norway Framework Agreement Concerning Cross-Border Petroleum Co-operation 2005.[53] This treaty mandates the joint development (through unitization) of cross-border fields, stating:

> Where the two Governments, after consultation with their respective Licensees, agree that a Petroleum reservoir is a Trans-Boundary Reservoir which should be exploited, *it shall be exploited as a single unit in accordance with the terms of this Agreement, unless otherwise agreed by the two Governments.*[54]

Article 3.1 is under the heading 'Unitisation and Authorisations'. Curiously, the framework agreement does not include an article on redetermination or provide guidelines for redetermination. Rather, it stipulates that it is in the licensee agreement that matters pertaining to the redetermination of the transboundary reservoir are to be addressed.[55] This approach is beneficial as it mitigates the bureaucratic delays that sometimes accompanies government-led redetermination. A notable example being the complex and lengthy Statfjord redetermination between the former UK Department of Trade and Industries[56] and the Norwegian Ministry of Petroleum and Energy.[57]

52 Norwegian Petroleum Directorate and Oil and Gas Authority, 'UK – Norway. Trans-boundary Oil & Gas Fields: Guidelines for Development of Trans-boundary Oil and Gas Fields' <https://www.npd.no/globalassets/1-npd/regelverk/forskrifter/en/transboundary-fields-1016.pdf>1 accessed 20 August 2022.

53 Framework Agreement between the Government of the United Kingdom of Great Britain and Northern Ireland and the Government of the Kingdom of Norway concerning Cross-Boundary Petroleum Co-operation. Oslo, 4 April 2005. The Agreement entered into force on 10 July 2007. <https://www.gov.uk/government/publications/framework-agreement-between-the-uk-and-norway-concerning-cross-boundary-petroleum-co-operation> accessed 7 July 2021.

54 Framework Agreement between the Government of the United Kingdom of Great Britain and Northern Ireland and the Government of the Kingdom of Norway concerning Cross-Boundary Petroleum Co-operation. Oslo, 4 April 2005. The Agreement entered into force on 10 July 2007. <https://www.gov.uk/government/publications/framework-agreement-between-the-uk-and-norway-concerning-cross-boundary-petroleum-co-operation> accessed 7 July 2021. Article 3.1 (emphasis added).

55 Framework Agreement between the Government of the United Kingdom of Great Britain and Northern Ireland and the Government of the Kingdom of Norway concerning Cross-Boundary Petroleum Co-operation. Oslo, 4 April 2005. The Agreement entered into force on 10 July 2007. <https://www.gov.uk/government/publications/framework-agreement-between-the-uk-and-norway-concerning-cross-boundary-petroleum-co-operation> accessed 7 July 2021. Article 3.3(2)(a).

56 This department was dissolved in 2007. It was replaced by the Department for Innovation, Universities and Skills and Department for Business, Enterprise and Regulatory Reform, on 28 June 2007 <https://www.gov.uk/government/organisations/department-of-trade-and-industry> accessed 28 August 2022.

57 For a discussion, see <https://statfjord.industriminne.no/en/2019/11/11/the-final-redetermination-1995-98/> accessed 7 July 2021. See also Daniel Fjærtoft and others, 'Unitization of Petroleum Fields in the Barents Sea: Towards a Common Understanding?' (2018) 9 Arctic Rev Law Pol 72, 79–81

Having considered the framework for intra-country and cross-border unitization, the next section discusses the UUOA.

10.6 The Unitization and Unit Operating Agreement in the UK

In the UK, as with other countries (save for the United States and Canada), the details of the unitization are typically recorded in a single UUOA.[58] To a large extent, the terms of the UUOA or unitization agreement are determined by the contracting parties (block participants), subject to the obligations of the licence with the host government, or host governments in a cross-border unitization.

The UK does not have a model UUOA, neither does it use the internationally renowned AIPN Model UUOA 2006 or 2020.[59] It is useful to note that the AIPN was renamed the Association of International Energy Negotiators (AIEN) at its September 2022 international energy summit.[60] In an email by this author to the formerly named Oil and Gas UK, which is the trade association who own and update the model contracts, dated 26 July 2021, a clarification was sought on the absence of a UUOA Model Clause and why the AIPN[61] Model is not utilized. The OGUK's[62] response, dated 26 July 2021, stated that '[A] model UUOA is not part of our current suite and there are no plans to introduce it. As our model contracts are optional and we are not party to them we would not be aware why the UK does not use alternative AIPN models'. The OGUK was renamed Offshore Energies UK (OEUK) in January 2022.[63]

<https://pdfs.semanticscholar.org/6e45/8e6f167870ca793596c53624d5da91ad692b.pdf> accessed 20 June 2021.

58 Jacqueline Lang Weaver and others, 'International Unitization of Oil and Gas Fields: The Legal Framework of International Law, National Laws, and Private Contracts' (Association of International Petroleum Negotiators) (2007) 5(2) Oil Gas Energy Law (OGEL) 1, 48. Weaver cites that in the USA and Canada, two documents are used to record the unitization: the unit agreement, and the unit operating agreement.

59 The AIEN Model UUOA is not utilised in the USA or Norway, either. Nina Howell and Lauren Kelsall, 'Unitization: Comments on 2020 AIPN Model International Unitization and Unit Operating Agreement' (6 March 2020) <https://www.energylegalblog.com/blog/2020/03/06/unitization-comments-2020-AIEN-model-international-unitization-and-unit-operating> accessed 10 June 2021.

60 AIEN, 'AIEN Approves 2023 Model International Joint Operating Agreement' <https://www.aien.org/aipn_news/aien-approves-2023-model-international-joint-operating-agreement/> accessed 28 December 2023.

61 The reference is to AIPN because it was so named at the date (26 July 2021) of the email exchange with the OGUK.

62 The reference here is to OGUK because it was so named at the date (26 July 2021) of the email exchange. The rebranding to OEUK took place in January 2022.

63 Shell, 'Offshore Energies UK (OEUK, formerly OGUK)' <https://reports.shell.com/climate-and-energy-transition-lobbying-report/2022/assessments/offshore-energies-uk-oeuk-formerly-oguk.html#:~:text=We%20welcome%20the%202022%20rebranding,routine%20flaring%20sooner%20than%202030.>; Energy Voice, 'Exclusive: North Sea Trade Body OGUK Drops 'Oil and Gas' from Name in New Energies Rebrand' (30 January 2022) <https://www.energyvoice.com/renewables-energy-transition/383604/oguk-rebrand-offshore-energies-uk-north-sea/> accessed 28 December 2023.

One explanation for the absence of a model UK UUOA is possibly that the UK oil and gas industry would appear to favour the OEUK standard joint operating agreement (JOA), and as a result would use a UUOA based on that model rather than the AIEN UUOA.

In negotiating the UUOA, the key clauses for licensees (and host governments if a cross-border unitization) would cover the common clauses in a JOA, from the appointment of the operator, voting, the default clause and so on. It would then cover specific clauses related to unitization such as the unit area, the method for calculating tract interest, dispute resolution, and redetermination.[64] Two key areas that give rise to disputes in UUOAs are tract calculation and redetermination. Although these complexities are not unique to the UK, there are distinctive features which make redetermination in particular a prominent issue in the UK.

In national and cross-border unitization, the various licensees have to determine the liabilities and benefits of each unit. At the commencement of unitized operations, the parties would typically only have a limited understanding of the characteristics of the reservoir and the percentage of production flowing from the various contract areas.[65] Although technological advancements have made this process a little less complicated, there remains a degree of uncertainty in the early stage of operations. To mitigate this, it is common for parties to include a redetermination clause in the unitization agreement, or as the case is in the UK, the UUOA. The redetermination process seeks to adjust the tract interests to better reflect the percentage of production from individual tracts into the common reservoir. Consequently, redetermination remains an important issue in unitization as anticipated profits and costs can be significantly (adversely or beneficially) affected by the adjustment of tract interest.

Typically, parties seek to use redetermination to increase their tract interest as more geological information is obtained on the reservoir. In the UKCS, there has been at least one instance where the redetermination process has been used by some licensees to reduce their unit interest in the face of increased exploration costs.[66] Another reason a party may seek a lower tract interest is linked to a prolonged period of low oil prices which may trigger early cessation of production and move decommissioning forward. This could motivate participants in one tract to seek a lower tract participation through redetermination so as to reduce their decommissioning liability. Whether or not this will be successful is another matter.

64 For a discussion on some of these clauses, see Jacqueline Lang Weaver and others, 'International Unitization of Oil and Gas Fields: The Legal Framework of International Law, National Laws, and Private Contracts' (Association of International Petroleum Negotiators) (2007) 5(2) Oil Gas Energy Law (OGEL) 1, 50–73.

65 This is not to suggest that the apportioning of production will always be based on that which flows from the unit area.

66 A prominent example is The Balmoral Field, Block 16/21, UK North Sea. Jim Ross, 'Industry Practice in Equity Redeterminations' (2004) 2 Transnatl Dispute Manag <https://www.transnational-dispute-management.com/article.asp?key=74> accessed 11 July 2021.

This chapter earlier noted that the NSTA can require that licensees enter into a UUOA prior to submitting a FDP,[67] as well as the fact that the NSTA's recommendation is for voluntary unitization early on.[68] The preference for early unitizations is one of the reasons where redeterminations in the UK are typically periodic, as it is the opportunity for parties to readjust tract participation to recover losses or increase profits.

However, where there is strong seismic and well data available from the outset, this may discourage redetermination, particularly in view of the significant costs and complexities. In some cases, the tract interest may be fixed for the life of the UUOA or redetermination cannot be requested by a single group, and must be agreed to by all groups. An example of the latter is the UUOA for the Peik Field (this field straddles the UK and Norway) where the adjustment of tract participation is only subject to unanimity by all parties.[69] Ultimately, the determination of whether to include a redetermination clause or not is not country specific. Rather, it is project specific, based on the data available, the financial considerations of the licensees and any peculiarities of the shared reservoir.

Given the complexities and significant costs of redetermination, the licensees would have strict criteria and guidelines for a redetermination.[70] This would cover the trigger, timing, frequency, effect and associated issues. Also, the UUOA would stipulate whether the redetermination is to have a retrospective effect (it is usually retrospective in the UK),[71] such that the unit that receives an increased production share is to be repaid certain volumes of gas/oil from the other units. That increased share would comprise the volumes that the unit newly assigned a larger tract interest had 'underlifted' from previous production. As expected, this brings with it other complications, related to the volume of repayment contractually allowed per lifting cycle, long-term sale obligations of the parties who are repaying agreed volumes and so on. However, the most significant issues pertain to tax where redetermination applies retrospectively. In the case of petroleum revenue tax, parties must consider whether they are legally required to re-declare their net gains for the adjusted periods.

67 Oil & Gas Authority, 'Requirements for the Planning of and Consent to UKCS Field Developments' (October 2018, updated October 2019) 1, 11, 19 <https://www.nstauthority.co.uk/media/6099/fdp_guidance_requirements-document-oct_update-2019v2.pdf> accessed 28 August 2022.

68 Oil and Gas Authority, 'Guidance Notes for Onshore Field Development Plans, Fdp Addendums and Cessation of Production' (August 2016) <https://assets.publishing.service.gov.uk/government/uploads/system/uploads/attachment_data/file/549118/OnshoreFDPGuidanceAug2016.pdf> accessed 9 May 2021; Oil & Gas Authority, 'Requirements for the Planning of and Consent to UKCS Field Developments' (October 2018, updated October 2019) 1, 11, 19 <https://www.nstauthority.co.uk/media/6099/fdp_guidance_requirements-document-oct_update-2019v2.pdf> accessed 28 August 2022.

69 Philip Weems and Nina Howell, 'Oil and Gas Unitization: Specific Considerations for Cross-Border Unitization' (King & Spalding, June 2016) <https://www.kslaw.com/blog-posts/oil-gas-unitization-specific-considerations-cross-border-unitization> accessed 22 May 2021.

70 In a cross-border unitization, each country would be concerned/invested in the guidelines surrounding unitization since this may affect expected profits for all sides.

71 Canadian Institute of Resources Law, 'A Note on Three UK Oil and Gas Unitization Cases' 78 Can Inst Res Law (Newsletter Spring 2002) 13, 14 <https://cirl.ca/sites/default/files/Resources/Resources78.pdf> accessed 14 June 2021.

Similarly, consideration must be given to whether the tax authorities will qualify the increased tract participation as a transfer of an interest in the field from one party to another. The combination of these factors may discourage retrospective rebalancing.

The UUOA would also indicate the mode and scale of repayment, be it in cash or in kind, although the latter is more common as it avoids disputes on the price payable. Disputes on the formula/data to be used for recalculating tract interest, as well as other issues surrounding the unitization, are typically resolved through the intervention of a third-party expert, whose decision is final.

10.7 Conclusion

Overall, the legal framework relating to in-country unitization in the UK can be described as a mixture of soft and strict measures. The NSTA's guidance and possibly preference is for licensees to voluntarily unitize. Yet, there are enough 'teeth' to the framework to ensure unitization is carried out where it is in the national interest. Where licensees fail to unitize voluntarily, the NSTA has two avenues for forcing unitization. The first is the requirement for the UUOA before consent is granted to the FDP, where the NSTA prescribes that licensees unitize.[72] The second avenue is the stricter position, whereby the NSTA can impose in-country unitization by relying on its powers in the model clauses.[73]

The UK has an extensive history with cross-border unitizations, as evidenced by the abundance of available transboundary agreements.[74] Therefore, with any discovery of straddling resources – no matter the complications – licensees can rely on the expertise and guidance of the NSTA to effect a workable development agreement.

A key feature in UK unitizations is the phase at which UUOAs are entered into. One cannot but note the emphasis on time in UK unitizations. There are at least two examples. Firstly, for FPDs involving a shared reservoir, the NSTA encourages licensees to voluntarily unitize 'early'.[75] Secondly, where a field has transboundary

72 Oil & Gas Authority, 'Requirements for the Planning of and Consent to UKCS Field Developments' (October 2018, updated October 2019) 1, 11, 19 <https://www.nstauthority.co.uk/media/6099/fdp_guidance_requirements-document-oct_update-2019v2.pdf> accessed 28 August 2022.

73 The Petroleum (Production) (Seaward Areas) Regulations 1988, Model Clauses for Production Licences in Seaward Areas, Schedule 4, Clause 28.1 <https://www.legislation.gov.uk/uksi/1988/1213/schedule/4/made>; The Petroleum (Production) (Landward Areas) Regulations 1995, Model Clauses for Petroleum Exploration and Development Licences in Landward Areas, Schedule 3, Clause 25.1 <https://www.legislation.gov.uk/uksi/1995/1436/schedule/3/made> accessed 4 July 2021.

74 Thirty-one of such agreements are listed on the NSTA's website. North Sea Transition Authority, 'Transboundary Fields' <https://www.nstauthority.co.uk/exploration-production/development/transboundary-fields/> accessed 28 August 2022. This chapter earlier cited that in an email response dated 26 July 2021, the then OGA noted to this author that there are two further treaties: 1976 Frigg Field Unitisation Treaty and 1973 Ekofisk Agreement. The total number of transboundary treaties is therefore 33.

75 Oil and Gas Authority, 'Guidance Notes for Onshore Field Development Plans, Fdp Addendums and Cessation of Production' (August 2016) <https://assets.publishing.service.gov.uk/government/uploads/system/uploads/attachment_data/file/549118/OnshoreFDPGuidanceAug2016.pdf> accessed 9 May 2021; Oil & Gas Authority, 'Requirements for the Planning of and Consent to

implications, the recommendation is for licensees to seek 'early' guidance from the NSTA.[76] A consideration for the future may be to examine whether early action in relation to unitization affects the process, complexity and outcome, for in-country and cross-border unitization.

Finally, the lack of a model UUOA in the UK should not be ignored. On the one hand, the non-use of the AIEN Model may be justified by the notion that the UK favours the OEUK standard JOA and as a result would use a UUOA based on that model, rather than the AIEN UUOA. On the other hand, there is an argument that an international model such as the AIEN UUOA can be amended to fit the specific needs of each country and its unitizations. Nevertheless, the use of the AIEN Model is not compulsory in any country, so the UK is free to choose whether or not to use the AIEN Model. However, it may be useful to consider whether there are justifications for the adoption of a UK model UUOA now or in the near future.

Key Findings of This Chapter

1. The legal and regulatory framework for unitization in the UK can be described as relatively robust. The NSTA has powers under the model clauses of the licence to mandate in-country unitization where it is in the national interest.
2. The UK through the NSTA employs a combination of soft and more stringent measures in the consent phase of a field development to direct or at least encourage licensees to unitize operations where it will optimize field development.
3. The UK has an emphasis on the timing of unitization, with the NSTA making clear its preference for early unitization. It is worthy of future consideration whether early action in relation to unitization affects the process, complexity and outcome, for in-country and cross-border unitization.
4. The UK utilizes the UUOA, but there is no model template. This does not appear to have adverse implications as UUOAs can be modelled on the UK Model JOA. Nevertheless, given the unique features of unitization, there is value to a consideration of whether the UK ought to adopt a model UUOA.

Bibliography

Treaties

1. Agreement Between The Government Of The United Kingdom Of Great Britain And Northern Ireland And The Government Of The Kingdom Of Norway Relating To The Delimitation Of The Continental Shelf Between The Two Countries. London, 10 March 1965

UKCS Field Developments' (October 2018, updated October 2019) 1, 11, 19 <https://www.nstauthority.co.uk/media/6099/fdp_guidance_requirements-document-oct_update-2019v2.pdf> accessed 28 August 2022.

76 North Sea Transition Authority, 'Transboundary Fields' <https://www.nstauthority.co.uk/exploration-production/development/transboundary-fields/> accessed 28 August 2022.

2. Agreement of 10 May 1976, as amended by the Agreement of 25 August 1998 and the Exchange of Notes dated 21 June 2001 relating to the exploitation of the Frigg Field Reservoir and the transmission of gas therefrom to the United Kingdom; and the use of the installations and pipelines for the exploitation and transmission of Hydrocarbons (also known as the Frigg agreement)
3. Agreement of 16 October 1979, as amended by the Exchange of Notes dated 24 March 1995, relating to the exploitation of the Statfjord Field Reservoirs and the offtake of petroleum therefrom (also known as the Statfjord agreement)
4. Agreement of 16 October 1979 and Supplementary Agreements of 22 October 1981 and 22 June 1983, as amended by the Exchange of Notes dated 9 August 1999, relating to the exploitation of the Murchison Field Reservoir and the offtake of petroleum therefrom (also known as the Murchison Field)
5. Agreement between the United Kingdom of Great Britain and Northern Ireland and the Kingdom of the Netherlands relating to the Exploitation of the ORCA Field 2013
6. Framework Agreement between the Government of the United Kingdom of Great Britain and Northern Ireland and the Government of the Kingdom of Norway concerning Cross-Boundary Petroleum Co-operation. Oslo, 04 April 2005

Legislation

1. The United Kingdom Petroleum Act 1998

Regulations

1. The Petroleum (Production) (Seaward Areas) Regulations 1988
2. The Petroleum (Production) (Landward Areas) Regulations 1995

Books

P Roberts, *Joint Operating Agreements: A Practical Guide* (3rd edn, Globe Business Publishing 2015).

E E Smith and others, *Materials on International Petroleum Transactions* (Rocky Mountain Mineral Law Foundation 2010).

United Nations, *Handbook on the Delimitation of Maritime Boundaries* (United Nations Division for Ocean Affairs and the Law of the Sea 2000) <https://www.un.org/depts/los/doalos_publications/publicationstexts/Handbook%20on%20the%20delimitation%20of%20maritime%20boundaries_Eng.pdf>

Book chapters

D Beggs and J Bremen, 'Unitisation and Unitisation Agreements' in Geoffrey Picton-Turbervill (ed), *Oil and Gas: A Practical Handbook* (Globe Law and Business 2009).

S Rush, 'Unitisation and Redetermination' in *Oil & Gas Handbook* (Sweet & Maxwell 2016) <https://www.seanrush.co.nz/wp-content/uploads/Chapter-4-Unitisation-and-Redetermination.pdf>

Journal

A E Bastida and others, 'Cross-Border Unitization and Joint Development Agreements: An International Law Perspective' (2007) 29 Houston J Int L 355–422.

Online Journals

Alex Procyk, 'Marigold Field to Undergo Joint Development' *Oil & Gas Journal* (19 September 2023) <https://www.ogj.com/exploration-development/article/14299160/marigold-field-to-undergo-joint-development> accessed 29 December 2023.

Canadian Institute of Resources Law, 'A Note on Three UK Oil and Gas Unitization Cases' (2002) 78 Can Inst Res Law (Newsletter Spring 2002) 13–16 <https://cirl.ca/sites/default/files/Resources/Resources78.pdf> accessed 14 June 2021.

R Chooramun, 'Unitisation – The Oil and Gas Industry's Solution to One of Geology's Many Conundrums' Notes From the Field – An English Law Perspective on the Oil & Gas Market (Andrew Skurth, August 2014) <https://www.andrewskurth.com/insights-1133.html> accessed 1 May 2021.

D Fjærtoft and others, 'Unitization of Petroleum Fields in the Barents Sea: Towards a Common Understanding?' (2018) 9 Arct Rev Law Polit 72–96. <https://pdfs.semanticscholar.org/6e45/8e6f167870ca793596c53624d5da91ad692b.pdf> accessed 20 June 2021.

N Howell and L Kelsall, 'Unitization: Comments on 2020 AIPN Model International Unitization and Unit Operating Agreement' (6 March 2020) <https://www.energylegalblog.com/blog/2020/03/06/unitization-comments-2020-aipn-model-international-unitization-and-unit-operating> accessed 10 June 2021.

J Ross, 'Industry Practice in Equity Redeterminations' (2004) 2 Trans Dispute Manag <https://www.transnational-dispute-management.com/article.asp?key=74> accessed 11 July 2021.

S Wade, 'Disputes Over Rights to Sub-sea Resources Implications for the Oil and Gas Industry' *Lexology: Stephenson Harwood* (12 November 2012) <https://www.lexology.com/library/detail.aspx?g=78f1856c-7040–4e1d-942e-f20f67ef2c7d> accessed 1 May 2021.

J L Weaver and others, 'International Unitization of Oil and Gas Fields: The Legal Framework of International Law, National Laws, and Private Contracts' (Association of International Petroleum Negotiators) (2007) 5(2) Oil Gas Energ Law 1–213 <https://www.ogel.org/article.asp?key=2405> accessed 20 June 2021.

P Weems and N Howell, 'Oil and Gas Unitization: Specific Considerations for Cross-Border Unitization' *King & Spalding* (June 2016) <https://www.kslaw.com/blog-posts/oil-gas-unitization-specific-considerations-cross-border-unitization> accessed 22 May 2021.

Websites

AIEN, 'AIEN Approves 2023 Model International Joint Operating Agreement' <https://www.aien.org/aipn_news/aien-approves-2023-model-international-joint-operating-agreement/> accessed 28 December 2023.

Department for Business, Energy & Industrial Strategy, 'North Sea Transition Deal: One Year On' (March 2022) <https://assets.publishing.service.gov.uk/government/uploads/system/uploads/attachment_data/file/1061986/north-sea-transition-deal-one-year-on.pdf> accessed 28 August 2022.

Department for Innovation, Universities and Skills and Department for Business, Enterprise and Regulatory Reform <https://www.gov.uk/government/organisations/department-of-trade-and-industry> accessed 28 August 2022.

Department of Energy and Climate Change, 'Guidance on the Content of Offshore Oil and Gas Field Development Plans' <https://assets.publishing.service.gov.uk/government/

uploads/system/uploads/attachment_data/file/265842/FDP_guidance_notes_November_2013_web.pdf> accessed 3 May 2021.

Energy Voice, 'Exclusive: North Sea Trade Body OGUK Drops 'Oil and Gas' from Name in New Energies Rebrand' (30 January 2022) <https://www.energyvoice.com/renewables-energy-transition/383604/oguk-rebrand-offshore-energies-uk-north-sea/>

GOV.UK, 'Department of Trade and Industry' <https://www.gov.uk/government/organisations/department-of-trade-and-industry> accessed 13 June 2021.

Industrial Heritage Statfjord <https://statfjord.industriminne.no/en/2019/11/11/the-final-redetermination-1995-98/> accessed 7 July 2021.

North Sea Transition Authority <https://www.nstauthority.co.uk/about-us/> accessed 28 August 2022.

North Sea Transition Authority <https://www.nstauthority.co.uk/exploration-production/development/field-determinations> accessed 28 August 2022.

North Sea Transition Authority, 'Field Determination' <https://www.nstauthority.co.uk/regulatory-information/exploration-and-production/development/field-determinations/> accessed 28 December 2023.

North Sea Transition Authority, 'Legislative Content' <https://www.nstauthority.co.uk/regulatory-framework/legislative-context/> accessed 28 August 2022.

North Sea Transition Authority, 'Licensing Consents' <https://www.nstauthority.co.uk/licensing-consents/overview/> accessed 28 August 2022.

North Sea Transition Authority, 'Regulatory Framework' <https://www.nstauthority.co.uk/regulatory-framework/> accessed 28 August 2022.

North Sea Transition Authority, 'Transboundary Fields' <https://www.nstauthority.co.uk/exploration-production/development/transboundary-fields/> accessed 29 December 2023.

Norwegian Petroleum Directorate and Oil and Gas Authority, 'UK – Norway. Transboundary Oil & Gas Fields: Guidelines for Development of Trans-boundary Oil and Gas Fields' <https://www.npd.no/globalassets/1-npd/regelverk/forskrifter/en/transboundary-fields-1016.pdf>1 accessed 20 August 2022.

Offshore, 'Unitization Deal Clears Path for North Sea Marigold, Sunflower Developments' (20 September 2023) <https://www.offshore-mag.com/field-development/article/14299208/unitization-deal-clears-path-for-north-sea-marigold-sunflower-developments> accessed 29 December 2023.

Oil & Gas Authority, 'Guidance Notes for Onshore Field Development Plans, Fdp Addendums and Cessation of Production' (August 2016) <https://assets.publishing.service.gov.uk/government/uploads/system/uploads/attachment_data/file/549118/OnshoreFDPGuidanceAug2016.pdf> accessed 9 May 2021.

Shell, 'Offshore Energies UK (OEUK, Formerly OGUK)' <https://reports.shell.com/climate-and-energy-transition-lobbying-report/2022/assessments/offshore-energies-uk-oeuk-formerly-oguk.html#:~:text=We%20welcome%20the%202022%20rebranding,routine%20flaring%20sooner%20than%202030>

Oil & Gas Authority, 'Requirements for the Planning of and Consent to UKCS Field Developments' (October 2018, updated October 2019) <https://www.nstauthority.co.uk/media/6099/fdp_guidance_requirements-document-oct_update-2019v2.pdf> accessed 28 August 2022.

Oil & Gas Authority, 'The Maximising Economic Recovery Strategy for the UK' <https://www.nstauthority.co.uk/media/1022/mer_uk_strategy.pdf> accessed 28 August 2022.

Oil & Gas Authority, 'The OGA Strategy' <https://www.ogauthority.co.uk/regulatory-framework/the-oga-strategy/> accessed 2 June 2021.

Oil & Gas Authority, 'The OGA Strategy' <https://www.nstauthority.co.uk/media/7105/the-oga-strategy.pdf> accessed 28 August 2022.

11 United States of America

Keith B. Hall

In the United States, the terms *pooling* and *unitization* are often used interchangeably.[1] But oil and gas scholars, and many of the more sophisticated oil and gas practitioners, use the two terms to refer to separate concepts.[2]

They use *pooling* to refer to a process that aggregates separately owned mineral interests to respond to the facts that (1) there is "private ownership of minerals" in the United States, meaning that the right to explore for and produce minerals typically belongs to the landowner; (2) private ownership of minerals often results in multiple tracts of land, each with separate mineral ownership, within an area that can be efficiently drained by a single well; and (3) the law governing "drainage" of oil and gas gives the owner of each tract an incentive to drill his own well (or perhaps multiple wells), giving rise to the possibility that parties will drill numerous wells in an area that could be drained by a single well.[3]

On the other hand, they use *unitization* to refer to schemes for coordinating production over a large area, such as the entirety of an oil and gas field or a major portion of it, in order to gain the efficiencies that can be achieved by a coordinated plan of development.

This chapter will first discuss pooling and then unitization. In the United States, pooling and unitization, like most oil and gas law, are governed by state law, rather than federal law. However, although some differences exist from one state to another, there also is significant similarity in the pooling and unitization statutes in the states that have oil and gas activity.

1 Bruce M Kramer and Patrick H Martin, *The Law of Pooling and Unitization* § 1.02; Patrick H. Martin and Bruce M Kramer, *Williams & Meyers Oil and Gas Law* § 901; Owen L Anderson and others, *Hemingway Oil and Gas Law and Taxation* § 7.13; Keith B Hall and Hannah J Wiseman, *Hydraulic Fracturing: A Guide to Environmental and Real Property Issues* (American Bar Ass'n 2017) 263.

2 *See, e.g.*, Bruce M Kramer and Patrick H Martin, *The Law of Pooling and Unitization* § 1.02.

3 Keith B Hall and Hannah J Wiseman, *Hydraulic Fracturing: A Guide to Environmental and Real Property Issues* (American Bar Ass'n 2017) 16, 17, 19, 20.

DOI: 10.4324/9781003491293-13

11.1 Pooling

"Pooling" is a term used to describe the aggregation of small tracts of land that individually would not be large enough to receive a drilling permit under conservation rules that require a minimum distance or "spacing" between wells, but which collectively have enough area to justify the granting of a permit to drill under the applicable spacing rules.[4] Pooling can be done by agreement or by order of a state's oil and gas regulator.

11.1.1 The Rule of Capture and Problems Arising From It

In the United States, the owner of a tract of land typically has the exclusive right to use the surface and subsurface of the land to explore for and produce minerals.[5] Further, the landowner generally will become owner of any minerals extracted from beneath the land. This follows from the *ad coelum* doctrine,[6] which provides that the owner of land owns not just the surface of the land, but also the airspace above it and the subsurface below it.[7]

This doctrine can be easy to apply with respect to solid minerals, but a more complex issue arises for substances that exist in a fluid state – either liquid or gas – such as oil and natural gas. Because fluids will move in the subsurface in response to differences in pressure, disputes can arise between neighbors. For example, suppose that the owner of a tract called Blackacre drills a well on his land, near the border with Whiteacre, a tract owned by his neighbor. The owner of Blackacre begins producing oil at a substantial rate, and the owner of Whiteacre concludes that much of the oil produced from the well located on Blackacre likely is being drained from beneath Whiteacre. Is the owner of Blackacre entitled to operate the well and keep all the proceeds, or is the owner of Whiteacre entitled to some type of relief – perhaps either an injunction to prohibit the owner of Blackacre from operating the well or a judgment requiring the owner of Blackacre to share the proceeds from such production?

4 Bruce M Kramer and Patrick H Martin, *The Law of Pooling and Unitization* § 6.01.

5 *Atlantic Richfield Co. v. Tomlinson*, 859 P.2d 1088, 1094 (Okla. 1993); *California Minerals v. County of Kern*, 62 Cal. Rptr. 3d 1, 6 (Cal. Ct. App. 2007); La. Rev. Stat. 31:6. An exception to the general rule is that, in most states, ownership of mineral rights can be severed from the ownership of land. This can occur if a landowner sells the right to explore for and produce minerals from the land, while otherwise retaining ownership of the land, or if the landowner sells the land, while retaining the right to explore for and produce minerals. Doing either of these things creates separate estates – a mineral estate and a surface estate. Patrick H Martin and Bruce M Kramer, *Williams & Meyers Oil and Gas Law* § 301; *Teel v. Chesapeake Appalachia, LLC*, 906 F. Supp. 2d 519, 522 (N.D. W.Va. 2012).

6 The doctrine's name comes from the Latin phrase *cujus est solum ejus est usque ad coelum et ad inferos*, which has been translated as "for whoever owns the soil, it is theirs up to Heaven and down to Hell." *Alyce Gaines Johnson Special Trust v. El Paso E & P Co., L.P.*, 773 F.Supp.2d 640, 645 (W.D. La. 2011). The doctrine has been stated by Lord Coke and by William Blackstone, and is repeated in Kent's Commentaries. *See* 1 Coke, *Institutes* (19th ed. 1832) ch. 1, § 1(4a); 2 Blackstone, *Commentaries* (Lewis ed. 1902) 18; 3 Kent, *Commentaries* (Gould ed. 1896) 621.

7 *Thrasher v. City of Atlanta*, 173 S.E. 817, 825 (Ga. 1934).

Courts began facing this issue in the late 1800s.[8] Across the United States, courts uniformly resolved such disputes by adopting what became known as the *rule of capture*.[9] The rule of capture provides that the owner of land acquires title to all of the oil and gas produced from a well drilled on his land, even if the well causes drainage of oil and gas from beneath a neighbor's land, and that the neighbor is not entitled to compensation for such drainage.[10] Courts justified the rule of capture of three grounds: (1) it was impossible to determine how much oil or gas drained from beneath a neighbor's land; (2) it would interfere with private property rights and development for a court to prohibit a landowner from drilling a well where he chose on his land; and (3) the neighbor had a self-help remedy – he could drill his own "offset wells" across the property boundary from the neighbor's wells, to capture oil or natural gas before it migrates across the property line.[11]

The rule of capture might have been the most practical rule that courts could develop on their own, but it also created certain problems. It created incentives for neighboring landowners to produce oil and gas as quickly as they could, before the neighbor did so. This often gave individuals an incentive to drill more wells than were needed to efficiently drain an area.[12] Some historic photographs show drilling derricks spaced so close together that the bases of the derricks are nearly touching one another. Some cases refer to operators drilling wells only about 30 feet from a property line and of operators drilling several wells, each only a few hundred feet apart, in a line along the boundary between two properties. This resulted in economic waste from excessive spending on drilling.

Further, too rapid a rate of production can result in inefficient use of the reservoir energy that can help transport oil up to the surface.[13] The inefficient use of such energy could result in less oil being produced from a field than could be produced if the reservoir energy was more efficiently used. Thus, more oil might be left in the ground, a form of physical waste. Finally, although a landowner always has the

8 *Kelly v. Ohio*, 49 N.E. 399 (Ohio 1897); *Barnard v. Monongahela Natural Gas Co.*, 65 A. 801 (Pa. 1907).

9 *See, e.g.*, Patrick H Martin and Bruce M Kramer, *Williams & Meyers Oil and Gas Law* § 204.4; Terence Daintith, *Finders Keepers? How the Law of Capture Shaped the World Oil Industry* 7 (RFF Press 2010).

10 Several sources provide excellent, comprehensive treatment of the Rule of Capture. *See, e.g.*, Bruce M Kramer and Owen L Anderson, 'The Rule of Capture – An Oil and Gas Perspective' 35 (2005) Envtl. L 899; Terence Daintith, *Finders Keepers? How the Law of Capture Shaped the World Oil Industry* (RFF Press 2010). For an interesting discussion of a suggested change from a traditional rule of capture analysis, see David E Pierce, 'Carol Rose Comes to the Oil Patch: Modern Property Analysis Applied to Modern Reservoir Problems' (2011) 19 Penn St Envtl L Rev 241.

11 *Kelly v. Ohio*, 49 N.E. 399 (Ohio 1897); *Barnard v. Monongahela Natural Gas Co.*, 65 A. 801 (Pa. 1907).

12 *Gadeco, LLC v. Industrial Comm'n of State*, 812 N.W.2d 405, 407 (N.D. 2012); *Nunez v. Wainoco Oil & Gas Co.*, 488 So. 2d 955, 960 (La. 1986) (rule of capture encouraged indiscriminate drilling).

13 *Nunez v. Wainoco Oil & Gas Co.*, 488 So. 2d 955, 960 (La. 1986) (referring to possible waste of reservoir energy and diminished ultimate recovery).

self-help remedy of drilling his own well, some people might question whether the rule of capture is fair.[14]

11.1.2 Voluntary Pooling

To avoid some of the problems associated with the rule of capture, the persons having operating rights might choose to operate their adjacent tracts in a coordinated manner. For example, suppose that a 40-acre area has been subdivided into four separately owned tracts of ten acres each. Further, suppose that oil can be recovered from a low-pressure formation that lies beneath the four tracts, and that a single well can efficiently drain 40 acres. The owners of the four tracts could each drill their own well. However, they might be better off if they agreed to combine their resources and drill a single well near the middle of the 40 acres, with the four owners sharing equally in expenses and revenue. That way, they spend substantially less on drilling, yet still manage to efficiently drain the oil beneath the 40 acres. Such an agreement would be an example of voluntary pooling.

Sometimes, the landowners or several mineral interest owners who have operating rights in nearby tracts enter voluntary pooling agreements. However, many voluntary pooling agreements are entered by oil and gas leaseholders. It is common for oil and gas leases to delegate to the leaseholder the authority to dedicate the leased tract to a voluntary pooling agreement. This can make it easier to reach a voluntary pooling agreement. There may be more than one oil and gas company holding leases in an area, but most tracts may be under lease, and there typically will be fewer leaseholders than tracts because leaseholders often hold leases over numerous tracts. Thus, assuming the oil and gas leases have clauses delegating pooling authority to the leaseholder, there will be fewer parties who need to reach agreement than if each landowner or severed mineral interest owner had to agree to pooling. Indeed, it is more common for voluntary units to be created by one or more oil and gas leaseholders than by multiple persons holding mineral interests as landowners or mineral estate owners.

11.1.3 State Conservation Statutes and Single Well Pooling

Starting in the early 1900s, states and the federal government began taking steps to avoid wasteful use of a wide variety of natural resources, including oil and gas. The enactment of conservation statutes and regulations directed toward avoiding waste of oil and natural gas resources started to become common by the 1930s and 1940s.[15] Common types of regulation included creation of allowables (maximum allowable rates of production from wells) and "spacing" rules that placed limitations

14 *Cf. Nunez*, 488 So. 2d at 960 (noting that one goal of conservation regulation can be "to insure a fair and reasonable participation, by the surface owners in the common pool within the producing area").

15 There are multiple articles discussing the history of conservation statutes. One is Leslie Moses, 'The Constitutional, Legislative and Judicial Growth of Oil and Gas Conservation Statutes' (1941) 13 Miss LJ 353.

on well density. The spacing rules included minimum distances between a well and the nearest property line, minimum distances between wells, and in some cases, a maximum number of wells in a specified area (e.g., no more than one well for a given number of acres).

But the spacing rules could create a problem. Suppose, for example, that a spacing rule prohibited drilling a well any closer than 330 feet from the nearest property line. Strict enforcement of such a rule would prohibit drilling altogether on small tracts. That could be unfair to the owner of small tracts. Further, given that the right to explore for and develop minerals is a property right, strict enforcement of such spacing rules could result in a taking of private property that might be unconstitutional in the absence of some compensation.[16] One response to this problem is pooling. In pooling, two or more separately owned tracts are "combined" for the purposes of creating an area large enough to obtain a well permit under applicable spacing regulations.[17]

11.1.3.1 Drilling and Spacing Units

Numerous states have statutes that authorize conservation agencies to issue orders creating drilling or spacing units – areas of land where the only well or wells allowed will be those authorized by the agency.[18] The statutes typically provide that the agency may create drilling or spacing units that will apply with respect to a common source of supply,[19] after notice and a hearing,[20] if the agency determines that such a unit is necessary to prevent waste,[21] avoid the drilling of unnecessary wells,[22] and protect correlative rights[23] (correlative rights are the rights of owners in a common pool to have the opportunity to produce their fair share of oil or gas from the pool[24]). The statutes often state that either that a drilling unit should be the

16 *See* U.S. Const. amend. V.

17 Patrick H Martin and Bruce M Kramer, *Manual of Oil and Gas Terms* at 272 (14th edn, LexisNexis 2009).

18 Colo. Rev. Stat. § 34-60-116(3); Wyo. Stat. § 30-5-109(c)(1). Often, "drilling unit" is contemplated to be the maximum area that can be drained by one well. *See, e.g.*, La. Rev. Stat. 30:9(C); Patrick H Martin and Bruce M Kramer, *Manual of Oil and Gas Terms* at 726 (definition of "drilling unit") and 918 (definition of "spacing unit") (14th edn, LexisNexis 2009).

19 La. Rev. Stat. 30:9(B); N.M. Stat. § 70-2-17(B) (proration units); N.D. Cent. Code § 38-08-07(1); Okla. Stat. 52 § 87.1(a); Utah Code § 40-6-6(1); Wyo. Stat. § 30-5-109(a).

20 Colo. Rev. Stat. § 34-60-116(1); Mont. Code 82-11-201; Okla. Stat. 52 § 87.1(a); Wyo. Stat. § 30-5-109(a).

21 Colo. Rev. Stat. § 34-60-116(1); La. Rev. Stat. 30:9(B); Mont. Code 82-11-201; N.M. Stat. § 70-2-17(B) (proration units); N.D. Cent. Code § 38-08-07(1); Okla. Stat. 52 § 87.1(a); Wyo. Stat. § 30-5-109(a).

22 Colo. Rev. Stat. § 34-60-116(1); La. Rev. Stat. 30:9(B); Mont. Code 82-11-201; N.M. Stat. § 70-2-17(B) (proration units); N.D. Cent. Code § 38-08-07(1).

23 Colo. Rev. Stat. § 34-60-116(1); Mont. Code 82-11-201; N.D. Cent. Code § 38-08-07(1); Okla. Stat. 52 § 87.1(a); Wyo. Stat. § 30-5-109(a).

24 Eugene Kuntz, 'Correlative Rights in Oil and Gas' (1958) 30 Miss LJ 1, 2; *Halbouty v. Railroad Commission*, 357 S.W.2d 364, 374 (Tex. 1962) ("It is an obvious result that if in a common reservoir

maximum size that can be efficiently drained by one well,[25] or that a drilling unit must be no smaller than that size.[26]

11.1.3.2 Statutory Pooling

In the United States, virtually all states with oil and gas activity have statutes that authorize the states' oil and gas regulators to issue orders to pool the separately owned tracts within a drilling unit. Perhaps the only exception is Kansas.

In some states, the state's oil and gas regulator frequently enters pooling orders. In other states in which the regulator has pooling authority, the regulator seldom enters pooling orders. In the states where the regulator's pooling authority is seldom used, there are different reasons why the authority is seldom used. Consider, for example, Texas and Pennsylvania. In Texas, oil and gas companies often consider it difficult to satisfy the requirements of the pooling statute. Accordingly, they typically include in their oil and gas leases a provision in which the landowner or mineral owner granting the lease delegates to the leaseholder the right to enter a voluntary agreement that commits the tract under lease to a voluntary pooling arrangement. Then, the leaseholder relies on this contractual pooling authority.

In Pennsylvania, the oil and gas regulator's authority to enter a pooling order only applies to subsurface formations deeper than the Onondaga formation, and most oil and gas activity in Pennsylvania is at depths shallower than the Onondaga formation. Thus, to the extent that pooling is used, it typically is done on a voluntary basis, rather than by order of the state's oil and gas regulator.

The language of statutes authorizing state conservation agencies to issue orders pooling interests and creating drilling units varies from state to state, but there are several features that are common. The language of pooling statutes typically suggests that the statutes apply only if two or more separately owned tracts or separately owned mineral interests exist within a drilling unit.[27] This makes sense because, unless there are separately owned interests, there is no need for a pooling of interests.

one tract owner is allowed to produce many times more gas than underlies his tract he is denying to some other landowner in the reservoir a fair chance to produce the gas underlying his land."); *Elliff v. Texon Drilling Co.*, 210 S.W.2d 558, 562–3 (Tex. 1948); *Higgins Oil & Fuel Co., Inc. v. Guaranty Oil Co.*, 82 So. 206, 212 (La. 1919) ("The rights of the several owners of the gas filed are coequal; one owner cannot exercise his own right so as to preclude his neighbor from exercising his, or so as to interfere with the neighbor."); La. Rev. Stat. 31:10 and cmt.

25 *See, e.g.*, N.M. Stat. § 70-2-17(B) (proration units). Until recently, Louisiana Revised Statute 30:9(B) contained this language, but the statute was amended in 2015 to state, "A drilling unit, as contemplated herein, means the maximum area which may be efficiently and economically drained by the well or wells designated to serve the drilling unit."

26 Colo. Rev. Stat. § 34-60-116(2); Utah Code § 40-6-6; Wyo. Stat. § 30-5-109(b).

27 *See, e.g.*, Colo. Rev. Stat. § 34-60-116(6)(a); La. Rev. Stat. 30:10(A); Miss. Code § 53-3-7(a)(a); Mont. Code 82-11-202(1)(a); N.M. Stat. § 70-2-17(C); N.D. Cent. Code § 38-08-08(1); 52 Okla. Stat. § 87.1(e); Tex. Nat. Res. Code § 102.011; Utah Code § 40-6-6.5(1); Wyo. Stat. § 30-5-109(f).

Pooling statutes typically anticipate that, if the parties who own mineral interests within a drilling unit wish, they may enter a voluntary agreement for pooling. Indeed, many pooling statutes state that the state's oil and gas regulator can enter an order pooling the separately owned interests in a drilling unit *if* the owners have not voluntarily agreed to pooling.[28] Most pooling statutes provide that any person owning an interest in an area can ask the oil and gas regulator to create a drilling unit and order pooling, or that the regulator itself can initiate a proceeding to create drilling units and order pooling.[29]

Because the creation of a drilling unit and pooling will affect property rights, state pooling statutes require that parties who will be affected must be given notice of the pooling proposal and that a public hearing be held, at which proponents and opponents of a pooling proposal have a right to be heard.[30] Pooling statutes typically state that, if the regulator enters an order requiring pooling, that the order must be on terms that are just and reasonable,[31] and the order must allow each person owning an mineral interest an opportunity to recover or receive, without unnecessary expense, his just and reasonable share of production from the common pool.[32] This is typically accomplished by allowing just one operator, but requiring that operator to share revenue on a specified basis – typically with each tract of land in the unit being attributed a share of production that is in proportion to the size of the tract.[33]

Pooling statutes typically state that, if a pooling order has been entered, operations incident to the drilling of a well for the drilling unit are deemed to be operations on each separately owned tract in the unit.[34] Further, the share of production allocated to each tract in the drilling unit will be deemed as having been produced

28 *See, e.g.*, Ark. Code § 15-72-302; Colo. Rev. Stat. § 34-60-116(6)(b); La. Rev. Stat. 30:10(A)(1); Miss. Code § 53-3-7(a)(a); Mont. Code 82-11-202(1)(b); N.D. Cent. Code § 38-08-08(1); N.M. Stat. § 70-2-17(C); Tex. Nat. Res. Code § 102.011; Utah Code § 40-6-6.5(2)(a); Wyo. Stat. § 30-5-109(f).

29 *See, e.g.*, Colo. Rev. Stat. § 34-60-116(6)(b); Mont. Code 82-11-202(1)(b); N.D. Cent. Code § 38-08-08(1); Tex. Nat. Res. Code § 102.012; Wyo. Stat. § 30-5-109(f).

30 *See, e.g.*, Ark. Code § 15-72-302; Colo. Rev. Stat. § 34-60-116(6)(b)(II); La. Rev. Stat. 30:10(A)(1)(a); Miss. Code § 53-3-7(a)(a); Mont. Code 82-11-202(1)(b) (after hearing, though not expressly referring to notice); N.D. Cent. Code § 38-08-08(1); N.M. Stat. § 70-2-17(C); 52 Okla. Stat. § 87.1(e); Tex. Nat. Res. Code § 102.016; Wyo. Stat. § 30-5-109(f).

31 *See, e.g.*, Colo. Rev. Stat. § 34-60-116(6)(b)(II); La. Rev. Stat. 30:10(A)(1)(a); Miss. Code § 53-3-7(a)(a); Mont. Code 82-11-202(1)(b); N.M. Stat. § 70-2-17(C); N.D. Cent. Code § 38-08-08(1); 52 Okla. Stat. § 87.1(e); Tex. Nat. Res. Code § 102.017; Utah Code § 40-6-6.5(2)(b); Wyo. Stat. § 30-5-109(f).

32 *See, e.g.*, Colo. Rev. Stat. § 34-60-116(6)(b)(II); La. Rev. Stat. 30:10(A)(1)(a); Miss. Code § 53-3-7(a)(a); Mont. Code 82-11-202(1)(b); N.D. Cent. Code § 38-08-08(1); N.M. Stat. § 70-2-17(C); 52 Okla. Stat. § 87.1(e); Tex. Nat. Res. Code § 102.017 (stating that pooling order must give each owner a chance to produce his fair share, but not referring to "without unnecessary expense").

33 Pooling statutes generally do not require that the sharing of revenue be done on a surface acreage basis, but that is the almost-universal practice.

34 *See, e.g.*, Colo. Rev. Stat. § 34-60-116(6)(c); Mont. Code 82-11-202(1)(b); N.D. Cent. Code § 38-08-08(1); N.M. Stat. § 70-2-17(C); Tex. Nat. Res. Code § 102.053; Utah Code § 40-6-6.5(3)(a); Wyo. Stat. § 30-5-109(f).

from that tract.[35] The significance of this is that the duration of many oil and gas leases is based in part on whether there is drilling on the tract covered by the lease and whether there is production from the lease. Thus, if there is unit production from a unit well on Tract 1, a lease covering some other tract in the unit can be kept alive by that unit production, even though the unit well is not located on that tract.

Typically, pooling statutes do not require the approval of any particular fraction of the landowners or mineral owners whose separately owned interests will be combined. Instead, the statutes merely require that the regulator find that the substantive requirements for pooling are met – with the most common requirements being that the creation of a drilling unit and the pooling of interests within the unit will prevent waste, avoid the drilling of unnecessary wells, and protect correlative rights.

11.1.3.3 Allocation of Production Under Pooling

The regulator has authority to allocate production to the various tracts within the pooled unit. Although most pooling statutes do not specify how production is to be allocated, regulators almost always allocate production based on surface acreage. That is, each tract will be allocated a fraction of production that is equal to that tract's fraction of the total acreage in the unit.[36]

11.1.3.4 Allocation of Costs Under Pooling

Drilling wells carries economic risk – often wells are either dry holes or wells that produce oil and gas, but not enough to recover the costs of drilling. Under pooling, the owner of mineral interests in a pooled unit is never forced to participate in that risk. They always have the right to refrain from participating. But this freedom leads to a question – if a particular owner chooses not to participate in that risk, what share (if any) of the proceeds from a productive well should the non-participating owner receive?

One possibility is a rule that an owner who refuses to participate in a well would be forever precluded from receiving a share of production or any other compensation. But arguably that is unfair because even the owners who do not participate in the well have "contributed" something to the pooled unit, namely their acreage, and no states have chosen to adopt such a rule.

35 *See, e.g.*, Colo. Rev. Stat. § 34-60-116(6)(c); La. Rev. Stat. 30:10(A)(1)(b); Miss. Code § 53-3-7(a)(a); Mont. Code 82-11-202(1)(b); N.D. Cent. Code § 38-08-08(1); N.M. Stat. § 70-2-17(C); 52 Okla. Stat. § 87.1(e); Tex. Nat. Res. Code § 102.053; Utah Code § 40-6-6.5(3)(b); Wyo. Stat. § 30-5-109(f).

36 *See, e.g., Anschutz Corporation v. Wyoming Oil and Gas Conservation Commission*, 923 P.2d 751, 757 (Wyo. 1996) ("surface acreage is perhaps the most frequently employed basis for allocating pooled production"); Tex. Nat. Res. Code Ann. § 102.051(a); *Panhandle Eastern Pipe Line Co. v. Corporation Commission*, 285 P.2d 847, 854 (Okla. 1955); *Traverse Oil Co. v. Chairman of Natural Resources Comm'n*, 396 N.W.2d 498, 500 (Mich. App. 1986).

Another possibility is that all persons who own mineral interests receive a share of gross production that is proportionate to their acreage, without the parties who incurred the costs of drilling being allowed to first recover their costs. But this would seem extremely unfair and no state has followed this approach.

Another possibility is that both parties who participated in the risk of drilling and those who did not participate in that risk can share in profits, but the persons who participated in the risk of drilling are entitled to a larger share. Most states follow this approach, but different states follow different schemes for giving a greater reward to those who participated in the risk of drilling.

A final possibility is that the proceeds of production first go to repaying the costs of drilling. Then, after "payout" is reached and the parties who paid the costs of drilling and recovered that costs, all parties (whether or not they participated in the costs and risks of drilling) will receive a share of the profits in proportion to the acreage they own. But most people would regard it as unfair because the persons who choose not to incur any risks would receive the same share of profits as those who participated in the risk of drilling. This is sometimes called the "free ride" approach because the persons who incur no risk get the benefit of the risks taken by others. Some states follow this approach, but not very many.

The following discussion describes three main approaches: (1) the risk-fee approach, one of the ways of giving greater compensation to the persons who participate in the risk of drilling; (2) the surrender of working interest approach, a second way of giving greater compensation to the persons who participated in the risk of drilling; and (3) the free ride approach.[37]

11.1.3.4.1 RISK-FEE APPROACH

The most common approach taken by states is to utilize a risk-fee, which is sometimes called a "risk charge" or a "risk-penalty."[38] Under this approach, state law authorizes the regulator or the operator to give the non-operators who own exploration and production rights within the compulsory pooling unit an opportunity to participate in the costs of drilling and completing the well. If a non-operator fails to participate, that non-operator's interest is treated as a "carried interest." That is, the parties who are participating in costs will "carry" the non-participating party's share of drilling costs, and the non-participating party will not be liable for any costs of drilling in the event that the well is a dry hole or fails to fully pay for itself.

Of course, if the well is productive, the operator may recover the non-participating party's share of drilling, completion, and operating costs from that party's share

37 For an excellent overview of these approaches, see Patrick Martin and Bruce M Kramer, *Williams & Meyers Oil and Gas Law* (abridged version, 4th edn, LexisNexis) § 944.

38 A prominent treatise uses "nonconsent penalty" and also "risk penalty." Patrick Martin and Bruce M Kramer, *Williams & Meyers Oil and Gas Law* at § 944 (using "nonconsent penalty") and § 973 n.3.1 (using "risk penalty"); Louisiana's relevant statute refers to a "risk charge." La. Rev. Stat. 30:10(A)(2)(b)(i). But the case *EOG Resources, Inc. v. Chesapeake Energy Corp.*, 605 F.3d 260, 263 (5th Cir. 2010) uses "risk-fee."

of production. But in addition, the operator may recover a risk-fee from the non-participating party's share of production. The risk-fee compensates the operator for the risk it took, but which the non-operator chose not to take. The risk-fee typically will be some multiple of drilling and completion costs or specified types of drilling and completion costs.

States that follow the risk-fee approach include Alabama,[39] Colorado,[40] Louisiana,[41] Michigan,[42] Mississippi,[43] Montana,[44] Nebraska,[45] Nevada,[46] New Mexico,[47] New York,[48] North Dakota,[49] Ohio,[50] Texas,[51] Utah,[52] and Wyoming.[53]

In some states that use the risk-fee approach, the amount of the risk-fee multiple (e.g., 50%, 100%, 200%, 300%) is set by statute.[54] In other states, the regulator is given the authority to set the risk-fee multiple.[55] Because the operator will be allowed to recover its reasonable costs associated with the well,[56] plus the risk-fee multiple of certain types of costs, it is important to define what types of costs are subject to the risk-fee. Some state statutes give somewhat detailed definitions, while others are more general.[57] The regulator typically will have authority to resolve disputes regarding whether costs are reasonable or subject to the risk-fee,[58] though parties will have a right to seek judicial review of the regulator's decision.

39 Ala. Code § 9-17-13.
40 Colo. Rev. Stat. § 34-60-116(7)(b).
41 La. Rev. Stat. 30:10(A).
42 Mich. Comp. Laws Ann. 324.61513(4); Mich. Admin. Code R. 324.1206(4).
43 Miss. Code Ann. § 53-3-7(2)(g).
44 Mont. Code Ann. § 82-11-202.
45 Neb. Rev. Stat. § 57-900(2).
46 Nev. R.S. 522.060(4).
47 N.M. Stat. Ann. § 70-2-17(C).
48 N.Y. Env. Cons. Law § 23-0901(3).
49 N.D. Cent. Code § 38-08-08(3).
50 Ohio Rev. Code Ann. § 1509.27.
51 Tex. Nat. Res. Code Ann. §§ 102.013 and 102.052.
52 Utah Code Ann. § 40-6-6(6).
53 Wyo. Stat. § 30-5-109(g).
54 La. Rev. Stat. 30:10(A)(2)(b)(i) (setting 200% penalty for unit wells, substitute unit wells, and cross unit wells, but 100% penalty for alternate unit wells); Nev. R.S. 522.060(4) (setting 300% fee).
55 N.M. Stat. Ann. § 70-2-17(C) (giving regulator authority to set risk-fee, but setting cap of 200%); Mich. Admin. Code R. 324.1206(4).
56 Virtually all pooling statutes expressly limit the operator to charging *actual* costs that are *reasonable*. Colo. Rev. Stat. § 34-60-116(7)(a)(I); La. Rev. Stat. 30:10(A)(2)(b)(i); N.M. Stat. Ann. § 70-2-17(C). This may include a reasonable charge for supervision. *See, e.g.*, Colo. Rev. Stat. § 34-60-116(7)(a)(I); La. Rev. Stat. 30:10(A)(2)(b)(i); Nev. R.S. 522.060(4); N.M. Stat. Ann. § 70-2-17(C).
57 For example, the Mississippi statute has significant detail, whereas the Nevada statute has considerably less. Miss. Code Ann. § 53-3-7(2)(g); Nev. R.S. 522.060(4).
58 *See, e.g.*, Colo. Rev. Stat. § 34-60-116(7)(d)(II); La. Rev. Stat. 30:10(f); N.M. Stat. Ann. § 70-2-17(C); Nev. R.S. 522.060(4); Tex. Nat. Res. Code Ann. § 102.052(b); Wyo. Stat. § 30-5-109(g).

11.1.3.4.2 SURRENDER OF WORKING INTEREST APPROACH

Some states, such as Oklahoma, use a "surrender of working interest" approach. Under this approach, each owner of a working interest is given the option to participate in drilling costs. An owner that fails to participate is deemed to have surrendered his working interest to the operator in return for compensation, such as a bonus, royalty, or both.[59] Effectively, this approach brings about an assignment of the non-participating lessee's lease rights or a lease of the unleased owner's interest. The amount of compensation to be paid for the surrender of a working interest is determined by the Oklahoma Corporation Commission. The Commission may, as an alternative, allow the non-participating working interest owner the option of paying a risk-fee,[60] though the Commission is not required to offer that option.[61] Oklahoma statutes do not expressly grant the Corporation Commission the authority to utilize the surrender-of-working-interest approach. Oklahoma's statute requires the Corporation Commission to allocate costs on a fair basis. The Corporation Commission developed the surrender-of-working-interest approach by way of its orders, and the Commission's use of the approach has been upheld by the Oklahoma Supreme Court.[62]

Several states have adopted the same general approach by statute, including Arkansas,[63] Idaho,[64] Illinois,[65] Kentucky,[66] Pennsylvania,[67] South Dakota,[68] and West Virginia.[69] Those statutes give the working interest owner the option to participate, surrender its working interest in return for compensation, or to be carried and pay a risk-fee out of its share of production.

11.1.3.4.3 FREE RIDE APPROACH

The final approach sometimes is called the "free ride" approach.[70] This approach applies when states have not adopted some other approach by statute or regulation.[71]

59 *Wakefield v. State of Oklahoma*, 306 P.2d 305, 308 (Okla. 1957); *Anderson v. Corporation Commission*, 327 P.2d 699, 700–1 (Okla. 1957).
60 Patrick Martin and Bruce M Kramer, *Williams & Meyers Oil and Gas Law* at §§ 944, 972.
61 *Wakefield v. State of Oklahoma*, 306 P.2d 305, 308–9 (Okla. 1957).
62 *Anderson v. Corporation Commission*, 327 P.2d 699, 700–1 (Okla. 1957).
63 Ark. Code Ann. § 15-72-304(b)(4).
64 Idaho Code § 47-322(c).
65 Ill. Comp. Stat. Ann. 725/22.2(f).
66 Ky. Rev. Stat. Ann. 353.640 (3).
67 58 Pa. Stat. § 408(c).
68 S.D. Codified Laws 45-9-33.
69 W. Va. Code, § 22C-9-7(b)(5).
70 *See, e.g.*, Patrick Martin and Bruce M Kramer, *Williams & Meyers Oil and Gas Law* (abridged version, 4th edn) § 944; *see also* Patrick H Martin, 'Unleased and Unjoined Owners – Forced Pooling and Co-Tenancy Issues' § 18.03[3], Proceedings of the Rocky Mountain Mineral Law Fifty-Sixth Annual Institute (2010).
71 Patrick H. Martin, *Unleased and Unjoined Owners – Forced Pooling and Co-Tenancy Issues* § 18.03[3], Proceedings of the Rocky Mountain Mineral Law Fifty-Sixth Annual Institute (2010).

In such circumstances, the various persons holding mineral interests within the pooled unit are treated as common law cotenants.[72] None may be forced to participate in the risk of drilling, and each is entitled to its proportionate share of drilling, subject only to a deduction of that owner's proportionate share of expenses from his share of production.[73] States that follow this approach include Alaska,[74] Arizona,[75] Indiana,[76] and Missouri.[77] There are other states that have failed to adopt some other approach in their statutes or regulations, but those states have little oil and gas activity and thus are less relevant in this context.[78]

11.1.3.4.4 DIFFERING TREATMENT OF LEASEHOLDERS AND OWNERS OF UNLEASED MINERAL INTERESTS

Some states give more favorable treatment to non-participating owners of unleased interests than to non-participating owners of mineral leaseholds.[79] For example, in Louisiana, non-participating lessees are subject to a risk-fee, but owners of unleased interests get a free ride, subject only to his payment of his proportionate share of costs out of his share of production.[80]

In Colorado, non-consenting (non-participating) owners of mineral leases are subject to a risk-fee.[81] A non-consenting owner of an unleased interest is treated as if he owned a landowner's royalty for 13% of natural gas produced and 16% of oil, along with a working interest of 87% (gas) or 84% (oil).[82] The non-consenting, unleased owner's share of costs and the risk-fee are recovered solely from production attributable to his 87% or 84% working interest. After his proportionate share of costs and the risk-fee have been recovered, he is entitled to all of the production attributable to his tract and, for purposes of costs he is treated as if he was a consenting owner.[83] Montana follows the same approach, except that that the deemed royalty for both oil and gas is one-eighth.[84] Utah also follows this approach, except that the deemed royalty is equal to the weighted average of the actual royalties applicable in the various leased tracts contained within the unit.[85]

72 Id.

73 Id.

74 Id.; *see also* Alaska Stat. Ann. § 31.05.100 (providing that non-participating lessee is responsible for reimbursing operator for non-participant's share of costs, but that reimbursement is required only out of production).

75 Ariz. Stat. Ann. § 27-505(A).

76 Ind. Code 14-37-9-3.

77 Vernon Ann. Missouri Stat. 259.110.

78 Patrick H Martin, *Unleased and Unjoined Owners – Forced Pooling and Co-Tenancy Issues* § 18.03[3], Proceedings of the Rocky Mountain Mineral Law Fifty-Sixth Annual Institute (2010).

79 Id.

80 La. Rev. Stat. 30:10(A).

81 Colo. Rev. Stat. § 34-60-116(7)(b).

82 Colo. Rev. Stat. § 34-60-116(7)(c).

83 Id.

84 Mont. Code Ann. § 82-11-202(2)(c).

85 Utah Code Ann. § 40-6-6.5(6).

11.1.3.5 Federal Lands

As noted above, most oil and gas regulation is based on state law. However, if the tracts of land at issue consist entirely of federal lands, federal rules that apply to the leasing of federal lands may apply, rather than state law. If some of the tracts at issue are federal lands, while other tracts are privately owned or owned by state government, state pooling law may apply if the federal government consents. The subject of federal lands is beyond the scope of this one-chapter review of United States law.[86]

11.2 Unitization

Unitization is the joint operation of all or a major portion of an oil or gas reservoir.[87] Because the term *unitization* is sometimes used interchangeably with "pooling," some people use the term *fieldwide unitization* to describe unitization, thereby emphasizing that they are not referring to pooling.[88] In the United States, unitization or fieldwide unitization is often used to help coordinate operations during gas injection or pressure maintenance operations, secondary recovery, and tertiary or enhanced recovery.[89] Unitization is seldom used during primary recovery in the United States, even though it sometimes would be possible to operate more efficiently if operations across a reservoir were coordinated.[90]

11.2.1 The Reasons for Unitization

In many situations, it is possible to recover more hydrocarbons or to recover them at lower cost (or both) if operations over an entire common source or a major portion of a common source of hydrocarbons is developed in a coordinated way. This is particularly true in secondary recovery operations and enhanced recovery operations. In such operations, it is common to use some wells as injection wells for the injection of water, steam, carbon dioxide, or some other substance that will help push oil toward production wells. The injected substance may also reduce the viscosity of the oil in the formation – either by increasing the temperature of the oil or (as in the case of carbon dioxide) by dissolving into the oil. In both secondary

86 For a more detailed discussion, see Keith B. Hall, *Single Well Spacing and Pooling: State Spacing and Jurisdiction over Conservation*, Special Institute on Federal Onshore Oil & Gas Pooling and Unitization, Rocky Mtn. Min. L. Fdn. (2014) and the sources cited therein, or Chapter 16 of Bruce M. Kramer and Patrick H. Martin, *The Law of Pooling and Unitization* (3rd edition).

87 Bruce M. Kramer and Patrick H. Martin, *The Law of Pooling and Unitization* § 6.02 (3rd edn, LexisNexis).

88 *Eads Operating Co., Inc. v. Thompson*, 646 So. 2d 948, 950 (La. App. 1st Cir. 1994); *Texas Pacific Oil Co., Inc. v. Petro Grande, Inc.*, 328 So. 2d 660, 661 (Miss. 1976).

89 Keith B Hall and Hannah J Wiseman, *Hydraulic Fracturing: A Guide to Environmental and Real Property Issues* (American Bar Ass'n 2017) 264.

90 Keith B Hall and Hannah J Wiseman, *Hydraulic Fracturing: A Guide to Environmental and Real Property Issues* (American Bar Ass'n 2017) 263.

and enhanced recovery, it is useful to coordinate operations over a large area. It is common to use unitization for secondary or enhanced recovery operations in the United States.

In some circumstances, it also can be useful to coordinate operations over a large area during primary recovery. For example, consider a formation that contains "wet" natural gas with large amounts of natural gas liquids (NGLs) such as ethane, propane, and butane. The NGLs often are contained in the gaseous phase when the natural gas (which is mostly methane) is at high pressure. When a well is drilled to such a formation and the natural gas reaches the surface, the pressure will be lower. At the lower pressure, some of the NGLs will condense into a liquid phase called "condensate." Those NGLs sometimes are very valuable. As natural gas is extracted from the subsurface formation, the pressure of the formation will drop. That can cause the NGLs to condense into a liquid while still in the subsurface formation. When that happens, it is difficult to extract the valuable condensate.

When such a gas-condensate field is encountered, one strategy is to extract the natural gas, separate the NGLs from the methane, and reinject the methane into the subsurface formation from which it was produced. The reinjection of the methane keeps the formation at a higher pressure than if the methane was not reinjected. This delays the pressure drop that will result in the NGLs condensing out of the gas while in the subsurface formation, while also allowing recovery of the valuable NGLs that can be separated from methane at the surface. In this way, a maximum amount of NGLs can be extracted from the pressure of the subsurface formation drops by an amount that will cause the NGLs to condense out in the subsurface, thereby becoming difficult or impossible to recover. At this point, the operator of the field can start extracting the natural gas.

Such a gas reinjection operation can maximize the value of the hydrocarbons recovered from the gas-condensate formation. But for such an operation to work as intended, it is important that all the methane be reinjected into the formation during the pressure-maintenance period of operations. If some operators are selling the methane that remains after NGLs have condensed out, rather than reinjecting that methane, the pressure of the formation will diminish more quickly, thereby hastening the time when NGLs begin to condense out in the subsurface formation. But an individual operator may have an incentive to sell the methane, rather than reinject it, because that operator will obtain all the benefit from the sale of the methane extracted by its wells, but the costs of failing to reinject (a hastening of the NGLs condensing out in the subsurface) will be shared amongst all operators in the field. Thus, coordinated operations under a unitization scheme can be useful to ensure that all gas is reinjected. For this reason, unitization is sometimes used in the United States in gas condensate fields.

Coordinating operations can also be useful sometimes in oil fields. In some cases, the oil in a formation is saturated with natural gas. When the oil flows into a well, some of the dissolved gas will begin to vaporize and expand. This helps drive the flow of oil into and up the well. But as oil is extracted from the formation, the pressure in the formation will drop and free gas will form in the formation.

Eventually, the free gas will begin to enter the well, leaving much of the remaining the oil behind and making it more difficult to recover. But if the gas is separated from the oil at the surface, and the gas is reinjected near the top of the oil formation (with wells extracting oil from a deeper depth), the pressure of the formation can be kept higher for longer. Thus, if the oil wells are extracting oil from a point in the formation below where free gas is being reinjected, those wells will recover oil that is still at a relatively high pressure and which is still saturated with gas that can vaporize and expand in the well, helping drive or expel oil from the well. But again, for such a scheme to work, it is important for there to be a coordinated operation in which natural gas from all oil wells is being reinjected.

In other oil fields, the force that helps push oil and up wells comes from a "gas cap" – a layer of higher pressure natural gas that is located above the oil in the subsurface formation. In such formations, as oil is produced, the gas cap will expand downward, resulting in the interface between oil and gas moving downward. In such formations, to maximize the recovery of oil, it can be helpful to focus on drilling wells to the deepest parts of the formation. If the formation is tilted, so that some parts of the formation are deeper than others, the strategy of drilling wells to the deepest parts of the formation – the "down-dip" portions – may mean that an optimum strategy for recovering the most oil with the least number of wells would require that no wells be drilled to recover oil from the "up-dip" portions of the formations. But persons who own mineral interests in tracts located "up dip" are not likely to consent to forgoing drilling and recovering oil from their tracts unless the field is unitized, so that those "up-dip" owners share in production from the "down-dip" wells.

In a water-drive field, the energy that drives oil into and up the wells is from a layer of compressed water located beneath the oil. As oil is extracted, the pressure in the formation will drop. The water in the formation will expand, causing the oil-water interface to move upward. Once the layer of water reaches any particular well, the well will "water out." That is, it will start producing too much water and too little oil for the well to be economic. To maximize recovery of oil from such a formation with the least number of wells, the best strategy would be to focus on drilling oil wells to the "up-dip" portion of the formation. But owners of the mineral interests in tracts located "down-dip" are not likely to forgo drilling on their tracts unless they get a share of the production from the "up-dip" wells. One way to achieve this would be unitization. Unitization is not often used in this situation in the United States, though in theory it might be efficient to do so.

11.2.2 Voluntary Unitization

Sometimes, parties create voluntary fieldwide units.[91] However, it often is difficult and time-consuming to secure agreement, if agreement can be reached at all.[92]

91 *See, e.g.*, *Palmer Exploration, Inc. v. Dennis*, 730 F. Supp. 734, 735 & n.3 (S.D. Miss. 1989).
92 Bruce M Kramer and Patrick H Martin, *The Law of Pooling and Unitization* § 17.01 (3rd edn).

One of the reasons for this difficulty is that numerous parties may be involved.[93] Another is that, in a large field, some tracts may still be recovering oil at substantial rate from primary production, while other tracts may already have exhausted the amount of primary production that is economically achievable. A third is that there are numerous factors that can be considered in a participation formula that will be used to determine what fraction of expenses and revenues will be attributed to each tract,[94] and often there is incomplete information regarding these factors.

The factors often considered in a participation formula include acre-feet of productive formation beneath each tract, which is determined by multiplying the size of the tract by the thickness of the productive reservoir beneath the tract; the porosity of the portion of the formation beneath a tract; the amount of oil initially in place beneath a tract; the amount recovered so far from the tract; the number of wells on existing on the tract that can be used in the unit operations; the productivity of any existing wells on the tract; the amount of additional oil that could be recovered from the tract if primary production continued; and the effect of any existing allowables or prorationing regulations.[95] There is not a standard formula that specifies how much weight to give to each of these factors, so each party is free to propose a formula that would work to its advantage.

Nevertheless, parties sometimes are able to reach agreement regarding a unitization scheme, for the same reason that parties are able to reach agreements in other contexts. Namely, even if an agreed participation formula is not one that each party thinks is ideal, the various parties may still be better off with the unitization agreement than without an agreement. This is because unitized operations often will increase the production of oil significantly compared to production without a unitization agreement. The increased production often can more than make up for the fact that a party may consider the unitization agreement's participation formula to be non-ideal. Also, conservation agencies sometimes use their leverage to push the parties toward an agreement.[96] Further, many oil and gas leases in the United States delegate to the leaseholder the authority to commit the leased tract to pooling or unitization or both. Such lease clauses may effectively reduce the number of

93 Bruce M Kramer and Patrick H Martin, *The Law of Pooling and Unitization* § 17.01 (3rd edn).

94 Bruce M Kramer and Patrick H Martin, *The Law of Pooling and Unitization* § 17.02[5][a] (3rd edn) (noting that it is difficult to reach agreement on a participation formula, that several factors often are considered, and that there often is incomplete information available regarding the relevant factors); *Trout v. Wyoming Oil and Gas Conservation Comm'n*, 721 P.2d 1047 (Wyo. 1986) (discussing difficulty in getting parties to agree to a participation formula).

95 Bruce M Kramer and Patrick H Martin, *The Law of Pooling and Unitization* § 17.02[5][a] (3rd edn) (noting that it is difficult to reach agreement on a participation formula, that several factors often are considered, and that there often is incomplete information available regarding the relevant factors); *Gilmore v. Oil & Gas Conservation Comm'n*, 642 P.2d 773 (Wyo. 1982).

96 The Texas Railroad Commission's efforts to encourage unitization are discussed in Jacqueline Lang Weaver, *Unitization of Oil and Gas Fields in Texas: A Study of Legislative, Administrative, and Judicial Policies* (Resources for the Future 1986). *See also* Bruce M Kramer and Patrick H Martin, *The Law of Pooling and Unitization* §§ 17.01, 18.01 (3rd edn).

parties that have to reach agreement because a particular company may hold leases covering numerous tracts within the oil field.

A unitization agreement will need to address numerous issues. It will need to identify the parties, acknowledge the agreement to enter a unitization agreement, and specify what areas are covered by the unitization agreement. In specifying the area covered, the agreement should go beyond specifying the tracts (or portions of tracts) covered, and should also indicate whether the agreement covers all depths or only certain depths and formations. Often, a unitization agreement will state that, although the parties intend to operate their separately owned interests in a coordinated manner, they do not intend to make a cross-conveyance of their interests.[97] That is, the parties do not intend to each convey to each other a fractional interest in their separately owned interests.

Often, unitization agreements state the purpose of the agreement. For example, an agreement may state that the parties intend to enter the unit agreement because unitization will increase total recovery of hydrocarbons and protect the interests of the parties. Like most commercial agreements, a unitization agreement often will contain a section with definitions of various terms used in the agreement. And, of course, the agreement will have to specify a participation formula.

The unitization agreement will need to designate an operator. The operator usually will be one of the parties owning a working interest[98] in the unit area, and it is common for the agreement to designate the party with the largest working interest as the operator.[99] In addition, unitization agreements frequently contains provisions that allow for enlargement of the unitized area or a change in the participation formula. Unitization agreements usually specify when unitization becomes effective, and often unitization agreements address termination of the agreement.

The parties also will need to reach agreement regarding the authority of the operator and how decisions relating to operations will be made. Often, these matters are covered in a separate agreement – a unit operating agreement, which is simply a joint operating agreement for the unitized area. Thus, the unit operating agreement should address such issues as any commitments that the parties make to indemnify the operator against third-party claims and any releases that the non-operator parties may give to the operator in advance. Often, operating agreements contain an exculpatory clause providing that each non-operator indemnifies and releases the operator for that non-operator's participation interest share of liability, except in cases of gross negligence or willful misconduct by the operator.

The operating agreement should also address resignation, removal, and replacement of the operator. Agreements typically give the non-operators the right to remove the operator, but there may be limitations on this right. Agreements also

97 Bruce M Kramer and Patrick H Martin, *The Law of Pooling and Unitization* § 17.02[3] (3rd edn).

98 A working interest is the right to conduct oil and gas operations. Most commonly, the term is used to designate operating rights that are derived from a mineral lease, as opposed to ownership of land or a severed mineral estate.

99 Bruce M Kramer and Patrick H Martin, *The Law of Pooling and Unitization* § 17.02[4] (3rd edn).

typically allow an operator to resign as operator, but agreements often provide that the resignation will not be effective until a certain period of time after the resignation, so that the parties have sufficient time to select a successor. The unit operating agreement also should specify how a successor operator is chosen.

11.2.3 Compulsory Unitization

Most states that have oil and gas activity have a statute authorizing the state's oil and gas regulator to enter an order requiring fieldwide unitization. An exception is Texas – a major oil and gas producing state – but voluntary fieldwide unitization agreements are often entered, sometimes at the urging of the state's oil and gas regulator, the Texas Railroad Commission.[100] Pennsylvania is another exception,[101] but all other states with significant oil and gas activity have a compulsory unitization statute,[102] as do some states with little or no oil and gas production.[103]

In the states that authorize their oil and gas regulator to enter orders creating fieldwide units, the statute authoring the regulator to do so is a different statute than the one that authorizes the regulator to create drilling units and order pooling. The unitization statutes typically are supplemented by regulations that help implement the statutes. The unitization schemes in the various states generally contain both substantive and procedural provisions, and although the schemes in the various states vary from one another, many of them have common features.

The substantive provisions generally require the regulator to make certain factual findings before issuing a unitization order. The required factual findings

100 *See* Bruce M Kramer and Patrick H Martin, *The Law of Pooling and Unitization* § 18.01 (3rd edn) (recognizing that Texas does not have a compulsory unitization statute). Although the Texas Railroad Commission used to regulate railroads in the state, it has not done so for several decades. The Railroad Commission's main job now is to regulate the oil and gas industry in Texas. For an interesting book describing the history of the unsuccessful efforts to enact a fieldwide unitization statute in Texas, and the ways in which the Railroad Commission sometimes has been able to push companies into entering voluntary fieldwide unitization agreements, see Jacqueline Lang Weaver, *Unitization of Oil and Gas Fields in Texas* (Resources for the Future 1986).

101 *See* Bruce M Kramer and Patrick H Martin, *The Law of Pooling and Unitization* § 18.01 (3rd edn).

102 *See, e.g.*, Ala. Code § 9-17-3; Alaska Stat. § 31.05.110; Ark. Code Ann. §§ 15-72-308 to 15-72-315; Cal. Pub. Res. Code § 3630-59; Colo. Rev. Stat. § 34-60-118; Fla. Stat. Ann. § 377.28; 225 Ill. Comp. Stat. 725/23.3 to 725/23.14; Ind. Code Ann. §§ 13-8-11-1 to 13-8-11-4; Kan. Stat. Ann. §§ 55-1301 to 55-1315; Ky. Rev. Stat. Ann. § 353.652; La. Rev. Stat. Ann. §§ 30:5B, 30:5C; Mich. Comp. Laws §§ 324.61701 to 324.61738; Miss. Code Ann. §§ 53-3-101 to 53-3-119; Mont. Code Ann. §§ 82-11-201 to 82-11-216; N.M. Stat. Ann. §§ 70-7-1 to 70-7-21; N.Y. Envtl. Conserv. § 23-0901; N.D. Cent. Code §§ 38-08-09.1 to 38-08-09.12; Ohio Rev. Code Ann. § 1509.28; Okla. Stat. Ann. tit. 52, §§ 287.1 to 287.15; Utah Code Ann. § 40-6-8; W. Va. Code §§ 22C-9-8, 22C-9-7a; Wyo. Stat. § 30-5-110.

103 Ariz. Rev. Stat. Ann. §§ 27-531 to 27-539; Ga. Code Ann. § 43-706(a)(2); Mo. Rev. Stat. § 259.120; Neb. Rev. Stat. §§ 57-910 to 57-910.12; Nev. Rev. Stat. §§ 522.082 to 522.090; Or. Rev. Stat. §§ 520.270 to 520.330; S.C. Code Ann. § 48-43-350; S.D. Codified Laws Ann. §§ 45-9-37 to 45-9-51; Tenn. Code Ann. § 60-1-202(M & N); Vt. Stat. Ann. tit. 29, § 505(15 & 20); Wash. Rev. Code § 78.52.330.

include such things as determinations that the proposed unitized operations are economically feasible, that the value of additional recovery of oil and gas that is made possible by unitization will exceed the estimated costs of the unit operations, and that such operations are necessary to support conservation goals such as promoting production, avoiding waste, and protecting correlative rights.[104]

The procedural rules are somewhat similar to those for pooling, with the additional requirement in almost all states that a certain fraction of the working interest owners and royalty owners – the required percentage varies by state, but typically is between 60% and 80% – consent to the proposed unitization.[105] Typically, it is most difficult to obtain the required level of consent to the participation formula. It generally is less difficult to secure agreement regarding the way in which unitized operations would be conducted.

The procedural rules typically allow any interested party to petition the regulator for a compulsory unitization order, though in some states only a working interest owner can file such a petition.[106] State rules generally require that a petition seeking a unitization order contain a map showing the proposed unit area, a statement describing the proposed unit operations and how the proposed operations would satisfy the substantive requirements for unitization (e.g., the requirements that unitization will protect correlative rights and result in an increase in production, the value of which exceeds any extra costs), and the names and addresses of all the owners of interest within the proposed unit boundaries.[107]

All of the compulsory unitization schemes within the United States require that a public hearing be held prior to the regulator issuing a unitization order.[108] Given that unitization orders will affect property rights, notice is probably constitutionally required to satisfy due process. The requirement for a hearing may be found in the unitization statutes themselves, the implementing regulations, or the general statutes governing actions of the oil and gas regulator. In addition, the various states' unitization schemes typically require that persons whose interests would be affected must be given notice of the unitization proposal and of any public hearings regarding the proposal. This may also be necessary constitutionally to satisfy due process.

104 *See, e.g.*, La. Rev. Stat. 30:5; Utah Code Ann. § 40-6-8-(2).

105 Alaska's statute seems to be an exception. *See* Alaska Stat. § 31.05.110. On the low end for the level of consent required, New York and South Dakota require 60%, N.Y. Envtl. Conserv. L. § 23-0901 and S.D. Comp. L. § 45-9-40, while Nevada requires 62.5%, Nev. Rev. Stat. § 522.0834, and Oklahoma Kansas require 63%, Okla. Stat. Ann. tit. 52, § 287.5 and Kan. Stat. Ann. § 55-1305. At the high end, Colorado requires 80%, Colo. Rev. Stat. § 34-60-118(5), and Wyoming generally requires 80%, though in some circumstances the regulator has authority to lower the required level of consent to 75%, Wyo. Stat. § 30-5-110.

106 *See* Bruce M Kramer and Patrick H Martin, *The Law of Pooling and Unitization* § 18.02 (3rd edn) (citing Kansas and New Mexico statutes, Kan. Stat. Ann. § 55-1303 and N.M. Stat. Ann. § 70-7-5).

107 *See* Bruce M Kramer and Patrick H Martin, *The Law of Pooling and Unitization* § 18.02 (3rd edn); Kan. Stat. § 55-1303; N.M. Stat. Ann. § 70-7-5.

108 *See* Bruce M Kramer and Patrick H Martin, *The Law of Pooling and Unitization* § 18.02 (3rd edn). *See also* Ark. Code § 15-72-308.

If a petition seeks unitization of only a portion of a common pool of hydrocarbons, the state's unitization statutes require that the proponent of the partial unitization must show that a partial unitization is justified. For example, New Mexico's pooling statutes require that, if only a portion of a common pool is to be unitized, the regulator must conclude that the unit operations "will have no adverse effect upon other portions of the pool."[109]

Many states' compulsory unitization statutes provide that a unit order may be amended to enlarge the unit area.[110]

11.2.4 Federal Lands

As with pooling, additional considerations arise if fieldwide unitization is contemplated for an area where all or a portion of the land at issue is federal land. Those issues are beyond the scope of this one-chapter overview of unitization in the United States.[111]

11.3 Issues Raised by Horizontal Drilling and Hydraulic Fracturing

Much of oil and gas law – both the common law rules regarding the rule of capture and the creation of drilling units and pooling to respond to problems arising from the rule of capture – developed in the context of *conventional*, vertical drilling to relatively permeable formations. But a significant portion of the oil and gas activity in the United States is *unconventional* development, which involves the combination of horizontal drilling and hydraulic fracturing in formations with very low permeability, and such unconventional development raises some different issues that those raised by conventional development.

For example, surface location of a conventional, vertical well typically will be located on a single tract of land, and often the subsurface portions of the wellbore will be located wholly beneath and in the subsurface of the same tract. Thus, assuming the well is located on a tract where the operator had authority to drill, there will be no trespass against neighboring tracts, but the well may drain hydrocarbons from an area that includes the subsurface of neighboring tracts. Spacing rules and pooling are a regulatory response in which multiple tracts are combined into a single "drilling unit" for purposes of oil and gas operations, with a portion of the costs and revenue from operations being allocated to each tract.

109 N.M. § 70-7-11; Mont. Code § 82-11-210.

110 *See, e.g.*, Okla. Stat. tit. 52, §287.10. Often, even if there is a unit order, there also will be a unitization agreement that was entered by the parties whose consent to unitization provided the requisite percentage consented needed in order for the regulator to have the authority to enter a unitization order. Unitization statutes may also provide for the amendment of unitization agreements and unit operating agreements. *See* Bruce M Kramer and Patrick H Martin, *The Law of Pooling and Unitization* § 18.02 (3rd edn).

111 For more information on unitization involving federal lands, see Chapter 16 of Bruce M. Kramer and Patrick H. Martin, *The Law of Pooling and Unitization* (3rd edition).

In contrast, when a horizonal well is drilled, the horizonal lateral may be very long – 2 miles or more in length (more than 3 km). Often, such a well will pass through the subsurface of multiple tracts of land. The fractures produced by hydraulic fracturing will typically extend perpendicularly to the horizontal lateral, but the fractures that run perpendicular to a particular portion of the horizontal lateral will not necessarily extend far enough to enter the subsurface of a property different than that through which that portion of the horizontal lateral is located. Further, the well typically will not drain any significant amount of hydrocarbons from areas outside those where fractures are located. Thus, a particular portion of the perforated wellbore may only drain hydrocarbons from the tract where that portion of the wellbore is located. However, the wellbore itself may pass through multiple tracts and comingle hydrocarbons from each of the tracts.

In such situations, it is difficult or impossible to know what portion of the horizontal well's total production was drained from beneath particular tracts. This raises questions regarding how much production should be allocated to each tract. Further, it can raise trespass issues. Suppose that the vertical portion of the well is on and beneath Tract 1. The wellbore then turns to a horizontal direction, with a portion of the perforated horizontal being beneath Tract 1, and a portion of the horizontal lateral being beneath Tract 2. Is it proper to transport oil or natural gas produced from the portion of the horizontal lateral located beneath Tract 2 through the portion of the horizontal lateral located beneath Tract 1, so that the oil can be transported to the surface? Or would that be a trespass?

If all the tracts through which the wellbore passes are pooled together, those tracts can be treated as one for purpose of production, with production allocated between tracts based on some formula to which the parties agreed (in voluntary pooling) or that the regulator imposed by an order (in forced pooling). Further, it is generally agreed that, when tracts are combined into a pooled drilling unit, the subsurface of any tract in the pooled drilling unit (and perhaps even the surface) can be used to support unit exploration and production. Thus, pooling can answer both the allocation question and eliminate the trespass issue. But pooling regulations and practices that were developed in the context of conventional, vertical wells may not always work well in the context of hydraulically fractured, horizontal wells.

Some jurisdictions have responded by creating drilling units that are narrower and longer than traditional pooled units, which often were square in shape. Some jurisdictions have stuck to using square units, but this raises another issue. In traditional pooling, it was often contemplated that a pooled drilling unit would be sized at the maximum area that could be drained by one well. But if a square unit is used, four to six horizontal wells may need to be drilled parallel to one another within the same drilling unit to drain the entire unit. But if this is done, it may be necessary to change the language of the pooling rules, which may state that a pooled drilling unit should be the maximum size that can be drained by a single well.[112]

112 The relevant Louisiana statutes used to say that a drilling unit should be the maximum size that could be drained by one well. The statute was amended to state that a drilling unit should be the

Further, another issue can arise at the edges of drilling units in which horizontal drilling and hydraulic fracturing is used. The issue is raised by a combination of three facts: (1) horizontal fractures tend to propagate in a direction perpendicular to the wellbore; (2) not much oil or natural gas will be drained from the portion of an unconventional formation that is not fractured; and (3) traditional spacing rules would have required that both the start and the end of each horizontal lateral satisfy spacing rules that might require the well not approach any closer than some specified distance to the boundary of the unit.

Given these facts, suppose that the terminal end of the horizontal lateral is some distance – say, 300 feet – from the unit boundary. Further, suppose that the fractures extend in a perpendicular direction to the wellbore, so that the fractures will not extend into the 300 feet past the end of the wellbore in the direction of the unit boundary. Finally, suppose that little or no hydrocarbons are drained from the unfractured area. The result is that there is no drainage of oil or gas from the 300 feet near the boundary of the unit. To address this issue, some states have authorized "cross unit" wells that actually cross the boundaries between two units.[113]

Conservation regulations are still adapting to the new issues and challenges being raised by the combination of horizontal drilling and hydraulic fracturing.[114]

Key Findings of This Chapter

In the United States, the right to explore for and produce minerals is privately owned—typically by the landowner—as opposed to being owned by the sovereign. For this reason, the right to explore for and produce minerals is highly fragmented for most oil and gas fields. Further, absent an agreement or a regulator's order to the contrary, the owner of exploration and production rights in each tract of land will be the owner of all the oil and gas produced from a well located on and bottomed beneath that tract, even if the well drains oil and gas from beneath neighboring tracts. This creates an incentive for each person who has exploration and production rights to drill his or her own well on the tract where the operating rights exist. This can lead to economic waste in the form of operators drilling more wells than are necessary to efficiently drain an oil or gas field. Also, sometimes the race to produce hydrocarbons at a rapid rate to recover the hydrocarbons before a neighbor does, can harm the reservoir and reduce the total amount of hydrocarbons that can be recovered.

Responding to this problem, most states (the main subnational jurisdictions within the United States) have enacted statutes that authorize an oil and gas regulator

maximum size that can be drained by the well or wells permitted in the drilling unit. *See* La. Rev. Stat. 30:9(B).

113 *See, e.g.*, La. Rev. Stat. 30:9.2.

114 For a discussion of some of these issues, see Keith B Hall, *Single Well Spacing and Pooling: State Spacing and Jurisdiction over Conservation*, Special Institute on Federal Onshore Oil & Gas Pooling and Unitization, Rocky Mtn. Min. L. Fdn. (2014); Bruce M Kramer and Patrick H Martin, *The Law of Pooling and Unitization* § 5.05 (3rd edn).

to create drilling units in areas with tracts that are smaller than the area that can be efficiently drained by a single oil and gas well. The regulator will name one person as the operator of the drilling unit. The classic conception is that the drilling units would each be the maximum size that could be efficiently drained by one well. And, if the owners of the separate tract did not enter an agreement to "pool" their interests in the drilling unit, the regulator would enter an order "pooling" the separately owned interests for purposes of sharing revenue and costs from drilling and operating a unit well. The creation of such drilling units and the issuance of pooling orders does not provide for coordination of operations over the entire oil and gas field, but it can prevent the drilling of unnecessary wells and the waste of financial capital that would result.

The fragmentation of interests in an oil and gas field also can make it difficult to obtain an agreement from everyone having operating rights for the coordination of operations over an entire oil and gas field. Further, there is often opposition to fieldwide unitization from the different persons who have operating rights in an oil and gas field. As a result, fieldwide unitization is seldom used during primary production in the United States. However, fieldwide unitization is used more often for types of operations that require coordination over a large area, such as pressure maintenance operations, secondary recovery, and tertiary recovery (enhanced oil recovery). Sometimes this is done by agreement, but other times fieldwide unitization is imposed by a regulator's order. Most state jurisdictions have statutes that give the state's oil and gas regulator the authority to enter orders requiring such fieldwide unitization and coordination. A notable exception is Texas, which is a very significant oil and gas state, but in Texas the oil and gas regulator has been able to use other authority that it has to nudge operators in some oil and gas fields into entering voluntary unitization agreements for coordinated fieldwide operations for such things as pressure maintenance, secondary recovery, or tertiary recovery.

Part III

Conclusion

12 Negotiating Risk-Free Unitization and Joint Development Agreements

Summary and Options for Policymakers

Eduardo G. Pereira, Marianthi Pappa, and Damilola S. Olawuyi

12.1 Background

This book set out to examine the legal framework for unitization and the underlying unitization and unit operating agreement (UUOA) in selected domestic law perspectives. With case studies from oil and gas jurisdictions across the world, the book explores the latest developments of law, regulations, policies and governance structures on unitization and joint development of oil and gas resources. The chapters highlight the necessity of exploiting petroleum to attain energy security while minimizing waste and examine the benefits of unitization, including lowering production costs, reducing waste, maximizing economic recovery and giving relevant parties a fair share of the common reservoir. The book also provides a comparison of the UUOA and similar arrangements like pooling, joint operating agreements, and joint development agreements (JDAs). The various chapters cover current and emerging laws on unitization, and its case studies cut across several continents of the world. This final chapter reviews salient themes that were discussed and identifies directions for future action and research.

12.2 Overview of Latest Developments in Legislation and Contracts

Over the last several decades, the need for the joint development of oil and gas resources in multiple units and wells to ensure the efficient, orderly and sustainable use of oil and gas resources has become widely recognized. Several scholarly studies and reports have provided a survey of the various concluded agreements (especially JDAs) with the aim of demonstrating the increasing application and use of these agreements in the oil and gas sector. What remained absent, however, was a systemic and multijurisdictional survey of the unique and underlying features of unitization and JDAs in diverse jurisdictions, with focus on the risk points and the contractual approaches and tools for avoiding and managing such risks. This book has filled a gap in this regard. This book provides an invaluable compendium of analyses and resources for a wide range of audiences. For those in the academic field, it provides significant resources given that it touches upon every aspect of

DOI: 10.4324/9781003491293-15

unitization and UUOA, including a view of its global use. It also provides a sturdy basis for further research in this subject matter.

In Chapter 4, 'Unitization in Brazil: Conflicting Legal Regimes and Non-unitized Areas Experience', André Lemos and Eduardo G. Pereira explore Brazil's substantial oil and natural gas reserves and production, and how unitizations in Brazil can be complex when involving various different legal regimes for exploration and production (E&P). The Brazilian Federal Constitution of 1988 established a state monopoly over the upstream, importation and exportation of oil and its by-products, oil refining, and maritime and pipeline transportation activities. However, this monopoly was loosened in 1995, and the Petroleum Law was enacted in 1997, creating the National Agency of Petroleum, Natural Gas and Biofuels (ANP) and allowing for private parties to contract with the government. The Pre-Salt Law was enacted in 2010, establishing the production sharing contract regime for all of the pre-salt polygon and other strategic areas, while the Transfer of Rights Law provided a mechanism for Petrobras to produce up to 5 billion barrels of oil equivalent in a specific prolific area of the pre-salt province. The current Brazilian E&P legal framework includes the production sharing contract regime for pre-salt and strategic areas, the transfer of rights agreement for specific fields of the pre-salt area, and the concession contract regime for all other areas. Unitizations in Brazil can be complex and challenging, involving different E&P legal regimes. Further improvements in applicable regulations are still necessary to increase the attractiveness of the Brazilian upstream market to investors.

In Chapter 5, Chi Iliya-Ndule examines unitization in Canada and provides an overview of the legal and regulatory regime governing unitization at both the federal and provincial levels, with a particular focus on Alberta. Although the majority of mineral rights within Canada's boundaries are owned by the government, the extent of privately owned mineral rights varies by province. Alberta is the largest producer of crude oil and marketable gas within Canada but is the only jurisdiction that has not made provision for compulsory unitization, leaving the decision to enter into a unit entirely up to the owners. However, the delay in establishing a unit can result in a costly deferral of revenue to owners and inefficient development of oil and gas resources. The Alberta government has been pressed to include compulsory unitization provisions in its legislation, but has yet to do so. The need for compulsory unitization was highlighted in the Butte Energy Inc. case, where waste and drainage problems could have been avoided with a compulsory unitization order. The chapter concludes by arguing that compulsory unitization will be required if Alberta is to fully meet the stated purposes of the Oil and Gas Conservation Act, reduce its industry footprint, and increase recovery rates for conventional reservoirs.

In Chapter 6, Thomas Kojo Stephens discusses the Republic of Ghana and its four sedimentary basins, with the Accra/Keta Basin being the only offshore basin currently producing oil. The Tano-Cape Three Points Basin is the most explored, followed by Saltpond, Accra/Keta, and the virtually unexplored inland Voltaian Basin. Ghana made a small-scale oil discovery in 1970 and a large-scale commercial discovery in 2007 in the Tano-Cape Three Points Basin. The unitization of parts of the West Cape Three Points Block and Deepwater Tano constituted Ghana's first and only unitization in its petroleum industry. This chapter focuses on the unitization of the Jubilee Field as a case study for unitization in Ghana. While there has been stagnation in Ghana's industry, the Jubilee Field unitization was pulled off successfully, and the field was brought into production in record time. However, the Afina-Sankofa is encountering difficulties due to the absence of the recognition of unitization.

In Chapter 7 on unitization agreements in Mexico, Dario G. Lamanna examines the Zama oilfield unitization process, a groundbreaking initiative that marked the first instance of a shared oilfield between a public and a private company in Mexico. The discovery of the Zama oilfield in 2015 not only prompted regulatory challenges but also catalysed discussions surrounding unitization in Mexico. The unitization process is outlined in various regulations, guidelines and agreements which inform the obligation to notify authorities of shared oilfields or reservoirs and the signing of a unitization agreement for joint and optimal hydrocarbon exploitation by the operators of both involved blocks. Despite the release of the new SENER Guidelines in March 2018, which provided a framework for the process, an official model contract was not approved, and the authors recommend that a model unitization agreement be established to expedite and maximize negotiations. Despite the progress made, legal ambiguity remains, necessitating comprehensive regulatory reform to enhance security and clarity for all stakeholders involved. Overall, this study provides valuable insights into the complexities and challenges of unitization in the Mexican hydrocarbon sector and highlights the urgent need for effective regulatory frameworks.

In Chapter 8, 'Unitisation in the Nigerian Oil and Gas Industry', Damilola S. Olawuyi and Olujobi Olusola Joshua explore the legal and institutional framework for unitization in the Nigerian oil and gas industry. Unitization in Nigeria, as in other countries, allows for the development of oil and gas fields that straddle two or more contracted areas as a unit. The chapter discusses the legal and regulatory framework surrounding unitization in Nigeria, including legislation, rules and guidelines. The legal challenges facing the effective implementation of unitization schemes in Nigeria are also evaluated, with legal innovations explored for addressing these gaps. The importance of unitization in achieving significant recovery of hydrocarbon reservoirs and combating waste and inefficiency in the sector is highlighted.

In Chapter 9 on unitization in Norway, Rune Omdahl explores the regulation of the concept of unitization and coordinated petroleum activities in the Norwegian continental shelf (NCS) under the Petroleum Activities Act of 29 November 1996 no. 72, and other associated rules and regulations. The provision stipulates that licensees must cooperate where a petroleum deposit spans multiple blocks with different licensees or onto the continental shelf of another state. Additionally, joint petroleum activities that would evidently be more efficient must be carried out in collaboration between licensees. The ministry has the authority to impose joint activities and establish the terms and conditions for a unitization agreement, including the apportionment of the reservoir. The obligation to coordinate petroleum activities reflects the state's perspective on the petroleum resources underlying the NCS, where resource management is to be conducted in a long-term perspective for the benefit of Norwegian society as a whole. Exploitation and production of petroleum are to be carried out in a manner that maximizes efficiency while minimizing costs. Overall, the chapter provides a comprehensive overview of the regulatory framework that governs unitization and coordinated petroleum activities in Norway.

In Chapter 10, Tolulope O Taiwo provides an assessment of the legislative and regulatory framework for unitization in the United Kingdom, focusing on both national and cross-border unitization. The concept of unitization, which refers to the coordinated operation of a common oil or gas reservoir by multiple parties with rights in different contract/licence areas (or state borders), has been adopted in the UK, where all rights to oil and gas are vested in the Crown. The chapter examines the legal measures in place to ensure voluntary unitization and mandatory unitization where in the national interest, and notes the importance of early action in relation to unitization, as well as the absence of a model UUOA in the UK. The UK's extensive history with cross-border unitizations is also highlighted, with available transboundary agreements providing guidance and expertise for workable development agreements.

In Chapter 11, Keith B. Hall outlines the differences between the practices of pooling and unitization, and provides an overview of the legal frameworks and practices relevant to unitization in the United States. Conceptually, the underlying purposes and effects of unitization in the United States are similar to those in other countries. However, in practice, the presence of multiple legal systems, practices and procedures have given rise to significant differences in when and how unitization is effected. Moreover, the advent and dominance of horizontal drilling and hydraulic fracturing have overturned even the semblance of order that existed with respect to the unitization of conventional operations. In the face of this uncertainty, the pace of activity remains the most defining factor of the oil and gas industry in the United States. Despite the differences in practice and procedure, the legal effects of unitization remain constant across jurisdictions. The pooled or unitized tracts are treated as unitary, and underlying leases or other granting instruments are conformed, insofar as they are located within the unit.

12.3 Maximizing the Full Value of Unitization and Joint Development Agreements

Several crosscutting lessons on how to maximize the full value of unitization and JDAs as tools for promoting resource efficiency and advancing energy security goals emerge from the different chapters. First is the need to establish clear boundaries when establishing units and development zones, especially for cross-border unitization. The clear delimitation of boundaries can enable parties to understand the nature and scope of their rights, while preventing a wide range of disputes that may occur from existing tensions or uncertainties, especially in conflict-prone regions.

Second is the need for a clear and comprehensive legal and institutional framework that clarifies the preconditions and procedures for unitization, especially in cases of compulsory unitization. As demonstrated in several of the chapters, while unitization and JDAs have grown in recognition and application as tools for securing the maximum and efficient recovery of oil and gas resources, lack of regulatory clarity in many countries on the procedures for structuring and applying unitization remains a key gap. For example, in many countries the circumstances under which regulators may mandate compulsory unitization remain unclear, while the procedures for securing regulatory approval even for voluntary unitization remains daunting and less straightforward. There is a need for clear, comprehensive and specific legislation and regulation on unitization in order to streamline the unitization process. A clear legal framework can enable licensees to better understand their rights and obligations when negotiating unitization agreements, while also providing guidance on the relationship between the parties and their respective environment, social and compliance obligations when coming together to jointly develop petroleum reservoirs.

Third is the need to improve local capacity for fiscal coordination and risk mitigation, especially at contract negotiation phases. One of the key factors that heighten contractual risks in the development and implementation of unitization arrangements is the failure to clearly define the respective roles and duties of the parties when negotiating the UUOA. The UUOA is the most important contractual mechanism that spells out the terms of the unitization process, how the common field will be governed or operated, and the rights and duties of each of the parties. However, weak domestic capacity, especially during contract negotiation phases, may result in ambiguous or lopsided contractual terms and provisions. While several countries in Africa, Latin America and the Middle East have increasingly outsourced contract negotiation work to law firms to match the expertise of international investors, there is a need to expand the domestic capacity of energy sector officials through local content development initiatives. The rise of local content development programmes provides timely tools for oil- and gas-rich countries to incorporate capacity development programmes in areas relating to contract negotiation and development to progressively improve the in-house expertise of national oil companies and entities that are involved in contract negotiation, procurement and management. Implementing clear local content policies that strengthen the abilities of local industries and individuals to negotiate clear and risk-free UUOA can help countries stimulate domestic value creation, economic diversification, and maximize the full value of UUOA as tools for promoting efficient and sustainable recovery and use of oil and gas resources to advance energy security.

Fourth and equally important is the need to integrate contractual provisions that ensure the timely, fair and efficient resolution of disputes that may arise in the context of unitization. While the importance of arbitration as a mechanism for ensuring the timely resolution of oil and gas disputes in a neutral and efficient manner has been increasingly promoted, without a clear and enforceable arbitration clause in a UUOA, disputes resulting from such agreements may end up being litigated in courts, which may result in delays. The UUOA and other related contracts must consist of a valid arbitration clause (arbitration agreement) in which the parties opt for a private dispute resolution procedure instead of going to court.[1] Furthermore, the arbitration agreement should clearly specify the number of arbitrators, the legal place or seat of the arbitration and the procedural rules that will govern the arbitration.[2] In the UUOA, the parties must decide on whether the arbitration will be conducted in accordance with the rules of a particular arbitration institution or will be ad hoc. A clear and comprehensive arbitration agreement is essential as it is the jurisdictional foundation of the arbitral tribunal. As such, a poorly drafted arbitration clause may endanger the validity and enforceability of an arbitral award, which may limit the application of the UUOA.[3] It is therefore imperative for parties to a UUOA to clearly integrate an arbitration clause that specifies that disputes resulting from the agreement are to be resolved by final and binding arbitration, the applicable arbitration rules, as well as the language and venue of arbitration, including the number of tribunal members.[4]

Fifth is the need for increased cooperation by countries to promote the effective implementation of cross-border unitization and JDAs. As several of the case studies demonstrate, while several JDAs have been put in place to promote orderly and less conflictive use of transboundary resources that straddle different countries, lack of solidarity and cooperation in the implementation of such agreements remain key issues. Conflictive geopolitics between countries, absence of clear implementation structures and lack of a regional knowledge-sharing platform on unitization best practices continue to weaken the effective design and wide implementation of unitization and JDAs. There is a need for countries to put in place adequate supervisory mechanisms and institutions to oversee the consistent and cooperative implementation of cross-border unitization and JDAs. Such institutions should also be provided the resources, tools and training to consistently monitor the implementation of the unitization agreements in a manner that eliminates conflicts. Similarly, greater emphasis should be placed on pursuing energy cooperation and trade that avoids competitive and conflictive geopolitics, but instead focuses on improving the availability, affordability and accessibility of energy resources for the people through maximizing the safe, orderly and efficient production of petroleum resources in jointly managed fields.

1 See Victoria Nalule and Damilola Olawuyi, 'Introduction to International Energy Arbitration Disputes in Africa' *The Palgrave Handbook of Arbitration in the African Energy and Mining Sectors* (Springer 2023) 1–15.

2 See Victoria Nalule and Damilola Olawuyi, 'Introduction to International Energy Arbitration Disputes in Africa' *The Palgrave Handbook of Arbitration in the African Energy and Mining Sectors* (Springer 2023) 1–15, see also P D Friedland, *Arbitration Clauses for International Contracts* (Juris Publishing, Inc. 2007).

3 Nalule and Olawuyi (2023) P D Friedland, *Arbitration Clauses for International Contracts* (Juris Publishing, Inc. 2007).

4 Nalule and Olawuyi (2023) P D Friedland, *Arbitration Clauses for International Contracts* (Juris Publishing, Inc. 2007).

12.4 Conclusion

While domestic legislation and bilateral investments agreements increasingly promote the joint development of petroleum resources in an efficient manner, the next step would be for stakeholders to develop comprehensive and holistic legal and contractual frameworks and tools that ensure that the implementation of unitization and JDAs proceeds in a risk-free manner.

The chapters in this book underscore the need for cooperation, clear rules and effective legal frameworks to explore and exploit transboundary oil and gas resources effectively. The book provides a wide-ranging, detailed and comprehensive analysis of the legal framework for unitization from both domestic and international law perspectives. The various chapters cover current and emerging laws on unitization, and case studies which cut across several continents of the world. The book provides an invaluable resource and tool to stakeholders ranging from those in academia to countries and entities faced with the challenge of common petroleum reservoirs and to those seeking to negotiate or draft a UUOA or a JOA.

Index

absolute ownership 25; oil and gas 13–15
Accra-Keta Basin 75
African Centre for Energy Policy (ACEP) 95–97
Agyemang, Mark 95
Alberta 72–74, 184; cooperation and sharing resources 68; Court of Queen's Bench 71n102; dispute resolution 72; financial resources and taxation 71; governing law 71; legal and regulatory framework 64–68; management 69; Mines and Minerals Act 64, 67; operatorship 69–70; Petroleum and Natural Gas Conservation Board 63–64; Petroleum Joint Venture Association (PJVA) model Unitization Agreements 64–65; primary legislation and regulatory body 63–64; restrictions 68–69; terms of PJVA's model unit agreement 68–72; Turner Valley Conservation Act 63; Turner Valley Conservation Board 63; unitization in 63–72; working interest (WI) owners 68–72; *see also* Canada
Alberta Energy 63, 64
Alberta Energy and Utilities Board 64
Alberta Energy Regulator (AER) 64
Algeria, Hydrocarbon Law (2005) 29
Anadarko West Cape Three Points Company 79, 80
Anasuria Hibiscus UK 144
Anglo-American ownership system 11
ANP *see* National Agency of Petroleum, Natural Gas and Biofuels (ANP)
arbitration agreement 188
Asmus, David 126
Association of International Energy Negotiators (AIEN) 34, 36, 103, 150, 154
Association of International Petroleum Negotiators (AIPN) 34, 35, 37, 39, 93, 103, 133n53, 150
Australia, unitization and unit operating agreement (UUOA) 30

Bankes, Nigel 73–74
Barnard v. Monongahela Natural Gas Co. (1907) 26
Barnhill, Kenneth 33
Borys v. C.P.R. (1953) 18
Brazil 43–44, 54; exploration and production (E&P) legal framework 44, 49–51; Law #12,276/2010 (Transfer of Rights Law) 44; Law #12,352/2010 (Pre-Salt Law) 44, 184; legislation and contracts 184; PPSA (state owned company) 51–52; unitization and unit operating agreement (UUOA) 29; unitization regulation in 44–48; unitizations in 53–54; unitizations involving conflicted legal regimes in 49–51; unitizations with open acreages in 51–53
Brazilian Civil Code 49
Brazilian Federal Constitution (1988) 43, 184
Breidablikk-case 130, 135n61, 138
Buhari, Muhammadu 113
Butte Energy Inc., Alberta 73
Butte Energy Inc. (2013) 73

Caldera Petroleum UK Ltd. 144
Canada 55–56, 74; Alberta and unitization 72–74; chief conservation officer 59–60; compulsory unitization 59–62; legal and regulatory framework governing unitization federally 58–63; legal and regulatory framework

governing unitization in Alberta 63–72; legislation and contracts 184; unitization 56–57; unitization and unit operating agreement (UUOA) 29; unitization of straddling resources 62–63; voluntary unitization 59; working interest owners 60–62; *see also* Alberta
Canadian Energy Regulator 58
Canadian Foundation of Dispute Resolution 72
Canadian Oil and Gas Operations Act (COGOA) 58, 59, 62
Cansearch Resources Ltd. v. Regent Resources Ltd. (2017), Court of Queen's Bench in Alberta 71n102
Certificate of Non-existence of Archaeological Remains (CIRA), Mexico 108
chief conservation officer, compulsory unitization in Canada 59–60
Chigwell Viking Units 73
Companies Income Tax, Nigeria 115
conquest 11
Constitution of the Federal Republic of Nigeria (1999) 112–113
contractual agreements, unitization and unit operating agreements (UUOA) and 31–34
cost sharing agreement, Norway 131–132
COVID-19 100
cross-border agreements, United Kingdom (UK) 147–150
cross-border unitization, UK 146–147

Deepwater Tano (DT) Block, unitization 76–80, 185
determination, unitization and unit operating agreement (UUOA) 36–37
drilling: conventional vertical 177; hydraulic fracturing 179; unconventional horizontal 177, 178–179

Energy Act (2016), UK oil and gas 142
Energy Resources Conservation Board, Alberta 64
energy security, term 3
English System, ownership 11
ENI Ghana Exploration and Production Ltd. 83n52; legal process and outcome 97–100; position of 88–92; Sanofa-Afina unitization issue 83–86; Springfield's position 86–88; Springfield's response to 92–93
Environmental Impact Assessment Act, Nigeria 114–115
Environmental Impact Study (EIA) 108
Exclusive Economic Zone Act, Nigeria 114
extraction, resources from deposit 4
Extractive Industries Transparency International (2003) 115

federal lands: pooling 170; unitization 177
Field Development Plan (FDP) 143
fieldwide unitization, term 170
Frigg Field Reservoir and the Transmission of Gas (Frigg Agreement) 123–125; *see also* Norway

gas *see* oil and gas
Gavin, James 95
Ghana 75, 100–101; Deepwater Tano (DT) Block 76–80; different perspectives in 94–97; governing law on unitization within 82; legal process and outcome 97–100; legislation and contracts 184–185; Petroleum Agreement (Article 24) 98, 98n118; Sankofa Field and Afina Fields Directive to unitize 83–86; Springfield's position 83, 86–88; unitization and unit operating agreement (UUOA) 77–80; West Cape Three Points (WCTP) Block 75–79
Ghana Exploration and Production Law (1984) 77
Ghana National Petroleum Corporation (GNPC) 75, 76, 78, 96–100
government approvals 7; absolute control and sovereign rights 20; license 20–22; ownership 20–24; production sharing agreements (PSAs) 22–23; risk service contract 23–24
Grane Unit Agreement (GUA) 130

Harmful Waste (Special Criminal Provisions) Act 115
Herbert Smith Freehills LLP 100
horizontal drilling, United States 177–179
hydraulic fracturing, United States 177–179
Hydrocarbons Revenue Law, Mexico 107

Indonesia, pre-initiation agreement 30–31
Institute for Energy Studies (IES), Ghana 95
international oil company (IOC): production sharing agreements 22–23; risk service contract 23–24

In the Matter of an UNCITRAL Arbitration between ENI Ghana of Ghana: Ghana National Petroleum Corporation 100
Ithaca Oil and Gas 144

Johan Sverdrup decision 134–135, 138, 138n75; Ministry of Energy 125, 125n19
Johan Sverdrup Resolution 135
Joint Authority, Australia 30
joint development agreements (JDAs) 6, 7, 8, 183; form of unitization 27; maximizing the full value of 186–188
joint operating agreements (JOAs) 28; Norwegian state 6, 7, 127; unitization and unit operating agreements (UUOA) and 32–34
Joint Petroleum Activities: Norway 128–129; Norwegian Offshore Directorate 129, 129n33; term 129n33
Jubilee Field: unitization in Ghana 75, 81, 93; unitization of 78

Katona, Viktor 94
Kelly v. Ohio Oil (1897) 26
Kosmos Energy Ghana Limited 75, 76, 79, 80, 81

Land Use Act (1978), Nigeria 114
legislation and contracts, overview of latest developments 183–186
license(s): ownership 20–22; United Kingdom 144–146
licensee, word 131

Mahogany 1 (M-1) Exploration well, Kosmos 76
Marigold Field: joint development 145; licensees in 144
Mexico 102; dispute between PEMEX and Talos Energy in Zama oilfield 108–109; environmental and social aspects 107–108; fiscal regime 107; Hydrocarbons Law 104; Hydrocarbons Revenue Law 107; legislation and contracts 185; National Hydrocarbons Commission (CNH) 103–105; PEMEX (state-owned company) 102, 105, 108–109; principles of regulation of unitization process 102–103; regulatory and legal framework 103–107; SEMER (Ministry of Energy of Mexico) 102, 103–106, 109; transboundary unitizations 106–107; Zama oilfield discovery 102
Mills, John Atta 81
mineral deed 14
mineral ferae, term 13
Mines and Minerals Act, Alberta 64, 67
Ministry of Energy: Johan Sverdrup decision 125, 125n19; Norway 126
Ministry of Petroleum and Energy, Norway 22
moveable oil originally in place (MOOIP) 36–37, 39, 134

National Agency of Petroleum, Natural Gas and Biofuels (ANP) 43, 184; Brazil 43; Local Content Superintendence 49; Round 1 (1999) 45; Round 2 (2000) 45; Round 3 (2001) 45–46; Round 4 (2002) 45; Round 5 (2003) 45; Round 6 (2004) 46; Round 7 (2005) 46; Round 8 (2006) 46; Round 9 (2007) 46; Round 10 (2008) 46; Round 11 to 16 (latest) 46; Round Zero 43, 45
National Council of Energy Policy (CNPE), Brazil 44, 47
National Development of Hydrocarbon Resources (ALNAFT) 29
National Environmental Standard and Regulations Enforcement Agency (NESREA) Act 119–120
National Hydrocarbons Commission (CNH), Mexico 102, 103–105, 108, 109
natural gas liquids (NGLs), United States of America 171
Niger Delta Development Commission Act 119
Nigeria 110–112, 122; Companies Income Tax 115; Constitution of the Federal Republic of Nigeria (1999) 112–113; domanial theory of ownership 110; Environmental Impact Assessment Act 114–115; Exclusion Economic Zone Act 114; hurdles militating against unitization in 117–118; Land Use Act (1978) 114; legal framework in oil and gas resources in 112–116; legal preparedness for sustainable unitization in Nigerian oil and gas industry 121–122; model unit agreement and unit operating agreement in 120–121; Nigerian Minerals and Mining Act (2007) 114; Oil Pipelines Act 115–116; Petroleum Industry Act (2021) 113–114;

regulatory bodies in Nigeria's oil and gas industry 118–121; unitization in 110–112; unitization in Nigerian Oil and Gas Industry 116–118
Nigeria Extractive Industries Transparency Initiative (NEITI) Act (2007) 115, 119
Nigerian Content Development and Monitoring Board (NCDMB) 118–119
Nigerian Midstream and Downstream Petroleum Regulatory Authority 110, 113, 117
Nigerian Minerals and Mining Act (2007) 114
Nigerian National Petroleum Company Limited 113
Nigerian National Petroleum Corporation (NNPC) 113
Nigerian National Petroleum Policy (2017) 4
Nigerian Oil and Gas (Industry Content Development) Act (2010) 118
Nigerian oil and gas industry: investment in 110–111; legal preparedness for sustainable unitization in 121; legislation and contracts 185; National Environmental Standard and Regulations Enforcement Agency (NESREA) (Establishment) Act 119–120; Niger Delta Development Commission (Establishment) Act 119; Nigeria Extractive Industries Transparency Initiative Act 119; regulatory bodies in 118–121; significant prerequisites of model union agreement and unit operating agreement 120–121
Nigerian Oil and Gas Industry Content Development (NOGICD) Act 115, 119
Nigerian Petroleum Industry Act (2021) 110
Nigerian Upstream Petroleum Regulatory Commission 110–112, 113, 118
North Sea Transition Authority (NSTA) 141, 142–146, 154
Northwest Territories (NWT), Oil and Gas Operations Act (OGOA) 58, 59, 62
Norway 123, 139; authority of the ministry 136–139; cost sharing agreement 131–132; Frigg Field Reservoir and Transmission of Gas (Frigg Agreement) 123–125; legal basis for unitization 127–129; legislation and contracts 185–186; Ministry of Petroleum and Energy 22; pre-unitization agreement 131–132; unitization 124–126; unitization (co-ordinated petroleum activities) 129–131; unitization agreement 132–136
Norwegian continental shelf (NCS) 123, 137, 139, 185–186
Norwegian Offshore Directorate (NOD) 129
Norwegian Petroleum Directorate (NPD) 149

Offshore Cape Three Points (OCTP) 83–84, 86–87, 98
Offshore Energies UK (OEUK) 150–151, 154
Oil & Gas Authority (OGA) 21, 141
oil and gas: absolute ownership 13–15; ownership of 12–20; qualified ownership 15–17; rule of capture 17–20
Oil and Gas Conservation Act, Alberta 64, 72, 73, 74
Oil and Gas Conservation Amendment Act, Alberta 73
Oil and Gas Conservation Board, Alberta 64
Oil and Gas Conservation Regulations, Alberta 73
Oil and Gas Operations Act (OGOA) 58, 59, 62; Northwest Territories (NWT) 58, 59, 62
Oil and Gas UK (OGUK) 150
Oil Pipelines Act, Nigeria 115–116
operating agreement 174–175
Organization of the Petroleum Exporting Countries (OPEC) 9
ownership 7, 9, 25; absolute 13–15, 25; Anglo-American system 11; concept of 10–12; English System 11; government approvals 20–24; Nigeria's domanial theory of 110; oil and gas 12–20; qualified 15–17, 25; real property 13; rule of capture 17–20; theories of 13–20

Pakistan National Petroleum Exploration and Production Policy (2012) 4
Papua New Guinea, pre-initiation agreement 30
Peik Field, UUOA 152
PEMEX (state-owned company), Mexico 102, 105, 108–109
permanent sovereignty, principle of 15
petroleum, energy security 3

Petroleum (Exploration and Production) Act (1984), Ghana 82
Petroleum (Exploration and Production) Act (2016), Ghana 82, 85, 89
Petroleum (Exploration and Production) Regulations (2018) 82
Petroleum Act 1934 14
Petroleum Activities Act (1985) 125
Petroleum Activities Act (1996) 125
Petroleum Act of Nigeria (2004) 19
Petroleum and Natural Gas Conservation Board, Alberta 63–64
petroleum deposit: definition 129; Norway 129–131
petroleum industry, rule of capture as 18–20
Petroleum Industry Act (2021) 111, 116, 117; Nigeria 111, 113–114, 116, 117, 118, 121
Petroleum Industry Fiscal Framework 113
Petroleum Joint Venture Association (PJVA) model: cooperation and sharing resources 68; dispute resolution 72; financial resources and taxation 71; governing law 71; key terms of Unit Agreement and Unit Operating Agreement 68–72; management 69; operatorship 69–70; restrictions 68–69; Unitization Agreements 64–68
Petroleum Law, Brazil 44–46
Petroleum Regulations, United Kingdom 27
petroleum resources, control and management of 9–10
pooling: allocation of costs under 165–169; allocation of production under 165; differing treatment of leaseholders and owners of unleased mineral interests 169; drilling and spacing units 162–163; free ride approach 168–169; risk-fee approach 166–167; spacing rules 161–162; state conservation statutes and single well 161–170; statutory 163–164; surrender of working interest approach 168; term 31, 159; unitization and 129n34; unitization and unit operating agreements (UUOA) and 31–32; voluntary 161; *see also* United States of America
PPSA, Brazil 51–52
Pre-Salt Law, Brazil 43–44, 46
Production Sharing Agreement (1992), Yemen 27
production sharing agreements (PSAs), ownership 22–23
property rights, rule of capture as 17–18
qualified ownership 25; oil and gas 15–17; principles of 16

redetermination, unitization and unit operating agreement (UUOA) 37–38
Republic of Ghana *see* Ghana
Responsible Energy Development Act, Alberta 64
Rich v. Donaghey (1918) 16
risk service contracts, ownership 23–24
rule of capture 7, 26; land owners 124, 124n7, 160; oil and gas ownership 17–20; problems arising from 159–161; unitization 27

Sabre Oil and Gas Limited 76, 79, 80
Saltpond/Central Basin 75
samordnet, term 128
Sankofa-Afina Fields: ENI's position 88–92; unitization in Ghana 75, 83–86
Sankofa Gye Nyame (SGN) 81
Scots law 16
Social Impact Assessment (EVIS), Mexico 108
solum a caelo usque ad centrum, common law principle of 14
Springfield Exploration and Production Ltd. 83–85; position 86–88
Springfield Exploration and Production Ltd. v. ENI Ghana Exploration and Production Ltd. and Vitol Upstream Ghana Ltd. (2020) 97
state ownership, principle of 15
statutory pooling 163–164, 164n33
Stockholm Chamber of Commerce (SCC) 100
stock tank oil originally in place (STOOIP) 36–37, 39, 134–135

Talos Energy 102; Mexico 108–109
Tano-Cape Three Points Basin 75, 184
Territorial Sea (TS) 15
Texas Railroad Commission 175, 175n100
Transfer of Rights Law, Brazil 44
Tullow Ghana Limited 75, 79, 80, 81
Turner Valley Conservation Act, Alberta 63
Turner Valley Conservation Board, Alberta 63

UK *see* United Kingdom (UK)
UK-Norway Framework Agreement Concerning Cross-Border Petroleum Co-operation (2005) 149
unit creation, unitization and unit operating agreement (UUOA) 35–36

United Kingdom (UK) 6, 140–141, 154; cross-border agreements 147–150; cross-border unitization 146–147, 153; legal framework for voluntary and mandatory unitization 142–146, 153–154; legislation and contracts 186; Ministry of Petroleum 22; model of license 21–22; objective of unitization 141–142; Oil and Gas Authority Strategy 2021 4; oil and gas exploration 140; Petroleum Licensing Regulations 2008 27; rights to petroleum 21; unitization 140–141, 154; unitization and unit operating agreement (UUOA) 29, 150–153
United Nations, 2030 Agenda for Sustainable Development 3
United Nations Commission on International Trade Law Rules 99–100
United Nations Convention on the Law of the Sea (UNCLOS) 107, 114; Article 2 of 15; exclusive economic zone (EEZ) 16
United States of America: allocation of costs under pooling 165–169; allocation of production under pooling 165; compulsory unitization 175–177; drilling and spacing units 162–163; federal lands 170, 177; issued raised by horizontal drilling and hydraulic fracturing 177–179; legislation and contracts 186; mineral exploration 179; oil and gas interests 179–180; pooling 129n34, 158, 159–170; statutory pooling 163–165; unitization 129n34, 170–177; voluntary unitization 172–175; *see also* pooling
unitization: compulsory 175–177; concept of 5–6; cross-border, in UK 146–147; federal lands 177; maximizing the full value of 186–188; process 27; reasons for 170–172; term 5, 125, 128, 158, 170; unit operating agreements and 28–31; voluntary 172–175; word 124, 126; *see also* Brazil; Canada; Ghana; Mexico; Norway; United Kingdom (UK)
unitization agreement 173–174; importance of 3; Norway 132–136
unitization and unit operating agreement (UUOA) 5–6, 7, 8, 28, 183; common clauses in 34–38; contractual arrangements 31–34; determination 36–37; Ghana 77–80; joint operating agreements and 32–34; pooling and 31–32; pre-initiation agreement 30–31; redetermination 37–38; standard form of 7; unit creation 35–36; United Kingdom (UK) 150–153; unitization and 28–31
US Securities and Exchange Commission (SEC) 76

Valenti, Giuseppe 91–92, 99
Vitol Upstream Ghana Ltd. 83n53, 83–84, 86–88; legal process and outcome 97–100; Springfield's response to 92–93
Voltaian Basin 75
voluntary pooling 161
voluntary unitization 59, 172–175

Weaver, Jaqueline 126
West Cape Three Points (WCTP) Block, unitization 75–79, 185
Wintershall DES and Premier Oil (former Sierra Oil & Gas) 102
Wood County Petroleum Co. v. West Virginia Transp. Co. (1886) 13, 18
Wood Mackenzie, Afina discovery 84
working interest (WI) owners: Alberta 68–72; compulsory unitization in Canada 60–62

Zama oilfield 106; discovery of 102; dispute between PEMEX and Talos Energy 108–109; unitization process 109, 185

For Product Safety Concerns and Information please contact our EU
representative GPSR@taylorandfrancis.com
Taylor & Francis Verlag GmbH, Kaufingerstraße 24, 80331 München, Germany

www.ingramcontent.com/pod-product-compliance
Lightning Source LLC
LaVergne TN
LVHW021128300926
849160LV00010B/911
9781032792668